Fathers And Sons: A Novel

Ivan Sergeevich Turgenev

FATHERS AND SONS

A NOVEL

BY

IVAN SERGHEÏEVITCH TURGENEF

TRANSLATED FROM THE RUSSIAN
WITH THE APPROVAL OF THE AUTHOR

BY

EUGENE SCHUYLER, Ph. D.

NEW YORK
LEYPOLDT & HOLT
1867

SEASONABLE NEW BOOKS.

I. A Russian Novel.—Fathers and Sons.

Translated from the Russian of IVAN SERGHEIEVITCH TURGENEF, by EUGENE SCHUYLER, Ph.D.   12mo., cloth, $1.50.

The publishers would state that this work has been issued upon its literary merits, without regard to the fact of its being, in some sense, a 'curiosity.' Purely as a novel, they believe it to rank with the best productions of our time.   As a picture of Russian life and institutions, it of course possesses more value than any work yet published in America.

II. Critical and Social Essays.

Reprinted from the NEW YORK NATION.   12mo., cloth, $1.50.

Some of the most valuable and successful books recently issued in England, have consisted of essays reprinted from the high-toned critical and literary weekly newspapers, which have hitherto been almost peculiar to that country. The publishers present this volume, composed from an American journal which the first scholars of the country have thought worthy to rank with the *Spectator*, the *Examiner*, and the *Saturday Review*, in the full assurance that it will obtain, as it deserves, equal favor and equal permanence with the English reprints of the same description.   THE NATION'S staff of contributors embraces so many distinguished names in our literature, that a dull or worthless collection could scarcely be made from the files of the paper.

III. The Man with the Broken Ear.

Translated from the French of EDMOND ABOUT.   12mo., cloth, $1.50.

One of those peculiar novels based on scientific theories, in which M. About has been distinctively successful. The chief feature of the book is a very humorous, though philosophical illustration of the fact that when a man dies, he will be apt to find it more comfortable to remain dead, than to return to life fifty years after his demise. The speculation in Natural Science on which the story is founded, is more interesting in itself, more elaborately developed, and more entertaining in its supposed consequences, than in any other of M. About's books. Another equally interesting feature is a humorous contrast of the spirit of the Napoleonic era with that of the present age.   The whole book is written in M. About's best vein.

Copies sent by mail, postpaid, on receipt of the price.

LEYPOLDT & HOLT, PUBLISHERS,

451 Broome Street, New York.

JOHN F. TROW & Co.,
PRINTERS, STEREOTYPERS, AND ELECTROTYPERS,
50 Greene Street, New York.

PREFACE.

RUSSIAN literature is of recent growth. The writers who enjoyed the patronage of the second Catherine, though many of them were learned and even brilliant men, gave to their writings no national tone, and were imitators and translators of what was then current in the rest of Europe. Lomonosof and Derzhavin, the two greatest writers of the last century, find no readers to-day, save those few who are interested in them from historical reasons. Of those belonging to the present century, even Karamzin and Zhukovski are seldom read, though one was the first of Russian prose-writers, and the second a really remarkable poet. With Pushkin Russian literature first became truly national. He was born in 1799 and died in 1837, in a duel : the duel has ended the lives of too many of Russia's brilliant young men. Pushkin has been often called the Russian Byron ; he was indeed strongly under Byron's influence, and in his finest poem, *Evgeni Onegin*, he imitated in form and in style Byron's *Don Juan*. Pushkin freed Russian poetry from the shackles of classicality which had been imposed on it by the Court poets of the preceding generation ; he adopted new metres and chose for his subjects Russian themes, especially old legends and traditions of popular life. At the age of twenty-one he published *Ruslan and Ludmila*, a romantic poem, which gained him great reputation and popularity. After this came his drama of *Boris Godunof*, his master-piece *Evgeni Onegin*, a novel of modern Russian life, in verse, the *Gypsies* (*Tsigani*), and various prose tales, of which the best is *The Captain's Daughter* (*Kapitanskaya Dotchka*), and some historical works. When he died he was the historiographer of the Government, and was engaged on a history of Peter the Great. The reign of Nicholas was adverse to literary eminence, but another writer of European fame soon followed. This was Lermontof, who was born in 1811, and first became known by a poem on the death of Pushkin, which was circulated for some time in manuscript, and caused his banishment to the Caucasus, where he served in the army until his death in 1841. Here most of his poems were written, all of them inspired by the surroundings. Many of them are very beautiful, but a more remarkable work is his melancholy novel, *A Hero of our Time* (*Geroi nashevo Vremeni*), which is generally considered as being in the nature of an autobiography. Its chief character, Petchorin, is a man who while still young has lost all the freshness of life, and who rushes into dangers merely for the sake of the excitements they yield. The story ends with a duel in a mountain pass between two precipices, so arranged that the wounded party necessarily falls over and is killed. A brother officer, thinking himself portrayed in Petchorin, challenged Lermontof to a duel of exactly this character, in which he killed the poet.

The continuator of Pushkin's and Lermontof's reputation was Nicholas Gogol, born in 1808 in Little Russia. He published several short stories, of which one, *Tarass Bulba*, a sketch of Cossack life, is remarkable for its power and beauty. His popularity and reputation were greatly increased by his witty and satirical comedy of *Revisor* or the *Inspector General*. In this he reviewed the series of Russian office-holders, and exposed their corruption. This comedy was often acted, the Government being apparently willing to allow public opinion to spend itself against vices of administration which it had vainly tried to correct. Soon after this appeared the first part of his great novel *Dead Souls* (*Mertbiya Dushi*), which is full of humor, satire, and excellent delineations of character, and is in no way inferior to a novel of Dickens. *Souls* was the technical name for *serfs*; and at that time the Government, through the Board of Guardians, lent money to proprietors on a mortgage of their serfs. This story tells the adventures of one Tchitchikof, who went about buying up dead souls, i. e., the right to serfs who had recently died but whose names had not yet been taken off of the registers, for the purpose of defrauding the Government by a fictitious mortgage. Russians first began to know themselves through Gogol's pictures. Owing to difficulties with the censure, Gogol soon left Russia, and went to Rome, where he resided several years. He finally returned home, bringing several works in manuscript, among them the concluding part of the *Dead Souls*. He soon died, very suddenly, and, it is said, by his own hand. Before his death, which was in 1851, he burned all his manuscripts.

The success of Gogol brought out a large number of romance-writers, who abandoned all imitation of German, French, and English novelists, and have founded a truly national school of romance. Among them are the Count Sollohub, though he is properly a little earlier in date; the Count Tolsloi, a writer chiefly of military novels; Grigorovitch, whose *Anton Goremika*, and *Fishermen (Ribaki)*, are pictures of the life of the lower classes; Gontcharof, the author of *Oblomof;* Pisemski, the satirical novelist; and Turgenef, who is easily their chief.

Ivan Serghei͏̈evitch Turgenef was born at Orel, on October 28 (Nov. 3), 1818, of noble parents who were in easy circumstances. He was educated at first at home, and afterwards at school at Moscow, subsequently passing three years at the University of St. Petersburg. In 1838 he went to Berlin, where he devoted himself to the study of metaphysics, especially the Hegelian philosophy, the classics, and history. He began his literary career in the year 1843, by the publication of *Panasha*, a small volume of poems, many of them of considerable merit. Turgenef's life on his estate, where he lived quietly for some years, devoted to reading and shooting, and various journeys and sporting tours through the interior of Russia, had familiarized him with the condition of the serfs, and had greatly interested him in their welfare. He contributed to the *Contemporary (Souremenik)*, a literary journal and review of Moscow, at various times from 1846 to 1851, sketches of serf-life, which were afterwards, with others, collected into a volume called *Memoirs of a Sportsman (Zapiski Okhotnika)*. This book had a very large circulation, and created an intense excitement in Russia—an excitement without parallel in that country, and only to be equalled in any other by that caused at about the same time by Mrs. Stowe's *Uncle Tom's Cabin.* It was somewhat strange that in two great countries, so diverse in character and then so utterly unacquainted with each other, the appearance of a popular novel should be raised to the importance of a public event. On two opposite sides of the world, in two countries popularly said, the one to be the freest, the other the most despotic government on the globe, human slavery received most vigorous blows dealt in a similar way. These two books are however quite different in form. The work of Turgenef is a collection of twenty-two sketches and stories, which from the freshness of their descriptions and the ease of their style had excited attention in the journal in which they were published, though from an unknown pen. Yet the effect which they were about to produce when brought together in a book was very far from being foreseen. These sketches presented a striking picture of Russian manners and life, when there was the least knowledge on the part of the Russian public, and in some way revealed the Russians to themselves. Each story helped the others, and the whole made a strong cumulative argument against serfdom. Yet there is no formal accusation, no declamation, no exaggeration for effect; simple photographs. The author writes in simple and sober style and is only seen in his work. The *Memoirs of a Sportsman* did much to stimulate Russian thought and exertion on the subject of emancipation, and its author may justly feel, as he does, that the happiest event of his life was the reading of this book by the present Emperor, who himself declared that it was one of the first incitements to the decree which gave freedom to thirty millions of serfs.

The amount of local color and veiled allusions in this book makes it almost untranslatable; yet it has been translated into German, twice into French, and a portion of it badly into English, under the title of "Russian Life in the Interior," by J. D. Meiklejohn, Edinburgh, 1855.

In 1852, nominally on account of a eulogy on Gogol, who had just died, but really on account of objectionable passages in his book, Turgenef was ordered by the Emperor Nicholas to be confined to his estate. After two years he was released at the earnest intercession of the crown-prince Alexander, the present Emperor. Since then he has resided chiefly abroad, in France and Germany. Meanwhile Turgenef continued writing short tales, and dramas, for various Russian reviews, and also for the *Revue des deux Mondes*—for he writes well in French ; the most remarkable of which are perhaps *Faust, Mumu,* and *Asya,* though it is difficult choosing where all are good. In 1858 he published a longer novel called *A Nest of Noblemen (Dvoryanskoe Gniyezdo)*, a French translation of which was published in the *Revue Contemporaine ;* in 1859 another called *The Evening before (Nakanunye)*, and in 1860 a charming little tale called *First Love (Pervaya Lioubof)*.

The novel which is here presented, *Fathers and Sons (Otsi i Dyeti)*, was published first in 1861 in the *Russian Messenger (Russkii Vyestnik)*, a Moscow review, and subsequently in book form. A tempest was raised in Russia by its appearance ; passionate criticisms, calumnies, and virulent attacks abounded. Russians are not the least susceptible people in the world, and a true picture of two generations of any society would scarcely please those whose portraits were drawn. Each generation found the picture of the other very life-like, but their own very badly drawn. The fathers protested, and the sons were enraged to see themselves personified in the positive Bazarof. Yet some, the party of *action*, were proud of the appellation of *nihilists* and chose it as their watchword ; even these, however, were indignant at the human weakness and susceptibilities with which Bazarof had been endowed by the author. The Government took up the word, and used *nihilism* to stigmatize all revolutionary, and ultra democratic and socialistic tendencies ; and we have seen it play its part in the recent investigations into the attempted assassination of the Emperor.

Of course the more the book was abused, the more it was read. Its success has been greater than that of any other Russian book.

It has therefore been selected as the best specimen of modern Russian literature to present to the American public. The author expresses his satisfaction at the choice, and his gratification if it shall in any way conduce to the more intimate acquaintance of two great nations. Mr. Turgenef has published nothing since this, but he has just finished a long romance which will soon be published at Moscow. This, with the favor of the public, will also soon be presented in an English dress.

The translator has endeavored to preserve as far as possible the flavor of the original, though he is conscious of only partial success. With the exception of some few more usual names, he has preserved the Russian sound of all the proper names. One change he has made which he now regrets, too late to correct it,—the change of the second person singular to the plural.

E. S.

New York, May 21, 1867.

FATHERS AND SONS.

I.

"WELL, Peter, do you see nothing yet?" asked, on the 20th of May, 1859, a man of forty odd years, dressed in a rusty overcoat and plaid pantaloons, who stood bare-headed on the threshold of an inn, on the high road of X., in Russia. The servant to whom he put this question was a young fellow with chubby cheeks, small, dull eyes, and a round chin, covered with a colorless down.

This domestic, in whom every thing, from his greased hair and his turquoise ear-rings to his studied gestures, revealed a servant of the new generation of progress, threw his eyes carelessly down the road, in deference to his master, and gravely replied :

" Nothing at all ! there is nothing coming."

" Nothing ? " asked the master.

" Nothing at all ! " repeated the domestic.

The master sighed and sat down on a bench.

While he remains there, with his legs crossed and looking around him with a pensive air, let us introduce him to the reader.

His name is Nicholas Petrovitch Kirsanof, and he owns, at fifteen versts from the inn, a fine property of two hundred souls ; or, to speak as he does since he has made his

1

arrangements according to the new regulations, and has established a "farm"—of two thousand desiatines. His father, one of the fighting generals of 1812, a man of an un-cultured, even rude nature, a pure-blooded and thoroughly good Russian, had grown gray in the harness. Appointed brigadier-general, and later commander of a division, he lived in the country, where, by reason of his rank, he played quite an important part. Nicholas Petrovitch, his son, was born in South Russia, as well as his elder brother Paul, of whom we shall speak later, and was educated at home until he was fourteen, by cheap tutors, surrounded with sharp but servile aids-de-camp, and other individuals belonging to the regiments and the staff. His mother, of the Koliazin family, who as a girl was called Agathe, when once married took the name of Agathokleïa Kuzminishna Kirsanof, and fell not at all short of the habits that characterized the "ladies" of the superior officers ; she wore magnificent bonnets and dresses of rustling silk ; at church went always the first to kiss the cross ; * talked much and very loud ; and gave her children her hand every morning and her benedic-tion every evening : in a word she was the great lady of the head-quarters. Although Nicholas Petrovitch was weak and timid, he was destined, as the son of a general, to enter the military service, as was also his brother Paul, but on the very day of his departure for his regiment, he broke his leg, and, after having passed two months in bed, limped all his life. Obliged to give up making him a soldier, his father became resigned to putting him into the civil service, and, as soon as he was eighteen, took him to St. Petersburg to have him enter the University. Paul got the same year the rank of lieutenant in the guards. The two young men took rooms together,

* At the end of the mass in the Russian Church every body kisses the cross.

and lived there under the very lax surveillance of a maternal uncle, Ili Koliazin, a high official. Their father went back to rejoin his division and his wife, and from time to time addressed to his sons enormous folds of gray paper covered with a writing that showed the practised hand of the regimental secretary. At the end of each letter stood, circled with carefully-made flourishes, the words—" Peter Kirsanof, *generale*-major."

In 1835, Nicholas Petrovitch graduated at the University with the title of candidate, and the same year General Kirsanof, having been retired after an unsuccessful inspection, came to fix himself at St. Petersburg with his wife. He had hired a house near the Tavrichesky Gardens, and had got admitted to the English club, when he suddenly died of a stroke of apoplexy.

Agathokleïa Kuzminishna did not long survive him. She had not been able to accustom herself to the quiet life she was forced to lead at the capital. Vexation at seeing herself put, as it were, on the retired list brought her quickly to the tomb.

Meanwhile Nicholas Petrovitch, while his parents were still alive, and to their great regret, fell in love with the daughter of a government clerk, the proprietor of the house he lived in. She was a young person with a pleasing face, and her mind did not lack cultivation; she used to read the most serious articles in the Reviews under the head of " Science." The marriage was celebrated at the end of the mourning, and the happy Nicholas Petrovitch, having left the Ministry of Domains, where the influence of his father had got him a place, went with his Masha* to a country place near the Institute of Forests; afterwards, having returned to town, he hired pretty little apartments, with a

* Diminution of Maria, Mary.

well-kept staircase, and a cool parlor ; finally he retired to
the country, where his wife soon gave him a son, Arcadi.
The married pair led a tranquil and happy life ; they almost
never quitted each other ; played four-hand pieces on the
piano, and sang duets. The wife cultivated flowers and
looked after the house-keeping ; the husband occasionally
went hunting and busied himself with farming ; Arcadi,
their son, grew up and lived likewise in calm and quiet. Ten
years passed thus like a dream. But in 1847 Madame Kirsanof died. Her husband bore up with difficulty under this
unexpected blow, and his hair whitened in a few weeks. He
was getting ready to go abroad to divert his thoughts when
the year 1848 rendered travelling impossible. Forced to
return to the country, he stayed there some time in complete
inactivity, then set about introducing reforms into the management of his property. At the beginning of the year 1855,
he took Arcadi to the University of St. Petersburg, where he
passed three winters with him, almost without going out of
his house, and cultivating the acquaintance of the young
comrades of his son. He could not rejoin him during the
winter of 1858, and we find him now, in the month of May
following, when our story begins, his head already quite
white, of full, slightly stooping figure, expecting his son who
has just graduated with the degree of candidate, as he himself had done in his time.

The domestic who had just spoken to him, went to the
door of the court-yard to light his pipe, either from respect,
or because he did not care to remain under the eye of his
master.

Nicholas Petrovitch lowered his head and began to look
at the marble steps of the staircase ; a fat cock with variegated plumage walked gravely up and down, striking the
steps with the spurs on his big yellow feet ; a cat, all

covered with ashes, looked at him with rather an unfriendly
air from the top of the balustrade where it was crouching.
The sun was burning hot ; from the low chamber that served
as the entry to the inn issued a smell of freshly-cooked rye
bread. Nicholas Petrovitch began to dream: " My son . . .
candidate . . . Arkasha* . . ." he kept saying to himself in a
low voice. He recalled to his imagination his wife : " She
left us too soon," he sadly murmured. At this moment a
fat pigeon lighted on the road and ran hastily to drink in a
puddle of water near the well. Nicholas Petrovitch began
to observe it ; but his ear already distinguished the noise of
a carriage approaching. . . .

" They must be coming," said his domestic, who all at
once came in from the doorway.

Nicholas Petrovitch rose abruptly and looked down the
road. A tarantass† drawn by three cart-horses showed itself without delay. In the tarantass appeared the visor of
a student's cap, shading the dear features of a well-known
face.

" Arkasha ! Arkasha ! " cried Nicholas Petrovitch, and
he started to run, holding out both hands. In a few moments his lips were glued to the beardless, hot, and dusty
cheek of the young candidate.

II.

" Let me shake myself, papa," said Arcadi, in a voice a
little hoarse from fatigue, but sonorous and young, while re-
sponding joyfully to the paternal caresses ; " I shall cover
you with dust."

" That is nothing, never mind," said Nicholas Petrovitch,
with a smile of emotion, trying with his arm to wipe off the

* Diminutive of Arcadi or Arcadius.
† A kind of Russian travelling carriage.

dust from the collar of his son's coat and from his own coat also. "Show yourself then, show yourself," he added, drawing back a little ; and immediately went with hasty steps to the court of the inn, crying : "Come ! here, here ! bring the horses right up !"

Nicholas Petrovitch appeared much more moved than his son ; he seemed at once troubled and somewhat intimidated. Arcadi stopped him.

"Papa," he said, "allow me to present to you my friend Bazarof, whom I have written to you about so often. He is so good as to promise to stay some time with us."

Nicholas Petrovitch returned immediately and advanced towards a tall young man who had just descended from the tarantass, enveloped in a long coat covered with frogs ; he shook very strongly and heartily the large red hand that was undemonstratively extended to him.

"I am very glad," he said, "to hear that you will visit us. I hope——allow me to ask you your name and your father's."*

"Eugene Vassilief," replied Bazarof, in a slow but manly voice ; and unbuttoning the collar of his coat, he let Nicholas Petrovitch see him full in the face. He had a long and thin face, with a broad forehead, a nose thick above and sharper towards the end, large greenish eyes, and long drooping moustaches of a sandy hue ; a quiet smile played on his lips ; his whole physiognomy expressed intelligence and confidence in himself.

"I hope, my dear Eugene Vassilief," added Nicholas Petrovitch, "that you won't get tired of us."

The lips of Bazarof opened a little, but he made no reply, and only lifted his cap. Notwithstanding his thick chestnut

* In Russia the word corresponding to Mr. is rarely used in addressing an equal. A person is called by his baptismal name, followed by the baptismal name of his father, with the termination *ef* or *of*, or *vitch*, the latter being more polite.

hair, it was easy to distinguish the prominent bumps of his large head.

"Arcadi," said Nicholas Petrovitch, all at once turning towards his son, "shall we harness up immediately, or do you want to take a little rest?"

"We will rest ourselves at home, papa: harness up."

"Directly, directly," replied Nicholas Petrovitch. "Ho! Peter, do you hear? Come, get us off as soon as you can."

Peter, who, in his quality of accomplished servant, in place of coming to kiss the hand of his young master, had contented himself with saluting him at a distance, disappeared anew under the doorway.

"I came in a calash," said Nicholas Petrovitch, hesitatingly, to his son, "but there are horses for your tarantass."

While he was speaking Arcadi was drinking some fresh water that the mistress of the inn had brought him in a tin dipper, and Bazarof, who had just lighted his pipe, approached the coachman who was putting in the horses.

"Only," resumed Nicholas Petrovitch, "there are but two places in my calash, and I don't know how your friend—"

"He will ride in the tarantass," replied Arcadi, in an undertone; "don't stand on ceremony with him, I beg of you; he is a first-rate fellow; he will make no trouble, you will see."

The coachman of Nicholas Petrovitch brought round the horses.

"Come! hurry up there, thick-beard," said Bazarof to the postillion.

"Did you hear, Mitouka," cried immediately another postillion, who stood some steps off, his hands buried in the hind pockets of his tulupe,* "the little master called you thick-beard; that's quite right."

* A coat of sheepskin with the wool inside.

Mitouka, giving for his only reply a nod of his head which shook off his cap, took the reins of his foam-covered horses.

"Quick! quick! good fellow! help us a little!" cried Nicholas Petrovitch, "I will give good drink-money."

Some few minutes after the horses were put in; the father and son mounted into the calash; Peter climbed up on the seat; Bazarof leaped into the tarantass, buried his head in a leather cushion, and the two carriages started off at a fast trot.

III.

"So, then, you are at last a candidate, and have come home," said Nicholas Petrovitch to his son, placing his hand affectionately sometimes on his knees and sometimes on his shoulder; "at last!"

"How is my uncle? Well?" asked Arcadi, who, notwithstanding the sincere and almost childish joy he felt, wished greatly, nevertheless, to give the conversation a calmer turn.

"He is well. He wished to come with me to meet you, but I don't know why he changed his mind."

"And did you wait long for me?" asked Arcadi.

"I was there nearly five hours."

"How good you are."

Arcadi turned quickly to his father's side and imprinted on his cheek a noisy kiss.

Nicholas Petrovitch replied with a restrained laugh.

"I have got you a very fine saddle-horse!" he began, "you will see! and I have had your room papered."

"Is there a room for Bazarof?"

"They will find one for him."

" Treat him as well as you can, I beg you. I can't tell you what good friends we are."

" Have you known him long ? "

" No."

" Then I did not see him the other winter ? What is he studying ? "

" Natural sciences principally. But he knows every thing. He intends to pass his examination for a doctor next year."

" Ah ! he is studying medicine," said Nicholas Petrovitch, and he was silent for some minutes.

" Peter ! " he asked all at once and pointed with his hand, "are not those our peasants that are passing down there ? "

The servant turned his head to the side that his master pointed out. Several carts, whose horses were unbridled,* were rapidly going over a narrow cross-road ; each carried one or two peasants in unbuttoned *tulupes.*

" Yes, indeed," replied Peter.

" Where are they going ? to town ? "

" Probably ; they are going to a drinking-house," added Peter, in a tone of disdain, leaning a little toward the coachman, as if to take him for witness. But the coachman did not give the least mark of assent ; he was a man of the old style, who did not share any of the ideas of the day.

" The peasants give me much trouble this year," said Nicholas Petrovitch to his son, "they do not pay their rent. What shall I do ? "

" Are you better satisfied with the day-laborers ? "

" Yes," replied Nicholas Petrovitch, between his teeth ; "but they get corrupted ; that is the trouble. Besides, they don't work with real heartiness, and spoil the tools. Nevertheless the fields have been sown. All will be arranged in time. Are you interested in agriculture now ? "

* A strange custom of the Russian peasants.

1*

" You lack shade ; I regret that," said Arcadi, without replying to the last question of his father.

" I have had a large awning placed over the balcony, on the north side of the house," replied Nicholas Petrovitch ; "we can now dine out of doors."

" That, perhaps, is a little too much like the villa. However, that makes no difference. How pure the air is one breathes here ! how sweet it is ! I really believe that this delicious odor is peculiar to our country ! and how the sky—"

Arcadi stopped short, threw a timid look behind the carriage, and was silent.

" No doubt," answered Nicholas Petrovitch ; "you were born here, and consequently in your eyes every thing ought to have—"

" The place where a man is born makes no difference," interrupted Arcadi.

" Notwithstanding—"

" No ; it really makes none at all."

Nicholas Petrovitch gave a side glance at his son, and they rode nearly half a mile without either of them opening their mouths.

" I don't know whether I told you," began Nicholas Petrovitch at last, " that your old nurse, Yegorovna, was dead."

" Indeed ! poor woman ! And Prokofitch ; is he still alive ? "

" Yes, and he is always the same ; always grumbling, as he used to. You will not find great changes at Marino, I forewarn you."

" Have you still the same overseer ? "

" That is, perhaps, the only change I have made. I sent him away after deciding not to have free *dvorovis** any longer

* Serfs employed in domestic service.

in my service ; or at least not to confide to them any duty that brings any responsibility."

(Arcadi gave a glance at Peter.)

"*Il est libre, en effet,*" answered Nicholas Petrovitch, in an undertone, " but he is a *valet de chambre.* I have now for overseer a citizen who appears to me an intelligent man. I give him two hundred and fifty rubles a year. However," he continued, slowly rubbing his forehead and eyebrows, a gesture that he was in the habit of making when he felt embarrassed, " I just said that you would not find any change at Marino. That is not absolutely true, and I believe it my duty to forewarn you, though . . . ."

He stopped, and began soon in French.

" A severe moralist would without doubt find my sincerity improper ; but, in the first place, what I am going to confide to you could not remain secret ; and, in the second place, you know that I have always had peculiar principles relative to the relations that exist between a father and his son. After all, I ought to admit that you would be right to blame me . . . at my age . . . in a word, this young girl . . . whom you probably have already heard spoken of—"

"Fenitchka ? " asked Arcadi in an easy way.

Nicholas Petrovitch blushed a little.

" Don't speak her name so loud, I beg you," he said to Arcadi. " Yes . . . well, she lives with me now ; I have taken her into the house ; I have given her . . . two little rooms. But all that can be changed."

" Why change, papa, I beg you ? "

" Your friend is going to stay some time with us ; it is embarrassing—"

"If you do it on Bazarof's account, you are wrong. He is above all that."

"On yours, too," said Nicholas Petrovitch. " Unluckily, the wing of the house is not in good order."

"Come, come, papa ! you seem to try to excuse yourself.
What, have you no conscience ?"

"Yes, doubtless, I ought to have a conscience," added
Nicholas Petrovitch, who blushed more and more.

" Come then, father, I beg you !" said Arcadi to him, smiling with amenity. "What an idea to excuse oneself for
that," said the young man to himself; and while thinking
thus, an indulgent tenderness for the good and feeble nature
of his father, joined to a certain feeling of secret superiority,
awoke in him—"Don't let us speak any more about that, I
beg you," he added, enjoying involuntarily that independence
of mind that raised him so high above prejudices of all kinds.

Nicholas Petrovitch, who continued to rub his forehead,
looked at him a second time through his fingers, and felt
pricked to the heart. He accused himself inwardly.

" Here our fields begin," he said, after a long silence.

" And don't this wood opposite also belong to us ?" asked
Arcadi.

" Yes, but I have just sold it, and it will be cut down before the end of the year."

" Why did you sell it ?"

" I needed money ; besides, all these lands will soon belong to the peasants."

" Who do not pay you their rent ?"

" That is their look-out ; besides, they must pay it in the
end."

" I am sorry about this wood," said Arcadi, and he looked
around him.

The country through which they were passing was not
exactly picturesque. A vast cultivated plain extended to
the horizon, and the soil rose slightly, to fall soon after.
Some little woods appeared at rare intervals, and ravines,
curtained with scattered low bushes, wound around a little

further, recalling with some faithfulness the drawings that represent them on the old maps dating from the reign of the Empress Catharine. From time to time were seen little brooks with bare banks, ponds kept in by bad dikes ; poor villages, whose low houses were surmounted by black thatched roofs, half off ; miserable barns, with walls formed of interwoven branches, with enormous doors gaping on empty spaces ; churches, some of brick, covered with a layer of plaster that was beginning to come off, others of wood, topped by a badly supported cross, and surrounded with ill-kept graveyards. Arcadi felt his heart compressed little by little. As if expressly, all the peasants they met had a wretched air, and rode little worn-out horses ; the willows that edged the road,* with their torn bark and their broken branches, resembled beggars in rags ; shaggy cows, lean and fierce, eagerly browsed on the herbage along the ditches. You would have said that they had just escaped with great diffi-culty some sharp murderous claws. The sight of these poor animals evoked, in the midst of the brilliancy of a spring day, the white phantom of an endless winter—of a pitiless win-ter with its ice and its whirlwinds of snow.

"No," said Arcadi, "this country is not rich ; it does not strike one with its prosperity, with the traces of assiduous labor ; it is impossible for it to remain in this state ; it asks to be transformed . . . but how start to do it ? "

While Arcadi reflected thus, the spring continued to ex-pand most beautifully around him. All grew green, all moved gently, and sparkled with a gilded splendor under the mild breath of a warm and light wind—trees, bushes, and grass. From all sides rose the interminable trills of the larks ; the lapwings cried as they hovered over the damp

---

* In accordance with a ukase of the Emperor Alexander I., all the high roads in Russia are planted with willows.

meadows, or ran silently over the clods of ground ; crows, whose black plumage contrasted with the tender green of the still short wheat, were seen here and there ; they were distinguished with more difficulty in the midst of the rye that began already to whiten ; their heads hardly rose for a moment above this waving sea. Arcadi admired this picture, and his melancholy thoughts vanished by degrees. He took off his cloak and gave his father such a glad and childish look that he could not help clasping him again in his arms.

"We are getting near home," said Nicholas Petrovitch ; "as soon as we have got up this slope we shall see the house. We will indulge ourselves a little when there. You must help me manage the estate, if that don't tire you too much. We must be closely united and know each other well ; must we not ?"

"Certainly," replied Arcadi ; "but what a lovely day !"

"It is to celebrate your arrival, my dear boy. Yes, the spring is in all its glory. Besides, I am of the opinion of Pushkin. You remember these lines in Eugene Onegin :

"' How thy sight saddens me,
  Spring, spring, season of love !
  What—'"

"Arcadi !" cried Bazarof from the tarantass, "send me a match ; I can't light my pipe."

Nicholas Petrovitch stopped, and Arcadi, who listened with some surprise, but not without interest, quickly drew a silver match-box from his pocket, and told Peter to give it to Bazarof.

"Would you like a cigar ?" cried Bazarof again.

"Very much," replied Arcadi.

Peter brought him back with the match-box a large black cigar, that Arcadi immediately began to smoke, the odor of which was so strong that Nicholas Petrovitch, who had never smoked in his life, involuntarily turned away his nose, at the same time trying to conceal this movement from his son, in order not to discompose him.

A quarter of an hour afterwards the two carriages stopped before the portico of a wooden house, still new, the walls of which were painted gray, and the iron roof red. It was Marino, otherwise called the "New Farm;" or, as the peasants named it, the "Orphan's House.'

IV.

No crowd of serfs now met the masters at the steps on their arrival, as would have been the case a short time before ; only a little girl about twelve years old appeared at the door ; and soon after a young fellow, very like Peter, was seen, wearing a gray livery, with white armorial buttons : he was the servant of Paul Petrovitch Kirsanof.

He silently opened the door of the calash, and unfastened the apron of the tarantass. Nicholas Petrovitch, followed by his son and by Bazarof, crossed a dark and almost unfurnished hall, at the end of which appeared for an instant the figure of a young woman ; then he introduced his guests into a parlor furnished in the latest style.

"We are at last at home," said Nicholas Petrovitch, taking off his cap and shaking his hair. "First of all we must have some supper, and then a nap."

"A bite, indeed, is not unwelcome," replied Bazarof, stretching himself; and he threw himself down on a sofa.

"Yes, yes, give us some supper, quick ! " replied Nicholas Petrovitch, and he began to knock his feet together, without really knowing why. "Here's Prokofitch now."

A man of about sixty, thin, with white hair and a tawny complexion, entered the room. He wore a cinnamon-colored

coat, with copper buttons and a pink cravat. Having kissed
the hand of Arcadi, he saluted Bazarof, and stood near the
door, with his hands behind his back.

"Here he is, Prokofitch," said Nicholas Petrovitch to
him. "He has returned to us at last . . . Eh, well! how
do you find him?"

"In the best state possible," replied the old man, smiling
anew; but he took again almost instantly his serious air,
and contracted his bushy eyebrows.

"Shall we cover the table?" he asked with an important
air.

"Yes, yes, I beg you. But Eugene Vassilitch would perhaps like to go to his room?"

"No, I thank you. I should only like to have this little
valise carried there,—and this rag," he added, taking off his
coat.

"Very well! Prokofitch, take the gentleman's coat."

The old servant took the *rag* in both hands, with an
astonished look, raised it above his head, and went out of
the room on his toes.

"And you, Arcadi, would you like to go to your room?"

"Yes, I should like to brush myself up a little," replied
Arcadi, and started towards the door, when a man of
middle height, wearing an English suit of a dark color, a
low cravat in the latest style, and varnished boots, entered
the parlor. It was Paul Petrovitch Kirsanof. He seemed
to be about forty-five years old : his gray hair, cut very short,
had the brilliant reflection of new silver ; his features, of a
bilious hue, but clear and without wrinkles, were very regular, and of extreme delicacy of contour. You soon noticed
that he had once been very handsome ; his eyes, black, clear,
and oval, were especially remarkable. The elegant exterior
of Paul Petrovitch preserved still the harmony of youth, and

his step had a kind of spring that usually disappears after a man is twenty.

Paul Petrovitch took out of his pantaloons pocket his beautiful hand, with long pink nails, a hand whose beauty was heightened by wristbands of a snowy whiteness, fastened at the wrist by large opals, and extended it to his nephew. After having given him the European " shake-hands," he kissed him three times in the Russian way, that is, he touched his cheek three times with his perfumed moustaches, and said, " Welcome."

His brother presented Bazarof to him ; he slightly bent his slim body and smiled, but did not extend his hand, and even replaced it in his pantaloons pocket.

" I had begun to believe that you would not arrive to-day," he said, in a head-voice, of an agreeable pitch, swinging himself with a graceful air, shrugging his shoulders, and showing his handsome white teeth. " Did any thing happen to you on the road ? "

" Nothing happened to us," replied Arcadi ; " we did not hurry; that was all. So we are as hungry as wolves. Hurry up Prokofitch a little, papa ; I shall be back soon."

" Wait, I'll go with you," cried Bazarof, rising suddenly from the divan.

The two young men withdrew.

" Who's that ? " asked Paul Petrovitch.

" A friend of Arkasha's, and a very intelligent young man, he tells me."

" He is going to stay here some time ? "

" Yes."

" That great hairy fellow ? "

" Yes, certainly."

Paul Petrovitch drummed lightly on the table with his nails.

" I find that Arcadi *s'est dégourdi*," he said. " I am very
glad to see him again."

The supper passed silently ; Bazarof especially said almost nothing ; but he eat much. Nicholas Petrovitch told
several incidents in his farmer's life, as he called it ; explained his views on the measures that the government,
according to him, ought to take in reference to the commit-
tees * and the deputations ; the necessity of having recourse
to machine-labor, &c. Paul Petrovitch walked slowly about
the room (he never took supper), drinking from time to time
a swallow of red wine from a small wine-glass, and still
more rarely throwing out a word, or rather an exclamation,
"ah ! eh ! hem ! "

Arcadi brought news from St. Petersburg, but he felt a little embarrassed, as every young man usually does who, when
he has hardly emerged from childhood, finds himself in the
places where it was customary to consider and treat him like
a child. He lengthened his phrases unnecessarily, he avoided pronouncing the word "papa," and even tried to replace
it by "father," which he stammered, it is true, between his
teeth ; he poured out for himself with an affected indifference
much more wine than he wanted, and felt himself obliged to
drink it. Prokofitch did not take his eyes from him, and did
not cease moving his lips, as if he were chewing something.
The supper ended, and all separated almost immediately.

"Your uncle is a queer body," said Bazarof, who had
seated himself on Arcadi's bed, and was smoking a ·very
short pipe. "What elegance in the country ! it is really
curious, and his nails too, his nails ! They could be sent
to the Exhibition."

" You do not know," replied Arcadi, " that he has been a
beau in his time. I will tell you his story some day. He

---

* It was just on the eve of the emancipation of the serfs.

was a charming man; he turned the heads of all the women."

"It is that then! he still recalls the good old time. Unfortunately there are no conquests to make here. I could not get tired of looking at him. What odd wrists! You would say they were marble; and how well shaved his chin is! Arcadi Nikolaitch, do you know how ridiculous all that is?"

"I don't doubt it; but nevertheless he is an excellent man."

"A true piece of antiquity! But your father is a fine man. He is wrong in liking to read poetry, and can't understand much about agriculture, but he is a good fellow."

"My father is a rare man."

"Did you notice how embarrassed he was? quite timid?"

Arcadi raised his head, as though he was not timid himself.

"What singular people," continued Bazarof, "all these romantic graybeards are! They give such a development to their whole nervous system that the equilibrium is broken. Come! we must go to bed. I have in my room an English washstand, and the door does not shut. All that ought to stir us up! I speak of the English washstand. That is a progress!"

Bazarof went to his own room, and Arcadi experienced a great feeling of comfort take possession of him.

It is sweet to go to sleep under the paternal roof, in a well-known bed, under a coverlet which was sewed by friendly hands, perhaps by those of the good nurse who took care of you in childhood, those affectionate and unwearied hands! Arcadi recalled Yegorovna, and he wished her the joys of the saints; he did not pray for himself.

The two friends were soon asleep ; but several other inhabitants of the house did not rest so quickly. Nicholas
Petrovitch had been very much agitated by the return of his
son. He went to bed, but did not put out the light; he
began to reflect at length, his head resting on his hand. His
brother remained in his cabinet till midnight, stretched out
in a large arm-chair, before a grate filled with feebly-
burning coal. Paul Petrovitch had not undressed himself,
he had only changed his varnished boots for red Chinese
slippers without heels. Hè held in his hand the last
number of *Galignani,* but he did not read it. His eyes
were fixed on the fireplace, where a bluish flame wavered
for moments at a time. . . God knows on what he thought
then, but it was not in the past alone that his imagination
wandered ; he had a sad and absorbed air, which is not the
case when one abandons one's self to recollections only.
At the end of a little room at the back of the house was
seated, wrapped in a blue *dushagreika,** with a white handkerchief over her black hair, a young woman, named Fenitchka ; although nodding with sleep, she held her hand to
her ear, and occasionally threw a glance at a half-open door,
that showed a little bed where slept a child whose equal
breathing was heard.

V.

The next morning Bazarof woke up first, and went out of
the house.

"Oh," he thought, looking around, "the place is not really
very pretty."

When Nicholas Petrovitch entered into an arrangement
with his peasants, he had to resign himself to take for his
new establishment ten acres of a flat and dried soil. He

* A kind of short cloak usually thrown over the shoulders.

built himself there a house, with outhouses and stables. He sketched out on one side a garden, dug a pond and two wells; but the trees he had planted did badly, the pond filled slowly, and the water in the wells was brackish. Yet the acacias and lilacs of the grove began to give shade, and dinner or tea was sometimes served there. Bazarof walked rapidly through all the paths of the garden, visited the farm-yard, the stables, and discovered two little *dvorovi*, with whom he soon got acquainted, and went with them to fish for frogs in a marsh, about a verst from the house.

"What do you want frogs for, master?" asked one of the children.

"I'll explain to you," replied Bazarof, who had the peculiar gift of inspiring confidence in persons of the lower class, although, far from showing them any condescension, he usually treated them rather disdainfully. "I open the frogs and see what goes on inside of them; for you and I are frogs too, but frogs that walk on two legs; that shows me what goes on in our own bodies."

"And why do you want to know?"

"In order not to be mistaken, if you fall sick and I have to cure you."

"You're a *dochtur* then?"

"Yes."

"Vaska, listen here; the master says that we are frogs!"

"I'm afraid of frogs," replied Vaska, a child of about seven, with hair white as flax, clothed in a sack of coarse gray cloth with a standing collar, and going bare-foot.

"Why be afraid? Do they bite?"

"Come, get into the water, philosophers," said Bazarof to them.

Hardly had Bazarof gone out, than Nicholas Petrovitch woke up in his turn,; and, as soon as he had risen, he went into Arcadi's room, whom he found all dressed. The father and son went out on the terrace, which was sheltered by an awning ; a lighted *samovar* * waited for them on a table set between large bushes of lilac. The little servant who had first met them the evening before in the portico, soon appeared, and said in a shrill voice :

" Fedossia Nikolaïevna is unwell and cannot come ; she told me to ask you if you would pour the tea yourself or if she should send Duniasha ? "

" I will pour it myself," replied Nicholas Petrovitch hurriedly—" what do you take in your tea, Arcadi, will you have cream or lemon ? "

" I prefer cream," said Arcadi ; and after a moment of silence he began in a questioning tone :

" Dear papa ? . . ."

Nicholas Petrovitch looked at his son with an embarrassed air :

" Well, what ? " he asked.

Arcadi dropped his eyes.

" Pardon me, papa," he continued, " if you find my question improper ; but the freedom with which you spoke to me yesterday authorizes me to do as much . . . you will not be angry . . . "

" Speak."

" You encourage me to ask a question . . . If Fen . . . If *she* does not come to pour tea, is it not on my account ? "

Nicholas Petrovitch turned his head a little.

" Perhaps," . . . he replied at last, " she supposes . . . she is ashamed."

Arcadi threw a rapid glance at his father.

" She is very wrong," he replied ; " you know my mode of thought. (Arcadi was very fond of this expression).

* A large vessel in which tea is made.

Besides, I should be very sorry to disturb you the least in the world in your habits of life. Independently of that, I am sure you can't have made a bad choice ; and if you have permitted her to live under our roof, it is because she is worthy of it. After all, a son is not the judge of his father, and I especially . . . and especially of a father like you who never troubled my freedom."

Arcadi pronounced the first words in a trembling voice ; he felt himself generous, and yet he understood at the same time that he had the air of lecturing his father. But the sound of our own voice gives us courage, and Arcadi ended his little speech with firmness, and even in a somewhat declamatory tone.

" Thanks, Arkasha," replied his father, in a hoarse voice, rubbing again his forehead and eyebrows ; " your supposi- tions are probably not without foundation. It is certain that if this young girl were not worthy . . . It is not a sim- ple caprice . . . In fact, I feel some embarrassment in speak- ing to you of all this ; but you ought to understand that it was hardly possible for her to present herself here, especi- ally on the first day after your arrival."

" If that is so, I am going myself to find her," cried Arcadi, in a new fit of generosity, and he leaped from his chair. " I will explain to her that she has no need to blush before me."

" Arcadi," cried his father, rising also, " do me the kind- ness . . . it is impossible . . . There . . . I have not yet told you . . . "

But his son was no longer in hearing ; he left the terrace and ran off. Nicholas Petrovitch looked after him as he went, and fell back into his chair with some anxiety. His heart beat quickly . . . Was he conscious of the strange re- lations that necessarily were to be established between his son and him ? did he think that Arcadi would have acted more respectfully toward him by avoiding all allusion to this affair ? or did he reproach himself with his feebleness? it would be hard to decide. All these feelings confusedly agitated his breast ; the blush that had covered his face was not dissipated yet, and his heart was still beating violently.

Hasty steps were heard, and Arcadi reappeared on the scene.

" We have got acquainted, father," he cried, with an air at once triumphant and affectionate. " Fedossia Nikolaïevna is really unwell, and she will not come till later. But why did you not tell me that I had a brother ? I would have kissed him last night with as much joy as I did just now."

Nicholas Petrovitch wished to reply; he wanted to rise and open his arms . . . Arcadi threw himself on his neck.

" What; embracing each other still ! " cried Paul Petrovitch behind them.

His arrival rejoiced father and son alike ; one is often not sorry to put an end to the most touching situations.

" Does that astonish you ? " replied Nicholas Petrovitch gaily. " Arkasha has come home after so long . . . I have not had time since yesterday to look at him leisurely."

" It does not astonish me at all," said Paul Petrovitch ; " I am even quite disposed to do as much."

Arcadi approached his uncle, who again touched his cheek with his perfumed moustache.

Paul Petrovitch sat down at the table. He wore an elegant morning gown in the English style ; a little fez covered his head. This head-dress and a cravat negligently knotted were a sort of index of the liberty allowed in the country ; but the stiff collar of his shirt, which was of the color prescribed by fashion for a morning toilette, compressed his well-shaved chin with the usual inflexibility.

" Where is your new friend ? " he asked Arcadi.

" He is not at home ; he usually rises very early and makes

some excursion. But there is no use of bothering oneself about him. He detests ceremony."

"Yes, you can easily perceive that."

Paul Petrovitch began to slowly spread butter on his bread.

"Does he intend to remain here long?"

"I don't know. He is going from here to see his father."

"Where does his father live?"

"He lives in our Government, about eighty versts from here. He has a little property, and used to be a military surgeon."

"Ti... ti... ti... ti... I was asking myself that; where have I heard that name. Bazarof? Nicholas, don't you remember Doctor Bazarof that was attached to our father's division?"

"It seems to me there was such a man."

"I am sure of it. Well!" said Paul Petrovitch, twirling his moustaches. "And what is this Mr. Bazarof, the son, at bottom?" he added slowly.

"What is he?" Arcadi smiled. "Uncle do you want me to tell you what he is *at bottom?*"

"Do me that pleasure, my dear nephew?"

"He is a nihilist."

"What!" asked his father. As to Paul Petrovitch, he raised his knife, on the end of which was a small bit of butter, and remained motionless.

"He is a nihilist," repeated Arcadi.

"A nihilist," said Nicholas Petrovitch. "This word must come from the Latin *Nihil*, nothing, as far as I can judge; and consequently it signifies a man who ... who recognizes nothing?"

"Or rather who respects nothing," said Paul Petrovitch; and he began again to butter his bread.

"A man who looks at everything from a critical point of view," said Arcadi.

2

" Does not that come to the same thing ? " asked his uncle.

" No, not at all ; a nihilist is a man who bows before no authority, who accepts no principle without examination, no matter what credit the principle has."

" And you find this all right ? " rejoined Paul Petrovitch.

" That depends on circumstances, uncle. Some people find it right, and others on the contrary very wrong."

" Really? well, I see we shall never understand each other, we old time people, we think that principles . . . (Paul Petrovitch pronounced this word with a certain softness, like French ; Arcadi, on the contrary, accented the first syllable strongly) principles admitted without examination, to make use of your expression, are absolutely indispensable. *Vous avez changé tout cela,* may God give you health and the rank of General ; * we will content ourselves with admiring you, Messrs . . . how do you call yourselves ? "

" Nihilists," replied Arcadi, dwelling on each syllable.

" Yes, before we had Hegelians ; now there are nihilists. We shall see what you will do to exist in nothingness, in the vacuum, as if under an air-pump. And now, my dear brother, have the goodness to ring the bell ; I should like my cocoa."

Nicholas Petrovitch rang and cried " Duniasha ? "

But instead of Duniasha, Fenitchka herself appeared on the terrace. She was a young woman of about twenty-three, white and plump, with black eyes and shining hair ; her lips were red and full like a child's, and her hands were small and delicate. She had on a white muslin dress, and a new blue neck handkerchief was thrown over her rounded shoulders ; she held in her hand a large cup of cocoa ; in placing it before Paul Petrovitch, she seemed a little ashamed, and the fine and transparent skin of her pleasing

* Russian Proverb.

face colored with a lively red. She cast down her eyes, and stood near the table, resting the ends of her fingers on it. One would have said that she reproached herself for having come, and felt at the same time that she had not come without a right.

Paul Petrovitch frowned with a severe air, and Nicholas Petrovitch was very much confused.

"Good morning, Fenitchka," he said at last between his teeth.

"Good morning," she replied in a low and sweet voice; and she went away slowly after having cast a side look at Arcadi, whó smiled at her with a friendly air . . . She walked with a little swing; but that suited her very well. When she had gone, a deep silence reigned during some instants on the terrace. Paul Petrovitch drank his cocoa; and slowly raised his head:

"Here is the nihilist, who deigns to come find us," he said in a half whisper. In fact Bazarof was coming through the garden, walking across the grassplats. His linen coat and pantaloons were drabbled: a marsh plant was twined about his old round hat. He carried a little bag in his right hand; something moved in it. He approached the terrace with great strides, bowed a little, and said:

"Good morning, gentlemen, you will pardon me if I come a little late for tea, I am coming loaded, I must get rid of my prisoners first."

"What have you, leeches?" said Paul Petrovitch.

"No, frogs."

"To eat or to raise?"

"For experiments," replied Bazarof with an indifferent air; and he went into the house.

"He is probably going to dissect them," said Paul Petrovitch; "he does not believe in principles, but he believes in frogs."

Arcadi threw a look of commiseration on his uncle, and
Nicholas Petrovitch imperceptibly shrugged his shoulders. Paul Petrovitch himself understood that his jest was
worth nothing, and so began to talk rural economy, and in that
connection said that the new overseer had come to complain
to him, with his usual eloquence, about the workman
Thomas, with whom he could do nothing. " He is a true
Æsop," said the overseer ; " he has made himself be talked
about as a bad fellow ; he is hardly at work, than he makes
silly speeches, runs off, and that is the last of him."

VI.

Bazarof reappeared soon ; he took his place and began
to drink his tea, as though he wanted to exhaust the samovar.
The two brothers looked at him in silence, and Arcadi observed them both from the corner of his eye.

" Have you been far ? " asked Nicholas Petrovitch at
last.

" As far as that little marsh that is near your aspen wood.
I started five or six snipes there ; you could kill them,
Arcadi."

" You are a sportsman then ? "

" No."

" You are studying physics particularly ?" asked Paul
Petrovitch.

" Yes, physics and the natural sciences in general."

" I have heard it asserted that the Dutch have made great
progress in these sciences in the last few years."

" Yes, the Germans are our masters in that respect," carelessly replied Bazarof.

Paul Petrovitch had employed the word Dutch with an
ironical intention ; but without producing much effect.

"You have a very high esteem for the Germans!" he replied with an affected politeness. He began to feel a dull irritation. His aristocratic nature could not support the self-possession of Bazarof. This surgeon's son did not only not appear embarrassed, but replied to him brusquely and with bad grace, and the very sound of his voice had in it something rude that bordered on insolence.

"The scholars of that country are fellows of merit," said Bazarof.

"That is true, that is true,—and you probably do not have such a flattering opinion of Russian scholars?"

"That is possible."

"Such impartiality does you much honor," added Paul Petrovitch, and he straightened up and threw his head back a little. "Yet Arcadi Nikolaïvitch told us that you recognized no authority in the sciences. How do you make that consistent with the opinion you have just expressed? Is it indeed true, that you recognize no authority?"

"Why should I? and what ought I to recognize? You show me a reasonable thing; I admit it, and that is all."

"Do the Germans then always say reasonable things?" murmured Paul Petrovitch; and his face took such an expression of indifference and impassibility that he appeared to be raised into a sphere perfectly inaccessible to worldly agitations.

"Not always," replied Bazarof, with a suppressed yawn, as if to let it be understood that this idle conversation was getting wearisome to him.

Paul Petrovitch gave Arcadi a look that seemed to say "You must admit that your friend is hardly polite."

"As to me," he continued in a loud voice, not without a certain effort, "I humbly admit that I do not much like the Germans. I mean true Germans and not German Russians; every one knows what they are good for. Yes, the Germans

of Germany do not suit me. A while ago one could endure
them ; they had well known men. . . . Schiller, Goethe, for
example. . . . My brother has a very particular esteem for
those writers. . . . But to-day I see among them no longer
anything but chemists and materialists."

" A good chemist is twenty times more useful than the
best poet," interrupted Bazarof.

" Indeed ? " replied Paul Petrovitch, raising his eyebrows
a little, as if wishing to wake himself up ; " Art then seems
to you utterly valueless ? "

" The art of gaining money, and of curing one's corns ! "
said Bazarof, with a smile of disdain.

" Wonderful ! You please to jest ! That is equivalent to a
complete negation. Well, well ! be it so. You then believe
in science only ? "

" I have already had the honor of telling you that I believe
in nothing. What do you mean by this word science, taken
in a general sense ? There are sciences as there are trades
and professions ; there is no science in the meaning you
give the word."

" That is all very well. And you deny equally all the
other principles on which our social order rests ? "

" Is this a political inquisition ? " asked Bazarof.

Paul Petrovitch grew a little pale. . . . Nicholas Petrovitch
thought it his duty to join in the conversation :

" We will chat about all that at length, at some other
time, my dear Eugene Vassilitch ; you will explain to us
all your opinions, and we will tell you ours. For my part I
am charmed to learn that you are studying the natural sciences. I have been told that Liebig has lately made some
astonishing discoveries concerning the cultivation of land.
You can come to my aid in my agricultural labors, and give
me excellent advice."

" With pleasure, Nicholas Petrovitch ; but let us leave

Liebig out of the question. Before opening a book, we must learn to read, and we do not yet know the *a b c.*"

"Well, you really are a nihilist," thought Nicholas Petrovitch. "However that may be," he replied, "allow me to have recourse to you at need. But is it not time, brother, to go talk to the overseer?"

Paul Petrovitch rose from his chair.

"Yes," he said, without addressing any one, "it is unfortunate to live in the country four or five years at a time, far from all great minds! One quickly becomes a real imbecile. You take great care not to forget all you have learned; but bah! you discover some fine day that these are follies, idle things that no rational man thinks of to-day, and that you are an old driveller. But what can you do? It seems that the youth of to-day are decidedly wiser than we old folks."

Paul Petrovitch turned slowly on his heel, and walked out with measured steps. His brother followed him.

"Is he always so forcible?" Bazarof coldly asked Arcadi, as soon as the door was shut on the two brothers.

"Look here, Eugene," said his friend to him, "you have been too severe with him; you have wounded him."

"Indeed? You are obliged, perhaps, to treat them gently, these provincial aristocrats. But all that is only self-esteem, habits of the former dandy, silliness! Why didn't he continue playing his part at St. Petersburg, since he felt himself called to it?... However, may the good God bless him! I have found a rather rare variety of the *Dytiscus marginatus*; you know it? I will show it to you."

"I had promised to tell you his history," began Arcadi.

"The history of the *Dytiscus?*"

"Don't joke, Eugene; the history of my uncle. You will see he is not the man you think. Instead of making fun of him you ought rather to pity him."

"Possibly! but why does this disturb you so?"

"One ought to be just, Eugene."

"I don't see the necessity."

"Well, listen to me. . . ."

Arcadi began to tell his friend the history of his uncle.
The reader will find it in the next chapter.

VII.

Paul Petrovitch Kirsanof had passed his early childhood at home, with his younger brother Nicholas ; afterwards he was placed in the corps of pages. Of remarkable beauty, conceited, somewhat scornful, and coquettishly
irascible, he could not fail to please. He had hardly received epaulets when he went into society. He was received everywhere with eagerness ; he took his ease, abused
his success, and committed a thousand follies ; but that did
did not hurt him. The women doted on him, the men
thought him a fool, and secretly envied him. He lived,
as we have already said, with his brother, whom he loved
very much, though he did not at all resemble him. Nicholas Petrovitch limped slightly ; he had a small, rather
pleasing, but sad face ; his eyes were small, black, and
mild ; his hair thin ; he was idle, but he liked to read,
and he hated fashionable society. Paul Petrovitch never
passed an evening at home ; he had made himself a well-
merited reputation for boldness and agility (he was the
first who made gymnastic exercises fashionable in his set),
and had not read altogether more than five or six books,—
French romances. Captain at twenty-eight, a brilliant
career was open to him, when all abruptly changed.

The Princess R—— is still remembered at St. Petersburg. She occasionally showed herself there at the time we

are speaking of. Her husband was a well-bred, but rather
stupid man, and they had no children. The princess went
suddenly on long journeys, returned suddenly to Russia,
and acted very strangely in everything. She was called
coquettish and fickle; she eagerly gave herself up to all the
pleasures of society, danced till she fainted from exhaus-
tion, jested and laughed with the young people whom she
received before dinner in the dusk of her saloon, and passed
nights praying and weeping, without being able to take an
instant of rest. She often remained till morning in her
room, wringing her hands with anguish, kneeling, bent, pale,
and cold, over the leaves of a psalter. Day came, and she
transformed herself again into an elegant woman, made
calls, laughed, talked and threw herself in the way of everything that could bring her the least distraction. She was
admirably made; her hair, of the color of gold and as heavy
as gold, fell in thick tresses below her knees; yet she was
not cited as a beauty; her eyes were the only good thing in
her face. Perhaps that is saying too much, for these eyes
were rather small and gray; but their lively and deep look,
careless to audacity, and dreamy to desolation, was as enigmatical as charming. Something extraordinary was reflected there, even when the most empty words came from her
mouth. Her toilette was always too "loud."

Paul Petrovitch met her at a ball, danced a mazurka with
her during which she did not make a single sensible remark,
and fell passionately in love with her. Accustomed to
rapid successes, this time, as always, he reached his objects
quickly enough; but the ease of this conquest did not chill
him. He attached himself on the contrary more and more
to this woman, who, even when she wholly gave herself
up, always seemed to have in her heart a mysterious fibre
that one vainly sought to understand. What did she hold in
reserve there? God knows! You would have said that she

2*

was under the rule of some supernatural powers that played
with her at their caprices, her mind of little extent not
being able to struggle against such adversaries. Her whole
life presented a succession of inexplicable actions ; she had
written to a man whom she hardly knew, the only letters
that could compromise her in the eyes of her husband, and,
when she loved, her love had a strange reflection of sadness ;
she no longer laughed or jested with him whom she had just
chosen ; she looked at him and listened to him with a sort
of astonishment.   Sometimes, and almost always unexpectedly, this astonishment became a mute terror, and her
face would then take a sad and wild expression ; she would
shut herself in her bed-room, and her maids putting their ears
to the door could hear her sob heavily. More than once in returning home, after having had a tender interview with her,
Paul Petrovitch felt in the depth of his heart the bitter
feeling that is given by a definite check.

" Have I not obtained all that I wanted ? " he asked
himself; yet his heart continued to pain him.   One day he
gave her a ring, containing a stone engraved with a sphynx.

" What is there on it ? " asked she : " a sphynx ? "

" Yes," he replied ; "and this sphynx is you."

" I ? " said she, turning slowly on him her indefinable look.
" Do you know that I am flattered by it ? " she added with a
forced smile, but without changing the expression of her look.

Paul Petrovitch suffered much while the Princess R——
loved him ; but, when she began to grow cold to him, and
that was not long in coming, he almost lost his mind.   He
was in despair, and felt consumed with jealousy ; he did not
leave her a moment of repose, and followed her everywhere.
Annoyed by his pursuit she went abroad.   Paul Petrovitch
gave in his resignation, in spite of the remonstrances of
his friends, in spite of the advice of his superiors, and followed the princess ; during nearly four years, that he

passed in travelling, he sometimes rejoined her, and sometimes quitted her with the intention of never seeing her
again; he blushed for his weakness and cursed her . . . but
did nothing. The image of this woman, this incomprehen-
sible image, almost senseless but truly magical, was too
deeply imprinted on his soul. They saw each other again at
Baden, their relations were reëstablished on the old footing;
she seemed more taken with him than ever, but that
lasted hardly a month; the flame which had just been re-
kindled was extinguished forever. Foreseeing an inevitable rupture, he wished at least to remain her friend, as if
friendship were possible with such a woman. She left
Baden secretly, and from that day she constantly avoided
Paul Petrovitch. He returned to Russia and tried to take
up his old mode of life, but vainly. He was constantly in
motion, and nowhere found repose; he still frequented
society and had preserved all the habits of a fashionable
man; he could even plume himself on two or three
new conquests; but he no longer expected anything
of himself, nor of others, and he attempted nothing.
He grew old quickly, he began to grow gray, he
took up the habit of passing his evenings at the club, where,
devoured by ennui, he mingled with a bitter indifference in
the conversation; that, as everybody knows, is a bad sign.
The idea of getting married naturally could not come into his
head. So with astonishing rapidity rolled on nearly ten
years of an idle existence. Time nowhere flies so fast as in
Russia; we are told, however, that it flies still faster in
prison. One evening when he was dining at the club Paul
Petrovitch learned that the Princess R—— had just died
at Paris in a state bordering on madness. He rose
from his chair, and walked a long while in the hall of
the club, stopping near the card table, where he stood
almost petrified; nevertheless he returned home at the

usual hour. Not long after he received a packet to his address, and found the ring he had given the Princess. She
had traced a cross on the sphynx, and had left the message for
Paul Petrovitch, that the cross was the key to the enigma.

The Princess died in the beginning of the year 1848, just
at the time when Nicholas Petrovitch, having lost his wife,
arrived at St. Petersburg. Paul Petrovitch had hardly seen
his brother since he had settled in the country. The marriage of Nicholas Petrovitch coincided with the first days
of his acquaintance with the Princess. On his return from
abroad he went to rejoin him, and proposed passing two or
three months with him, to enjoy his happiness ; but he left
him at the end of a week. His brother and he were too different from each other then. This dissimilarity had much
diminished in 1848 ; Nicholas Petrovitch had become a
widower, and Paul Petrovitch, who had just lost the object
of his recollections, tried not to think of them any more.
But Nicholas had still the satisfaction of having led a regular life ; his son was growing up under his eyes ; Paul, on
the contrary, a sad bachelor, was entering the twilight of
life, in that evil period of regrets that resemble hopes, and
of hopes that resemble regrets, when youth is already
passed and old age is not yet come. This time must have
appeared more painful to Paul Petrovitch than to any one
else ; having lost his past, he had lost all.

"I no longer ask you to come to Marino !" said Nicholas
Petrovitch to him one day, (he had given the name of Marino
to this country place, in memory of his wife) ; "you got tired
of it when Mary was alive ; it would be worse now."

"That was because I was then too vain and too preoccupied," replied Paul Petrovitch ; "I am calmer now, if not
wiser. So I would not hesitate to follow you and fix myself
near you forever, if you would permit me."

Instead of replying Nicholas Petrovitch embraced him.

More than a year rolled by, nevertheless, before Paul Petrovitch decided to carry out his resolution. But once fixed in the country he no longer quitted it, even during the winters that Nicholas Petrovitch spent at St. Petersburg with his son. He read much, especially English books; his whole manner of living was ordered in the English style; he seldom visited the landlords of the neighborhood, and hardly went out except to assist at the elections, when he was almost always silent, opening his mouth only to frighten by his liberal sallies and pleasantries the proprietors attached to the old *régime*, without drawing any nearer to the representatives of the new generation. He was generally accused of haughtiness; but he was respected on account of his aristocratic manners and his reputation for success with women; he was respected too because his dress was so careful, and because he always stayed in the finest chambers of the best hotels; because he usually lived well, and one day had even dined with Wellington at the table of Louis Philippe; because he never started on a journey without taking chamber utensils of silver and a travelling bath-tub; because he used particular perfumes very "*distingués*;" because he played whist to perfection and always lost; finally, he was also much respected on account of his perfect honor. The ladies of the district considered him as a melancholy person of great attractions; but he never showed them the slightest attention.

"Now you see, Eugene," said Arcadi, in finishing his tale, "that you have judged my uncle wrongly. I don't speak of the services that he has often done my father, in giving him all the money he could dispose of; you are doubtless ignorant that their lands are undivided; he is always ready to oblige any one, and always takes the side of the peasant, although he never goes near them without fortifying himself with a bottle of Cologne water."

" I should know that," replied Bazarof.   " Nerves ! "

" Perhaps ; but he has an excellent heart, and he does not lack mind ; he has often given me excellent advice, especially. . . . especially with reference to women."

" Ah ! ah ! he has got burned with *his* milk and blows on the water *of others* ! * That's an old story."

" In a word," continued Arcadi, "he is very unhappy, that is certain.   One would be really wrong to despise him."

" Who speaks of despising him ? " replied Bazarof.   " But I no less affirm that a man who, having staked his whole life on the card of a woman's love and having lost that card, is so overwhelmed by it as to be good for nothing, is not a man, an individual of the masculine species.   You tell me that he is unhappy, and I readily believe it ; but he has not yet exhaused all his folly.   I am persuaded that he thinks himself an accomplished man, because he reads *Galignani*, and occasionally spares a peasant a flogging."

" Don't forget the education he had, and the age in which he lived," Arcadi answered.

" His education ! " cried Bazarof, "every man ought to educate himself, as I have done. . . . As to the age, I don't see why we should depend on that.   On the contrary, the age ought to be dependent on us.   No, my friend, all that is nothing but feebleness and vanity !   And then, what are these mysterious relations that become established between a man and a woman ?   We know the true nature of these relations, we physiologists !   Study the structure of the eye, I should like to know where you will find the material of that enigmatical look you were talking about.   All that is nothing but romanticism, nonsense, artistic phrases.   Let us rather go examine my beetle."

* A Russian proverb says : He that has burned himself with hot milk blows on cold water.

The two friends went to Bazarof's room, where already reigned a medico-chirurgical smell, mixed with that of cheap tobacco.

VIII.

Paul Petrovitch did not stay long at the interview between his brother and the overseer; this latter, a tall, thin man, with a crafty eye, a soft and honeyed voice, replied to every observation of Nicholas Petrovitch with an "assuredly! without any doubt!" and was always trying to represent the peasants as drunkards and thieves. The new mode of management that had just been adopted did not yet work smoothly, but creaked like a badly greased wheel, or a piece of furniture made of damp wood by a village carpenter. That did not at all discourage Nicholas Petrovitch, but he sighed and often remained thoughtful; he understood that things would not go rightly without money, and he had no money. Arcadi had told the truth. Paul Petrovitch had come more than once to the help of his brother; more than once, seeing him racking his brain, to find a way of getting out of his embarrassment, he had slowly approached the window, and putting his hands in his pockets, stammered between his teeth: "*Mais je puis vous donner de l'argent,*" and he had in fact given it to him; but this time he himself had none to spare, and he had thought best to go away. Domestic discussions caused him an insurmountable disgust; besides it always seemed to him that Nicholas Petrovitch, with all his zeal and all his efforts, did not pursue the right course; though it would have been impossible for him to show what ought to be done. "My brother is not practical enough," he used to say to himself; "they deceive him."

Nicholas Petrovitch, on the contrary, had a very high idea

of the practical mind of Paul Petrovitch, and always asked his advice.

" I am a weak, irresolute man; I have passed my life away from the world," he would say : " while you who have long lived among men, you know them well; you have an eagle's vision."

Instead of replying, Paul Petrovitch would turn away; but he did not attempt to undeceive his brother.

Leaving Nicholas Petrovitch in his cabinet, he followed the corridor that traversed the house, and arriving at a little door, he stopped, appeared to hesitate a moment, pulled his moustache, and knocked gently.

" Who is there ? " said Fenitchka; " come in."

" It is I," replied Paul Petrovitch, and he opened the door.

Fenitchka jumped up from the chair on which she had been sitting, her child in her arms. She gave the child to a woman, who carried it off immediately, and hastily arranged her neckerchief.

" Excuse me; I have disturbed you," said Paul Petrovitch to her, without looking at her, " I simply wanted to ask you. . . . I believe they send to town to-day; . . . will you have some green tea bought for me."

" Green tea," repeated Fenitchka, " how much would you like ? "

" Half a pound will be enough. But you have made a change here, if I am not mistaken," added he, throwing around him a rapid look, that took in also the figure of Fenitchka; " I mean these curtains," he said, seeing that she did not understand him.

" Yes : Nicholas Petrovitch made us a present of them; but they have been up for a long time."

" It is a long time since I have been to see you. You are very comfortable now."

"Thanks to Nicholas Petrovitch," said Fenitchka in a low voice.

"You are better off here than in your old rooms at the end of the court?" asked Paul Petrovitch with politeness, but without losing any of his seriousness.

"Certainly ; much better."

"Who lives now in the rooms that you used to have in the wing?"

"The laundresses are there now."

"Oh !"

Paul Petrovitch was silent. "He is going to go," thought Fenitchka ; but he did not go, and she remained without moving, except a slight trembling of her fingers.

"Why did you send your baby away?" said Paul Petrovitch at last. "I like children ; show it to me."

Fenitchka blushed with confusion and pleasure. She was afraid of Paul Petrovitch ; he very seldom spoke to her.

"Duniasha !" she cried, "bring Mitia." (Fenitchka never said *thou* to the servants.) "But no, wait ; he ought to be dressed ..." and she started for the next room.

"There is no need of that," said Paul Petrovitch.

· "It won't take long," replied Fenitchka ; and she went out hurriedly.

When alone, Paul Petrovitch began to look attentively about him. The little room in which he found himself was very neat. You smelled there at once chamomile, balm, mint and odor of paint, for the floor had been lately painted. Along the walls were chairs with lyre-shaped backs ; they had been captured in Poland by the late general in his last campaign. At one end of the room was a bed with muslin curtains, by its side a trunk bound with iron and a rounded top. In the opposite corner a copper lamp burned before

a large and sombre image of St. Nicholas ; a little porcelain
egg fastened to a red ribbon passed over the aureole of the
image, hung on the saint's breast; on the window-shelf
were jars of sweetmeats, prepared the year before, and carefully covered ; Fenitchka had written in large characters on
the paper that covered them " Gooseberry."   Nicholas Petrovitch liked these sweetmeats better than any others.
From the ceiling, hung by a long string a cage, in which
was a greenfinch with a clipped tail ; the bird chirped and
hopped about incessantly, and swung the cage by jerks ;
hemp seeds kept falling on the floor with a slight noise.
On the wall, between the two windows, above a dressing-
table, hung several photographs of Nicholas Petrovitch, in
different attitudes ; they had been taken by a travelling artist.
On one side there was also a photograph of Fenitchka herself ; a face without eyes, and smiling with a constrained
air, stood out on a black background ; that was all that
could be distinguished in this last portrait.   General
Yermolof, * wrapped in a Circassian cloak, was looking
with a frown at the Caucasus mountains, dimly seen in the
horizon ; a little silk slipper, which hung on the same wall,
fell over his face.   ·

During nearly five minutes, a noise of steps and whisper-
ings was heard in the neighboring room.   Paul Petrovitch
took a well-used book from the dressing-table, an odd volume of Masalski's *Strelits*, and turned over some pages of
it.   The door opened and Fenitchka appeared holding Mitia
in her arms.   The child wore a little red shirt, edged round
the neck with braid ; his mother had washed his face and
combed his hair ; he breathed loudly, moved his body and
his arms about as healthy children do ; young as he was, the
elegance of his dress had an effect on him ; his swollen

---

* A general who commanded in the Caucasus, in the first year
of the reign of Nicholas. ·

features expressed satisfaction. Fenitchka had not forgotten her own toilette, and had put on a fresh collar; but she might well have remained as she was before.

Is there in truth anything in the world more charming than a young and pretty mother holding a child in her arms?

" What a big fellow!" said Paul Petrovitch, with a benevolent air, and he tickled the double chin of Mitia with the end of the pointed nail of his forefinger; the child looked at the greenfinch and began to laugh.

" It is your uncle," said Fenitchka, inclining her head toward him and shaking it lightly, while Duniasha furtively put a lighted fragrant pastille on the window, under which she placed a piece of copper.

" How many months old is he?" asked Paul Petrovitch.

" Six; he begins his seventh soon, on the eleventh of this month."

" Isn't it his eighth, Fedossia Nicolaïevna?" Duniasha asked, not without hesitation.

" No; his seventh; I am sure of it."

The child looked at the trunk, and began to laugh, and all at once seized with his hand the nose and lips of his mother.

" Little darling!" said Fenitchka, not taking her face out of reach of his fingers.

" He looks like my brother," said Paul Petrovitch.

" Whom should he look like, if not him?" thought Fenitchka.

" Yes," continued Paul, as if he had spoken to himself, " the likeness is incontestable."

He began to look at Fenitchka with an air of attention, almost with sadness.

" It is your uncle," she repeated, but this time in a voice that could hardly be heard.

" Why ! Paul ! I was looking for you," cried all at once the voice of Nicholas Petrovitch.

Paul Petrovitch turned round quietly, and his features contracted ; but the face of his brother expressed such happiness and gratefulness, that it was impossible not to reply by a smile.

" Your child is superb," he said, looking at his watch ; " I had come in here to speak about some tea. . . ."

Paul Petrovitch took again his usual indifferent air, and went out of the room.

" Did he come of himself ? " Nicholas Petrovitch asked Fenitchka.

" Yes ; he knocked and came in."

" And Arkasha ? has he been back to see you ? "

" No. Perhaps I had better go back to my old rooms, Nicholas Petrovitch ? "

" Why so ? "

" I believe that it would be better for some time."

" But . . . no," replied Nicholas Petrovitch to her, with some hesitation. " It is too late in any case. . . ." " Good morning, my pretty one," he continued, with a sudden animation ; and drawing near the child, he kissed it on its cheek ; then he bent over further and rested his lips on the hand with which Fenitchka held Mitia, and which, white as milk, was relieved by the red dress of the child.

" Nicholas Petrovitch ! what are you doing ? " she murmured, and cast down her eyes ; then she raised them little by little. . . . The expression of her eyes was charming when she looked at you from under her eyelids, smiling at the same time with a naïve and caressing air.

Nicholas Petrovitch had got acquainted with Fenitchka in this way. Three years before he was obliged to pass the night in a little provincial town, at some distance from his estate, and slept at an inn. The cleanness of the room that

was given him, and the whiteness of the sheets, caused him
an agreeable surprise. "The landlady must be a German,"
he thought, but he was mistaken. She was a Russian
woman, about fifty years old, dressed with care ; her face
was intelligent and pleasant, and her conversation grave.
He chatted with her while taking his tea, and she pleased
him very much. He had just got established in his new
house, and, no longer wishing to have serfs in his service,
he was seeking for free servants ; the hostess, on her part,
was complaining of the small number of travellers, and of
the hardness of the times ; he proposed to her to become
his housekeeper ; she consented. Her husband had died
long before, leaving her with an only daughter, Fenitchka.
Two or three weeks after the return of Nicholas Petrovitch,
Arina Savishna (that was the name of the new housekeeper)
arrived at Marino with her daughter, and installed herself
in the wing of the house. Chance had served Nicholas Petrovitch exactly according to his wishes. Arina put his
establishment on an excellent footing. Nobody troubled
themselves then about Fenitchka, who was already seven-
teen, and who was hardly ever seen ; she lived tranquilly,
like a mouse in her hole ; on Sundays only, Nicholas Petrovitch sometimes happened to notice, in a corner of the village church, the delicate profile of a young girl's white face.
More than a year passed thus.

One morning Arina came into the cabinet of Nicholas
Petrovitch, and, after having made a low curtsy, according
to her habit, asked him if he could not show her a way of
relieving her daughter, who had just got a spark from the
oven in her eye. Nicholas Petrovitch, like all proprietors
living on their estates, was a little of a doctor, and had even
bought himself a case of homœopathic remedies. He told
Arina to bring Fenitchka at once. Fenitchka, when she
knew that the master had sent for her, was very much fright-

ened ; notwithstanding, she followed her mother. Nicholas Petrovitch led her to a window, and took her head between his hands. Having carefully examined her red and inflamed eye, he directed her to bathe it in water, which he prepared himself; then he took a piece from his handkerchief, and showed how it ought to be applied. When he had finished, Fenitchka was going away. "Kiss the master's hand, you foolish girl," said Arina to her. Nicholas Petrovitch did not let her do that; and, quite confused himself, he kissed her on her forehead, while she had her head bent over. Fenitchka's eye was not long in curing; but the impression that she had produced on Nicholas Petrovitch was not so readily effaced. He seemed still to hold her fine and soft hair between his hands ; he was always thinking that he saw that white and pure face timidly raised in the air, and her half-open lips showing teeth that shone in the sun like little pearls. From that moment he began to look at her more attentively in church, on Sundays, and tried to speak to her. She answered his advances at first with wildness, and once meeting him in the early evening in a narrow path that crossed a rye-field, to avoid him, she threw herself into the midst of the tall rye, mixed with poppies and wormwood. He perceived her head through the net of golden ears, from behind which she was observing him like a little fawn, and cried to her with an air of good humor :

"Good day, Fenitchka ! I don't bite."

"Good day," she murmured, without quitting her shelter.

Notwithstanding, she was beginning by degrees to get used to him, when her mother suddenly died of the cholera. What was going to become of her ? She had already the spirit of order and the good sense that distinguished her mother ; but she was alone, and Nicholas Petrovitch appeared so good and so delicate. . . . It is useless to relate what followed.

" You say, then, that my brother came in like that, without ceremony," said Nicholas Petrovitch ; "he knocked and came in ? "

" Yes."

" Well, that is good. Let me take Mitia a little while."

And Nicholas Petrovitch began to toss his son up almost to the ceiling, to the great joy of the baby and to the great inquietude of its mother, who, every time that she saw it go up, held her arms out towards its little naked feet. As to Paul Petrovitch, he had regained his elegant cabinet, the walls covered with handsome paper, with a trophy of arms, arranged on a Persian rug, with walnut furniture, covered with a bright green stuff, a *renaissance* book-case of old oak, bronze statuettes on a magnificent writing table, and a marble chimney piece. He threw himself down on the sofa, put his hands under his head and remained motionless, looking at the ceiling with an air almost of despair. Whether to hide in obscurity the expression that could be read on his face, or from some other motive, he rose almost immediately, let down the heavy curtains that hung at the windows, and threw himself down again on the sofa . . .

IX.

The same day Bazarof also made the acquaintance of Fenitchka. He was walking in the garden with Arcadi, and was explaining to him why certain trees, especially certain young oaks, had not taken root.

" You ought to plant here more poplars and savins, even lindens, if you wish, provided you bring earth for them. Here is a clump that has started well," he added, "because the acacias and lilacs are good fellows ; they don't need care. Holloa ! there is some one there."

It was Fenitchka who was there with Duniasha and Mitia. Bazarof stopped, and Arcadi nodded to Fenitchka as to an old acquaintance.

"Who is that?" asked Bazarof when they were a little away; "she is very pretty."

"Which do you mean?"

"*Which* is evident; there is only one who is pretty."

Arcadi explained in a few words, and without embarrassment, who Fenitchka was.

"Bah!" replied Bazarof, "your father seems to like nice girls. Do you know, I like your father. Really he is a good fellow! But we must get acquainted," he added; and he started again towards the clump.

"Eugene!" cried Arcadi frightened; "be prudent, for God's sake!"

"Don't be alarmed," replied Bazarof, "I have lived in cities. I know the world"; and, being near Fenitchka, he took off his cap.

"Allow me to present myself," said he, saluting her politely; "I am a friend of Arcadi Nikolaïtch, and a peaceable man."

Fenitchka rose and looked at him without replying.

"What a handsome child!" continued Bazarof. "Don't be uneasy. I have never brought ill-luck to any one.* Why are his cheeks so red? Is he toothing?"

"Yes," said Fenitchka, "he has four already, and his gums are swelling again."

"Show me, and don't be afraid; I am a doctor."

Bazarof took the child in his arms, who, to the great astonishment of Fenitchka and Duniasha, did not resist at all, and did not seem frightened.

"Really! I see . . . that will be nothing; he will have a

---

* It is a Russian superstition that praises bring ill-luck.

famous set of teeth. If anything happens to him call me. And you, are you well?"

"Yes, indeed, thanks to God."

"It is always well to thank God; health is the best of good things. And you?" added Bazarof, addressing Duniasha.

Duniasha, a girl very reserved in the house, and very silly out of doors, burst into laughter instead of replying.

"Good, that is well. Stop! I will give you back your big boy."

Fenitchka took the child again in her arms.

"How quiet he has been with you," she said, in a low voice.

"All children are when I hold them," replied Bazarof, "I have a secret for that."

"Children feel who love them," said Duniasha.

"That is true," added Fenitchka. "Mitia will not let everybody hold him."

"Would he come to me?" asked Arcadi, who had kept at a distance, as he came up to the group.

He offered to take Mitia, but Mitia threw back his head and began to cry, to Fenitchka's great confusion.

"He will come to me some other time, when he is used to me," said Arcadi pleasantly, and the two friends went away.

"What did you tell me her name was?" asked Bazarof.

"Fenitchka,—Fedossia," replied Arcadi.

"And her paternal name? It is always well to know that."

"Nikolaïevna."

"*Bené*, what pleases me in her is that she does not appear too much embarrassed. Some people, you know, would think that wrong. That is absurd. Why should she be embarrassed? She is a mother, then she is right."

"Doubtless," replied Arcadi, "but my father?"

3

"He is right, too."

"That is not my opinion."

"You don't like a divided inheritance."

"Are you not ashamed to suppose such a thought of me!" cried Arcadi with fire. "I don't place myself in that point of view at all to blame my father; I think he ought to have married her."

"Ho! ho!" said Bazarof, in a calm tone; "what magnanimity! You still give then some meaning to marriage; I did not believe that of you."

The two friends walked some steps without speaking.

"I have gone over your estate with some attention," resumed Bazarof. "The stock is in a bad state, and the horses not much better. I could say as much of the building; and the day laborers seem to me idlers. As to your overseer, he is an idiot or a rascal; I have yet no decided opinion with regard to him."

"You are very severe to-day, Eugene Vasilitch."

"And your fine peasants will twist your father round their fingers, I am sure of it. You know the saying: 'The Russian peasant would skin God.'"

"I begin to believe my uncle is right," said Arcadi to him. "You have decidedly a bad opinion of the Russians."

"What consequence? The only merit of the Russian is that he has a very poor opinion of himself; besides, that matters very little. What is of importance is that two and two make four; all the rest is of no account."

"What! nature herself of no account?" replied Arcadi, casting a dreamy smile over the variegated fields that the rays of the setting sun illuminated with a soft light.

"Nature also is of no account, in the sense that you give it now. Nature is not a temple, but a workshop, and man is a workman there."

At this moment the slow modulations of a violoncello struck

their ears as they approached; these sounds came from the house. The musician played with feeling, though with an unpractised hand, *Die Erwartung* of Schubert, and this sweet melody spread like the smell of honey in the air.

" Who is that ? " said Bazarof, with a surprised air.

" That is my father."

" Your father plays on the violoncello ? "

" Yes."

" But how old is he, then ? "

" Forty-four."

Bazarof burst out laughing.

" Why do you laugh ? "

" What ! a man forty-four years old, a *pater familias* in the district of X——, plays on the violoncello ? "

Bazarof began to laugh heartily ; but Arcadi, in spite of the respect he had for his teacher, did not feel the least wish of imitating him this time.

X.

About two weeks passed thus. Life at Marino flowed on with uniformity ; Arcadi played the sybarite, and Bazarof worked. All in the house had become used to him, to his want of ceremony, to his short and abrupt speeches. Fenitchka, especially, had got so familiar with him, that one night she had him waked up ; Mitia had been taken with convulsions. Bazarof came ; stayed nearly two hours, sometimes laughing, sometimes yawning, and relieved the child. But, on the other hand, Paul Petrovitch began to detest Bazarof, with all his soul ; he considered him insolent, shameless, cynical, a true plebeian ; he suspected that Bazarof had little esteem for him,—for him, Paul Petrovitch Kirsanoff,—and perhaps even went so far as to despise him. Nicholas Petro-

vitch feared the young "nihilist" a little, and doubted
, whether he exercised a happy influence over Arcadi; but
he listened to him with pleasure, and willingly assisted at
his physical and chemical experiments. Bazarof had brought
with him a microscope, and passed entire hours with his
eye at that instrument. The servants had also become used
to Bazarof, though he treated them cavalierly; they saw in
him rather a man of their own class than a master. Duniasha liked to giggle with him, and threw him sly meaning
looks, when she tripped before him like a little quail; Peter,
a man swollen up with his own importance, with a face perpetually careworn, whose merits were that he had a polite
attitude, knew how to spell, and often brushed his coat—
unbent and even smiled as soon as Bazarof showed him the
slightest attention; the little domestics followed the "doctor" like young dogs. The old Prokofitch was the only one
who did not like him; he waited on him at table with a
sulky air, called him a "butcher," a "go-bare-foot," and
said that with his long moustache Bazarof looked like a
pig in a bush. Prokofitch was not less aristocratic in his
way than Paul Petrovitch himself.

It was at the beginning of June, the finest season of the
year. The weather was magnificent; it is true the cholera
was approaching, but the inhabitants of the government of
X—— no longer feared it much. Bazarof used to rise early
and ramble two or three miles from the house, not to walk,
(he could not endure walking for pleasure,) but to collect
plants and insects. Arcadi sometimes accompanied him;
on returning the two friends often disputed, and Arcadi was
ordinarily beaten, though he talked much more than his
companion. One day, when they were late in coming back,
Nicholas Petrovitch went to meet them in the garden; when
he got near the arbor he heard the hasty steps and the
voices of both the young men. They passed on the other
side of the arbor and did not see him.

"You do not know my father," said Arcadi.

Nicholas Petrovitch remained motionless.

"Your father is a good fellow," replied Bazarof; "but he is only good now to be put on the retired list; he has gone out of active service; he has sung his song."

Nicholas Petrovitch listened. . . . Arcadi was silent. The man thus *retired* stayed yet a few moments in his concealment; then he cautiously came out and regained the house.

"The other day I noticed that he was reading Pushkin," pursued Bazarof. "Make him understand, I beg you, how absurd that is. He is no longer a calf, and ought to throw to the dogs all that nonsense. Who in our days is interested in romanticism, in poetry? Give him some good book to read."

"What can I give him?" asked Arcadi.

"You could commence, I think, with Buchner's *Stoff und Kraft*,* for example."

"I was thinking of that," replied Arcadi; "*Stoff und Kraft* is written in popular language."

"Well, we are judged," said Nicholas Petrovitch the same evening to his brother in his cabinet, whom he had just come to find; "we are only good now to be put on the retired list, we have sung our songs. After all, Bazarof is perhaps right. What chagrins me in all this is that I was hoping to come nearer to Arcadi, and be on friendly terms with him, and now I find myself behind him; he has got ahead of me, and we can no longer understand each other."

"How has he got ahead of you? and what is it that distinguishes him so much from the rest of us?" cried Paul Petrovitch, impatiently; "it is this fellow, this nihilist that has stuffed all that in his head! I cannot suffer this saw-

* A work intended to popularize the principles of the modern German materialist school.

bones ; in my opinion he is a true charlatan. I am sure that, notwithstanding all his frogs, his knowledge does not go far, even in physics."

"No, brother, do not say that," replied Nicholas Petrovitch, "Bazarof is intelligent and learned." "And what self-esteem ! It is truly revolting !" continued Paul Petrovitch.

"He does not lack self-esteem, I admit," replied his brother ; "It is inevitable, to all appearances. But here is a thing that goes beyond me. I do all I can to keep along with the age ; I have given my peasants a position, and have established a farm on my lands, which has made me be called a *red* in the whole government. I read, I study, and make every effort to be on a level with the wants of the country, and they say that my song is sung. After all, it is very possible they are right."

"How so?"

"Listen ; to-day I was sitting reading Pushkin ; I had just commenced *the Gypsies* . . . when all at once Arcadi came up to me silently, with a sort of caressing compassion ; he gently took away my book, as he would have done from a child, gave me instead another, a German book, . . . then he smiled and went away, carrying off Pushkin."

"Indeed ! and what book did he leave you ?"

"Here it is."

Nicholas Petrovitch drew out of the tail pocket of his coat the ninth edition of Buchner's famous brochure.

Paul Petrovitch turned over some pages of it.

"Hush !" he exclaimed, "Arcadi is busy with your education ; have you tried to read this ?"

"I have tried."

"Well ?"

"I must either be very stupid or the author has not common sense. But doubtless I am stupid."

"You have not forgotten your German?" asked Paul
Petrovitch.

"I remember my German."

Paul Petrovitch turned the book in his hands, looking at
his brother with a side glance. They were both silent for
some minutes.

"Apropos," said Nicholas Petrovitch, who wished to
change the conversation, "I have received a letter from
Koliazin."

"From Matvei Ilitch?"

"Yes. He has come to X——, to make the inspection
of the government. He is now quite a personage; he tells
me that as a relation he is very desirous of seeing us, and
invites me to come to town with you and Arcadi."

"Shall you go?" asked Paul Petrovitch.

"No; and you?"

"Not I. I do not see the necessity of dragging myself
fifty versts for his favor. *Mathieu* wants to show himself
to us in all his glory; the devil take him! He ought to content himself with administrative incense. He is now a
privy counsellor; very important! If I had continued in
the service, wearing the collar of misery, I should now be
general aid-de-camp; besides, we are on the retired list."

"Yes, brother. It is time, to all appearances, to order
our coffins and cross our hands over our breasts," said
Nicholas Petrovitch with a sigh.

"As to me, I shall not give up so easily," replied Paul
Petrovitch; "I shall have yet one battle with this fine doctor; you can count on that."

The battle took place that very evening, while they were
taking tea. Paul had come down into the parlor already
much irritated and ready for the combat. He waited only
for a pretext to throw himself on the enemy; but he had to
wait some time. Bazarof habitually spoke little in presence

of the "two old fellows," as he called the two brothers;
besides, he felt unwell this evening, and swallowed one cup
of tea after another in the most complete silence. Paul
Petrovitch was beside himself with impatience; notwithstanding he found at last the opportunity he was looking for.

Some conversation arose about a proprietor of the neighborhood. "Trash, a vile aristocrat," quietly said Bazarof,
who had known him at St. Petersburg.

"Allow me to ask you," said Paul Petrovitch, with a
trembling motion of his lips, "if the words *trash* and *aristocrat* are, in your opinion, synonymous?"

I said "*vile aristocrat*," replied Bazarof, negligently sip-
ping his tea.

"That is true; but I suppose you put aristocrats and
vile aristocrats on the same footing. I think I ought to
give you to understand that such is not my opinion. I dare
say I am generally regarded as a liberal man and a lover of
progress, but that is precisely the reason why I esteem
aristocrats, true aristocrats. Recall, my dear sir (at these
words Bazarof looked up at Paul Petrovitch), recall, my
dear sir," he repeated with dignity, "the English aristocrats. They do not yield an iota of their rights, and do not
less respect the rights of others; they exact what is due
them, and never fail themselves in their duties. The aristocracy has given liberty to England, and is its firmest
support."

"That is an old song that we have often heard," replied
Bazarof; "but what do you intend to prove by that?"

"I intend to prove by that,* my dear sir—(Paul Petrovitch,
when he became angry, used certain familiar phrases, though
he knew very well they were improper. This habit goes
back to the reign of the Emperor Alexander. The great

* In the original *eftim* instead of *etim*.

lords of the time, when they happened to speak their native language, affected a vicious pronunciation, to let it be understood, that in their quality of great lords they were allowed to disdain the rules of grammar imposed on scholars. For *eto* some would say *efto*, others *ekto*)—I intend to prove by that, that without the consciousness of personal dignity, without self-respect, and these feelings are familiar to the aristocracy, there could not exist solid foundations for the ... *bien public* ... for the public edifice. The individual, the personality, my dear sir, that is the essential part; the human personality ought to be as resisting as a rock, for all rests on this basis. I know very well that you find my manners, my dress, even my habits of neatness, ridiculous; but all that comes from self-respect, from the feeling of duty, yes, yes, sir, of duty. I live in the interior of the country, but I don't abandon myself for that; I respect man in my own person."

"I beg your pardon, Paul Petrovitch," replied Bazarof; "you say that you respect yourself, and you remain seated with folded arms; what advantage does that procure for the *bien public*? Supposing that you did not respect yourself, what would you do different?"

Paul Petrovitch grew pale.

"That is quite another question," he replied; "I do not care to explain to you now why I remain with folded arms, as you are pleased to say. I should like to confine myself to recalling to you that aristocracy reposes on a principle, and that immoral or worthless men are the only ones that can live in our day without principles. I said it to Arcadi, the day after his arrival, and I only repeat it to you to-day. Is it not true, Nicholas?"

Nicholas Petrovitch nodded assent.

"Aristocracy, liberalism, principles, progress," repeated Bazarof, meanwhile. "What strange words in our lan-
3*

guage, and perfectly useless ! A true Russian has no use for them."

" What does he need then, according to you ? To understand you, we are outside of humanity, outside of its laws. That is too much ; the logic of history exacts. . . ."

" What need have we of that kind of logic ? We can get on very well without it."

" How ? "

" Ah ! Look here. I think that you do very well without logic in putting a piece of bread in your mouth when you are hungry. What is the good of all these abstractions ? "

Paul Petrovitch raised his hands.

" I do not understand you at all ! You insult the Russian people. I don't understand that one can help recognizing principles and rules ! What then directs you in life ? "

" I have already told you, uncle, that we do not recognize any authority," interrupted Arcadi.

" We act in view of what we recognize as useful," added Bazarof ; " to-day it seems to us useful to deny and we deny."

" Everything ? "

" Everything."

" How ! not only art, poetry, but even . . . I hesitate to say it. . . ."

" Everything," repeated Bazarof, with an inexpressible calmness.

Paul Petrovitch looked at him fixedly ; he did not expect such a reply ; Arcadi blushed with pleasure.

" Allow me, allow me," interrupted Nicholas Petrovitch ; " you deny everything, or to speak more exactly, you destroy everything. . . . Notwithstanding, it is also necessary to rebuild. . . ."

" That does not concern us. . . . It is necessary in the first place to clear off the ground."

"The actual condition of the people exacts it," added Arcadi, with a grave air; "we ought to fulfil this duty; we have no right to give ourselves up to the satisfactions of personal selfishness."

This last phrase displeased Bazarof; it savored of philosophy, that is romanticism, for he gave that name also to philosophy; but he did not deem it expedient to contradict his young pupil.

"No, no," cried Paul Petrovitch, in a sudden outburst. "I do not wish to believe that you, gentlemen, have a just opinion of the Russian people; that you express what it demands, its secret wishes! No, the Russian people is not such as you represent it. It has a holy respect for tradition; it is patriarchal; it cannot live without faith. . . ."

"I shall not try to contradict you," replied Bazarof. "I am even ready to admit that you are right this time."

"But if I am right. . . ."

"That proves absolutely nothing."

"Absolutely nothing," repeated Arcadi, with the assurance of an experienced chess player, who having foreseen a move that his adversary believes dangerous, does not appear at all disconcerted.

"How does that prove nothing?" said Paul Petrovitch, with stupefaction. "You separate yourself then from your people?"

"But do not you also? The people believe that when it thunders, the prophet Elijah is driving his chariot through heaven. Well, shall I share its opinion in that respect? You believe that you will confound me by saying that the people is Russian; and I, am I not Russian, too?"

"No; after all that you have just said, you are not Russian! I can no longer recognize you as such."

"My grandfather drove a cart," replied Bazarof, with a superb pride; "ask the first one of your peasants which of

us two, you or me, he would most gladly recognize as his
fellow citizen.   You do not even know how to talk with
him."

"And you, who know, talk with him and despise him at
the same time."

"Why not, if he deserves it? You blame the direction
of my ideas; but who tells you that it is accidental, that it
is not determined by the general spirit of this people that
you defend so well?"

"Come now! Nihilists are very useful indeed!

"Whether they are or not is not for us to decide.   Do
not you suppose yourself also good for something?"

"Gentlemen, gentlemen, no personalities, I beg of you,"
. said Nicholas Petrovitch, rising.

Paul Petrovitch smiled, and laying his hand on his
brother's shoulder, compelled him to sit down.

"Be quiet," he said, "I shall not forget myself, precisely
by reason of that feeling of dignity that our friend . . . the
doctor, quizzes.   Allow me," he continued, addressing Bazarof again; "you believe, perhaps, that your way of seeing
is new? that is your error.   The materialism that you pro-
fess has already been in honor more than once, and has
always shown itself inadequate. . . ."

"Still a foreign word," replied Bazarof.   He began to be
vexed, and his face had taken a coppery tinge, very unpleasant to see.   "Besides, I will tell you that we do not
preach; that is not one of our habits . . ."

"What do you do then?"

"I am going to tell you.   We have begun by calling
attention to the bribery of office holders, to the want of
roads, to the absence of trade, to the manner in which justice is administered."

"Yes, yes, you are denouncers, convictors*; that is the

* This term was used to designate the literary movement of the

name that has been given you, if I am not mistaken. I agree with you in a great number of your criticisms; but . . ."

"Then, we have not delayed to recognize the fact that it was not enough to talk about the sore spots that annoyed us, that that resulted only in platitudes and doctrinarism; we perceived that our advanced men, our *convictors*, were worth absolutely nothing; that we were busy with foolishness, such as art for art's sake, the creative power that is ignorant of itself, parliamentarism, the need of lawyers, and a thousand other trifles, while it was necessary to think of our daily bread, while the most gross superstition was smothering us, while all our coöperative societies were becoming bankrupt, and that only because there was a dearth of honest people, while the very liberty of the serfs, that the government is so busy with, will perhaps do no good, because our peasant is ready to steal from himself to go and drink poisoned drugs in the taverns."

"Well," replied Paul Petrovitch, "very well. You have discovered all that and you are not less decided not to undertake anything seriously."

"Yes, we have decided not to undertake anything seriously," repeated Bazarof in a brusque tone.

He reproached himself all at once for having said so much on that subject before this gentleman.

"And you confine yourself to insult?"

"We insult at need."

"And this is what is called nihilism?"

"This is what is called nihilism," repeated Bazarof, but this time in a tone peculiarly provoking.

Paul Petrovitch winced a little.

"Very well!" he said with a forced calm that was rather

first years of the reign of Alexander II., to which allusion is made in this passage.

strange. "Nihilism ought to remedy everything, and you
are our saviours and our heroes. Wonderful! But why
do you insult so much the rest,—those that you call talkers?
Don't you talk like them?"

"Well, come now! If we have anything to reproach
ourselves with, it is not that," responded Bazarof between
his teeth.

"How! Do you maintain that you act, or only prepare
for action?"

Bazarof remained silent. Paul Petrovitch trembled, but
he calmed himself almost instantly.

"Hum! . . . act, destroy," he said; "but how can one
destroy without even knowing why he destroys?"

"We destroy because we are a force," said Arcadi
gravely.

Paul Petrovitch raised his eyes to his nephew's face and
smiled.

"Yes, force has no account to render," added Arcadi
straightening himself up.

"Unhappy boy!" cried Paul Petrovitch, unable to contain himself longer. "If you would only render account
of what you support in Russia with your ridiculous opinions! That is really too much; one would have to have
the patience of an angel to endure all that! Force! the
savage Kalmuk and the Mongol have force; but in what
can they help us? What ought to be precious to us is civilization; yes, yes, my dear sirs, the fruits of civilization.
And do not tell me that these fruits are insignificant; the
most wretched sign-dauber, *un barbouilleur*, the miserable
player of polkas and waltzes that earns five kopecks an
evening, are more useful than you; because they are representatives of civilization, and not of the brute force of
the Mongols! You believe yourselves advanced men, and

your place would be in a Kalmuk's kibitka*! Force! Remember, forcible sirs, that you are perhaps a dozen in all, while the rest are counted by millions, and will not permit you to tread under foot their most holy beliefs; they will crush you!"

"If they crush us, the road is theirs," replied Bazarof; "but you are far out of the way in your calculation. We are not so few as you suppose."

"How! You seriously believe that you can bring the entire people to reason?"

"A penny candle, you know, was enough to burn the whole city of Moscow,†" answered Bazarof.

"That is it, that is it; first an almost satanic pride; then irony in very bad taste. This is what allures the youth; this is what seduces the inexperienced hearts of these boys! Stop, here is one who holds to your side; he is almost in ecstacy before you! (Arcadi turned away and frowned.) And this contagion has already extended far and wide. I am assured that at Rome our painters no longer set foot in the Vatican; they treat Raffaelle as an idiot, because he is an authority, as they say, and those who express themselves thus are powerlessness personified; their imagination does not get beyond the 'young girl at the fountain'‡; they may do as they please, their efforts do not get beyond that! and take notice that this picture even is detestable. Yet you have these fellows in high esteem, do you not?"

"As to me," replied Bazarof, "I would not give two kopecks for Raffaelle, and I don't think them worth any more than him."

"Bravo! bravo! do you hear, Arcadi... That is the way our young contemporaries ought to express themselves!

---

* A four-wheeled cart. † Russian proverb.
‡ The majority of young Russian painters who go to Rome at the government expense choose this subject for their first picture.

Oh ! I understand very well that they press on your steps !
Once they felt the need of learning; not caring to pass for
ignorant people, they were forced to work; now they can
content themselves with saying, ' All is only nonsense and
folly in this world,' and the trick is played. They have
indeed reason to rejoice; formerly they were only block-
heads, but now they are transformed into nihilists."

" It seems to me that you forget the feeling of personal
dignity that you make so much of—" Bazarof phlegmatically
replied, while indignation colored the brow and animated the
eyes of Arcadi.

" Our discussion has carried us much too far, and I believe that we should do well to stop here. I shall agree
with you," he added rising, " when you have pointed out to
me in our society a single institution, not more, that does
not deserve to be completely and perfectly abolished."

" I could cite you a million," cried Paul Petrovitch, "a
million ! Hold, the community * for example."

A cold smile contracted the lips of Bazarof.

" As to the community," he replied, "you would much
better speak to your brother about it. I suppose he ought
to know what is the truth about the community, and the
strict mutual protection societies of the peasantry, their
temperance † and many other pleasantries of that kind."

" And the family ! the family, such as we find it among
our peasants," said Paul Petrovitch.

" There is also a question that " you would do well in my
opinion not to sound. Follow my advice, Paul Petrovitch,
give yourself two or three days of reflection; you will not
find anything on the spot. Pass in review all our classes

* The Russian "community" has still the indivisibility of
property as its basis.
† Six or seven years ago temperance societies were started
among the peasants but they were soon given up.

one after the other, and reflect well on them; during this time, Arcadi and I will ..."

" Turn all to ridicule," answered Paul Petrovitch.

" No, we will busy ourselves with dissecting frogs. Come ! Arcadi. Good night, gentlemen."

The two friends went out. Paul Petrovitch and his brother remained alone and confined themselves, during some minutes, to exchanging looks in silence.

" Well then," said Paul Petrovitch at last, " where is our youth gone ! Heavens—our successors ! "

" Our successors ! " repeated Nicholas Petrovitch with a deep sigh. He had remained all the time of the discussion as if on burning coals, and was contented with throwing from time to time a melancholy glance on Arcadi. " Do you know, brother, what recollection this brings back to me ? One evening I was disputing with my mother; she cried out and would not listen to me ... I ended by saying to her : ' You cannot understand me, we belong to two different generations.' These words wounded her deeply; but I said to myself; ' what would I do ? The pill is bitter; but it must be swallowed.' In our turn now our successors can say to us also : ' You are not of our generation, swallow the pill.' "

" You are too modest and kind-hearted," answered Paul Petrovitch ; " I am persuaded on the contrary that we are much more in the right than all these little gentlemen, though our tongue has perhaps grown old, a little *vieilli*, and we have not their arrogance ..... Besides that they are so affected ! If you ask them at table : ' Will you have white or red wine ? ' they reply to you : ' I have the constant habit of preferring the red,' and that in a loud voice and with an air so ridiculously important ! You would say that they posture before the whole universe."

" You do not wish any more tea ? " said Fenitchka, half-opening the door; she had feared to enter the parlor during the discussion.

"No, you can have the samovar taken away," answered Nicholas Petrovitch, and he rose to go before her. Paul Petrovitch abruptly said *bon soir* and went to his cabinet.

XI.

Half an hour after, Nicholas Petrovitch went into the garden, and turned to his favorite grove. Sad thoughts possessed his mind. For the first time he had measured the distance that separated him from his son; he felt that it would increase every day. It was then useless that for two winters at St. Petersburg he had passed whole nights reading new works; useless that he had lent an attentive ear to the talk of the young people; the eagerness with which he had mingled in their animated discussions had been in vain. "My brother maintains that we are right," he thought, "and putting all egotism aside, it seems to me myself that they are further from the truth than we ... and yet I feel that they have something we lack, a sort of superiority over us .. Is it youth? No, it is not youth alone. Does not this superiority consist in the fact that they have less than we the impress of lordly habits?"

Nicholas Petrovitch bent down his head, and passed his hand over his face.

"But to disdain poetry?" said he soon after; "not to sympathize with art, with nature? ...."

He looked about him, as if he had sought to understand how it was possible not to love nature ... The day was rapidly declining; the sun was hid behind a little aspen wood situated half a verst from the garden, and was casting an endless shadow on the moveless fields. A peasant mounted on a white horse trotted along a narrow path which skirted the wood; although he was in the shadow, his

whole person was distinctly seen, and a patch on his
shoulder was even noticeable; the horse's feet moved with
a regularity and a cleanness that was pleasing to the eye.
The rays of the sun penetrated into the wood, and, travers-
ing the thicket, colored the trunks of the aspens with a
warm tint which gave them the appearance of savin trunks,
while their almost blue foliage was surrounded by a pale
sky, slightly reddened by the evening twilight. The swal-
lows were flying very high; the wind had entirely ceased;
belated bees were feebly buzzing in the lilac flowers; a
swarm of gnats danced above an isolated branch that stood
out into the air. "How beautiful it is, my God!" thought
Nicholas Petrovitch; and verses that he loved to repeat
almost escaped from his lips, when he remembered Arcadi,
Stoff und Kraft, and he was silent; but he remained seated,
and continued to abandon himself to the mild and sad
pleasure of solitary revery. His sojourn in the country had
given him the taste for it; it was not long ago that he had
dreamed as to-day, while waiting for his son in the inn
court, and what a great change had worked already since
then! His relations with Arcadi, then still uncertain, had
been determined ... and how? His wife, whom he had
lost, presented herself to his mind, not such as he had
known her in the last years of her life,—not as a good housekeeper with a serene and affable air,—but under the form of
a young girl of a slim figure, with an innocent and inquiring
look, her hair rolled in great tresses over a childlike neck—
such in a word, as he had seen her for the first time, while
he was attending the University. Having met her on the
staircase of the house that he was living in then, he involuntarily jostled her, turned to make excuses, and in his confusion said to her: "Pardon, sir!" She looked down,
smiled, and began to run as if she was suddenly frightened;
then at the turn of the staircase, she threw a rapid glance

at him, then took a serious air and blushed. Then the first visit, reserved and discreet, the half words, the half smiles, the moments of doubt, of sadness, then the transports of passion, and finally the intoxication of happiness . . . what had become of all that? Once married he had been as happy as possible . . . "but nothing equals these first and sweet moments of felicity," he said to himself; "and why is it not permitted for them to endure always and not become extinct with life ! "

He did not try to clear up his thoughts; but he would have been glad to retain, to arrest that happy time by some means more powerful than memory; he would have been glad to find himself once more near his good Mary, feel the warmth of her cheek and her breath, and it seemed to him already that over his head . . .

"Nicholas Petrovitch ? " said Fenitchka very near the bushes, "where are you ? "

He started. Not that he felt a feeling of shame or of reproach . . . The idea had never occurred to him of making the least comparison between his wife and Fenitchka; but he regretted that she came to surprise him at that moment. Her voice recalled to him in an instant his gray hair, his early old age, his present state . . . The fairy world to the bosom of which he had been transported, this world that already stood out from the confused mist of the past, became troubled and disappeared.

"I am here," he answered; "I am going to come; go on." "Well," he said to himself almost immediately, "here are the lordly habits I was speaking of just now."

Fenitchka looked silently into the bushes and went away. He perceived then only, to his great astonishment, that night had surprised him in his reveries. All was sombre and quiet around him, and the form of Fenitchka had appeared to him so pale and so frail, during the few seconds that she had shown herself under the arbor. He rose to return; but his agitated heart had not yet had time to become quiet, and he began to walk slowly in the garden, sometimes looking down, sometimes looking up to the sky, which sparkled already with twinkling stars. He walked a long time, till he was nearly tired; and, in spite of his inner trouble, the secret inquietude that agitated him could not be dissipated. Oh! how Bazarof would have ridiculed him if he had known his state! Arcadi himself would have blamed him. His eyes were wet with tears, tears that ran without motive; for a man forty years old, a land-owner and an agriculturist, this was a hundred times worse than to play on the violoncello. Nicholas Petrovitch continued to walk, and could not decide to return to his peaceable house, to this house that recalled him so affectionately by its lighted windows; he did not feel the courage to leave the garden and darkness, to give up the feeling of the fresh air on his face, this sadness, this agitation. . . . He met Paul Petrovitch at a turn of a path. "What is the matter with you?" he asked him, "you look as pale as a ghost; are you going to be sick? You would better go to bed."

Nicholas Petrovitch explained what he felt in a few words, and went in. Paul Petrovitch went on to the end of the garden; he also began to meditate and raised also his eyes to heaven. . But his beautiful black eyes reflected only the light of the stars. He was not romantic, and reverie did not suit his passionate nature; he was prosaic, although accessible to tender impressions; he was a misanthrope of the French school.

"Do you know?" said Bazarof to his friend the same evening, "a magnificent idea has come into my head. Your father told us to-day that he had received an invitation from that grand personage, your relation. He will not go; what if we should take a turn at X——? You are comprised in this gentleman's invitation. You see how the wind blows here; the trip will do us good, we shall see the town. That will only take five or six days at most."

" And you will come back here with me ? "

" No. I must go see my father. You know he lives about thirty versts from X——. It is a long time since I have seen them, him and my mother; I must give them this pleasure. They are good people, and my father is a droll fellow in his way. Besides, they have only me; I am an only son."

" Will you stay long ? "

" I think not. I suppose I should get tired of it."

" Then you will come to see us on your way back ? "

" That depends on circumstances; I don't know. Well, is it agreed ? we depart ? "

" Very well," replied Arcadi, carelessly.

At heart he was very glad of the proposition his friend had just made ; but he believed it necessary not to let him see it ; that was to act like a true nihilist.

The next day he and Bazarof left for X——. The young people of Marino regretted their departure ; Duniasha even shed some tears, . . . but Paul Petrovitch and his brother, *the old fellows*, as Bazarof called them, breathed more freely.

XII.

The city of X——, to which the two friends went, had for governor a man still young, at once progressive and despotic, as so many are in Russia. During the first year of his entrance on duty, he had found ways to embroil himself, not only with many others, but also with the marshal of the nobility, who was a captain in the guard on the staff, a great breeder of horses, a man besides very hospitable, even to his own clerks. The differences that had resulted had taken such proportions, that the minister at St. Petersburg found himself obliged to send to the spot a confidential functionary to set matters straight. He entrusted this mission to Matveï Ilitch Koliazin, son of the Koliazin who had once been tutor of the brothers Kirsanof. He was equally an officer of the new school, although he had passed forty; but he proposed to become a statesman, and already wore two crosses on his breast. One was, to tell the truth, a foreign decoration, which was very little esteemed. Like the governor, whom he came to judge, he passed for a progressive, and important as he was, he resembled other officers of his class very little. He had, it is true, a very high opinion of himself; his vanity was without bounds, but he had simple manners, his look seemed to encourage you; he listened with kindness, and laughed in such a natural tone, that you would be tempted at first to take him for "a good fellow." Yet he knew very well how to use severity when circumstances demanded it.

"Energy is indispensable," he used to say, "*L'énergie est la première qualité d'un homme d'état.*"

Yet, notwithstanding this proud language, he was almost always duped, and every functionary of a little experience could lead him by the nose. Matveï Ilitch thought very highly of M. Guizot, and tried to insinuate to any one who would listen to him, that he was not one of these old fogy bureaucrats, friends of routine, like so many; that none of the phenomena of social life escaped his observation. . . . Terms of this kind were familiar to him. He even followed the literary movement, but affected to do it with a majestic condescension, as a man at ripe age sometimes follows in the street for some minutes a procession of young rascals. In reality Matveï Ilitch had not much advanced beyond the statesmen of the reign of Alexander I., who, in preparation for a soirée at Madame Swetchine's, who was then living at St. Petersburg, used to read in the morning a chapter of Condil-

lac ; only he had other and more contemporary forms. He
was a skilful courtier, a very shrewd man, and nothing
more ; he had no idea of business, and lacked mind, but he
knew very well how to watch over his own interests ; besides, no one could change his resolution, and that is a
talent that has its merits.

Matveï Ilitch received Arcadi with the kindness that
belongs to an enlightened officer ; we should say even with
playfulness. Yet he fell from his height when he found that
his other guest had remained in the country ; "Your papa
was always an original fellow," he said to Arcadi, playing
with the tassels of his magnificent velvet dressing gown ;
and turning all at once to a young clerk dressed in an
undress uniform, rigorously buttoned, he called out with a
busy air ; "Eh, well?" The young man, whose lips were
glued by long silence, rose and looked at his superior with
a surprised air. But Matveï Ilitch, after having thus stu-
pefied him, did not give him the least attention. Our dig-
nitaries generally love to stupefy their inferiors ; the
means to which they have recourse to produce this effect are
quite various. Here is one which is very often used, "is
quite a favorite" as the English say. The dignitary all at
once ceases to understand the most simple words, and
seems attacked with deafness. He asks for instance, the
day of the week, they reply to him respectfully : "Friday,
your excellency."

"Hey ? what ? what is that ? what do you say ?" replies
the dignitary with effort.

"To-day is Friday, your excellency."

"How ? what ? what is Friday ? what Friday ?"

"Friday, your excellency, the day of the week.'

"Come, do you pretend to give me a lesson ?"

Matveï Ilitch, with all his liberalism, was yet a dignitary
of this kind.

" I advise you, my dear friend," he said to Arcadi, " to go call on the Governor. " You understand me ; if I give you this advice, it is not because I have remained faithful to the old traditions that command you to pay court to the authorities, but because the Governor is very clearly a man of the right stamp; besides you probably intend to go into society ... I hope indeed that you are not a bear ? The Governor gives a grand ball day after to-morrow."

" Shall you be there ? " asked Arcadi.

" He gives it for me," said Matveï Ilitch almost in a tone of regret. " Do you dance ? "

" Yes, but badly."

" That is bad. There are some pretty women here, besides it is shameful for a young man not to know how to dance. It is not, I repeat it to you, that I hold to old usages. I do not at all suppose that the mind is in the feet, but I find Byronism ridiculous ; *il a fait son temps.*"

" Do you think, uncle, that that is Byronism which ... "

" I will make you acquainted with our ladies, I take you under my wing," replied Matveï Ilitch, laughing with a satisfied air. " You will be warm there ? hey ? "

A servant entered and announced the President of the Bureau of Finances, a pleasant-faced old man with pinched lips, who raved about nature, especially in summer, when he used to say, " The diligent bee sips a little pot of wine in every little flower."

Arcadi withdrew.

He found Bazarof at the inn where they had stopped, and urged the case so well that he decided him to go to see the Governor ; " Well," said Bazarof, " there is nothing else to do, if you have once said A, you must also say B. We have come to see the lords of the region, let us see them." The Governor gave the young people a good reception, but he did not invite them to sit down, and remained standing

4

himself. He always had a busy air; hardly up, he put on
a full-dress uniform, tied round his neck a very tight cravat,
and did not give himself time to finish his breakfast, so as
to go to work without relaxation at his administrative duties. In the government he had got the surname of Bour-
daloue, not in allusion to the celebrated French preacher,
but to the word *burda.** He asked Kirsanof and Bazarof to
come to his ball, and two minutes after repeated this invitation, taking them for two brothers, and calling them Kaïzarof.

On leaving the Governor's house they met a droschky
that immediately stopped; a young man of middle height,
wearing an overcoat trimmed with frogs in the fashion of the
slavophiles, leaped out, and crying out "Eugene Vasilitch,"
ran up to Bazarof.

"Ah! it is you, then, Sitnikof," said Bazarof to him, continuing to walk. "What brings you here?"

"It is all by accident," he replied, and turning toward
the droschky he beckoned five or six times with his hand,
crying out: "Follow us, follow us!" "My father," he
continued, jumping over the gutter, "has some business
here, and he asked me. . . . I heard of your arrival to-day,
and I just came from your hotel. . . . (In fact the two
friends found on their return a card with the corners bent
down, having on one side the name of Sitnikof in French,
and on the other in Slavonic characters.) I hope you are
not coming away from the Governor's."

"Do not hope it; we have just been there."

"Ah! in that case I am going to go there also. . . . Eugene Vasilitch, make me acquainted with your . . . with
this gentleman."

"Sitnikof, Kirsanof," grumbled Bazarof, without stopping.

"I am charmed," began Sitnikof, with a gracious smile,
walking alongside and hurriedly taking off his gloves, which

* Sauce, bad beer.

were too elegant for the occasion. " I have often heard you
spoken of. . . . I am a very old acquaintance of Eugene
Vasilitch, and I can even call myself his pupil. I owe to
him my transformation. . . ."

Arcadi looked at the transformed pupil of Bazarof. His
little face, with its smooth skin and its regular features, expressed an unquiet and obtuse attention; his small eyes,
which seemed wandering, looked fixedly and at the same time
uneasily; his very laugh, short and dry, had something wild.

" You will easily believe me," he said; "when Eugene
Vasilitch declared to me for the first time that we ought
not to recognize any authority, I felt such a joy. . . . I felt
myself born again, to a new existence ! 'At last,' I said to
myself, 'here is a man !' By the way, Eugene Vasilitch, you
really must go see a lady here who is quite up to your level,
and for whom your visit would be a real festival ; you must
have heard her spoken of ? "

" Who is she ? " unwillingly answered Bazarof.

" Kukshin,—Eudoxia,—Eudoxia Kukshin. She has a remarkable nature, *émancipée* in the whole sense of the term, a
woman truly in advance, you know. Come, let us go see
her now, all together. She lives two steps from here. We
will lunch there. . . . You have not lunched yet ? "

" Not yet."

" Just the thing. She lives, you understand, separate
from her husband, and is quite independent."

" Is she pretty ? " asked Bazarof.

" N—, no, I cannot say she is."

" Then why in the devil should you take us to see her ?"

" Come, jester, she will give us a bottle of champagne."

" Indeed ! the practical man soon shows himself. By
the way, is your father still in the brandy trade."

" Yes,' Sitnikof hurriedly answered, with a shrill laugh.
" Well ! are you coming ? "

"My faith, I don't know."

"Since you wished to make observations on people, said Arcadi in a half whisper.

"And you then, Mr. Kirsanof?" added Sitnikof; "you come too. We shall not go without you.

"We cannot fall on her all three of us like that. . . ."

"That is nothing; the Kukshin is a good child."

"She will give us a bottle of champagne?" asked Bazarof.

"Three!" cried Sitnikof; "I'll answer for it."

"On what?"

"On my head."

"Your father's purse would have been a better pledge. But never mind; let us go."

XIII.

The little manor-house, in the Muscovite style, in which Avdotia Nikitishna (or *Eudoxia*) Kukshin lived, was situated in a street that had been recently burned; nobody is unaware that our country towns burn down every five years. At the entry door, and near a visiting card that was nailed across it, hung the handle of a bell; a woman, with a cap on, holding an intermediate position between a servant and a companion, came to meet the visitors in the anteroom. All that gave to understand, plainly enough, that the mistress of the house was a friend of progress. Sitnikof asked for Avdotia Nikitishna.

"Is that you, Victor?" cried a shrill voice in an adjoining room; "come in."

The woman in a cap immediately disappeared.

"I am not alone," said Sitnikof; and, briskly taking off his Hungarian overcoat, which brought to view something like an English sack, he threw Arcadi and Bazarof a glance full of assurance.

"That makes no difference," replied the voice.—"*Entrez.*"

The young men obeyed. The room in which they found themselves looked more like a work room than a parlor. Papers, letters, many numbers of Russian reviews, whose pages were generally uncut, lay strewn over the dust-covered tables; ends of half-smoked cigarettes were scattered on all 'sides. The mistress of the house was reclining on a leathern divan; she was still young, had fair hair somewhat dishevelled, and was dressed in a not entirely clean silk; a lace handkerchief covered her head, and large bracelets set off her hands which had very short blunt fingers. She rose from the divan, and putting negligently over her shoulders a velvet cape, lined with yellowish ermine, she said in a languishing voice to Sitnikof: "Good morning, Victor," and shook his hand.

"Bazarof, Kirsanof," he said in an abrupt tone, imitating the manner of Bazarof in introductions.

"Be welcome," replied Madame Kukshin; and fixing on Bazarof her round eyes, between which rose a poor little red pug nose, she added; "I know you;" and shook his hand also.

Bazarof made a slight grimace. The insignificant little figure of the emancipated woman had nothing positively ugly; but the expression of her features was disagreeable. You would gladly have asked her "What is the matter with you? are you hungry? are you tired? are you afraid of anything? why these efforts?" She also like Sitnikof felt something that continually *scraped*, as it were, her soul. Her movements and her language were at once unconstrained and awkward; she considered herself doubtless as a good and simple creature, yet whatever she did, she always seemed to you to have intended doing something else.

"Yes, yes, I know you, Bazarof," she replied (following a usage peculiar to country women and some ladies of Moscow, she called men that she saw for the first time by their family name). "Would you like a cigar?"

"A cigar, yes!" said Sitnikof, who had had the time to throw himself into an arm-chair and place his leg over his knee; "but you must also give us some lunch. We are dying of hunger; offer us at the same time a bottle of champagne."

"Sybarite!" answered Eudoxia, and she began to laugh. (When she laughed, her upper gum showed above her teeth.) "Is it not true, Bazarof, that he is a Sybarite?"

"I love comfort in life," said Sitnikof with an important air. "That don't prevent me from being liberal."

"Not at all!" said Eudoxia, and she ordered her maid to prepare lunch and to bring some champagne.

"What do you think of it?" she asked Bazarof. "I am sure you share my opinion."

"You are mistaken," replied Bazarof: "a piece of meat is worth much more than a piece of bread, even from the standpoint of analytical chemistry."

"Ah! you are busied with chemistry? That is my passion! I have even invented a mastic."

"A mastic? You?"

"Yes, I myself, and do you know why? To make dolls, heads of dolls, so as not to break; it is more solid. I am a practical woman. But I haven't finished yet. I must consult Liebig. By the way, have you read in the *Moscow Gazette* the article of Kisliakof on the work of women? Read it, I beg of you. You ought to be interested in the women question? and in schools also? What does your friend do? What is his name?"

Madame Kukshin threw out these questions one after the

other with a mincing negligence, without waiting for an answer; spoiled children talk so to their nurse.

"My name is Arcadi Nikolaïvitch Kirsanof," said Arcadi, "and I do nothing."

Eudoxia began to laugh.

"That's charming! Don't you smoke? Victor, do you know that I am vexed with you?"

"Why?"

"I am told that you have begun to praise George Sand again. She is a woman that is behind the age, and nothing more! How do you dare compare her to Emerson! She has no ideas, either on education, or physiology, or on anything! I am sure she has never heard of embryology, and how would you get on without that science to-day? (Eudoxia opened her arms when pronouncing these last words.) Ah! what an admirable article Elisevitch has written on this subject! That gentleman is a genius! (Eudoxia always said "gentleman" for "man.") Bazarof, sit down by my side on the divan. Perhaps you don't know that I am horribly afraid of you."

"Why so? I am curious to know."

"You are a very dangerous gentleman; you criticise everybody. Ah! my God! I speak like a true country girl. After all I really am a country girl. I manage my estate myself, and, would you think it, my stanosta Erofeï is a wonderful character; he makes me think of Cooper's *Pathfinder*. I find him so primitive. Well I'm fixed here for ever; what an insupportable town, is it not? But what can I do!"

"One town is much like another," said Bazarof coldly.

"People are only busy with little interests here. That is what is terrible! Formerly, I used to pass all my winters at Moscow ...; but the venerable Mr. Kukshin has just established himself there. Besides Moscow is now ... I don't know ...; everything is changed there now. I should like to travel; last year I was even on the point of starting."

" For Paris doubtless ?" asked Bazarof.

" For Paris and Heidelberg !"

"Why for Heidelberg ?"

" How ? Since Bunsen lives there !"

Bazarof found nothing to say to this exclamation.

" Pierre Sapozhnikof ..., you know him ?"

" No, not at all."

" Is it possible ? Pierre Sapozhnikof ... he is constantly with Lydia Khostatof."

" I do not know her either."

" Well ! he offered to accompany me. I am alone, thank God ! I have no children ... What did I say then: 'Thank God ?' Well that is of no consequence."

Eudoxia rolled a cigarette between her fingers which were yellow with tobacco, passed it over her tongue, sucked the end of it and began to smoke.

The servant entered with a tray.

" Ah ! here's our lunch ! Won't you eat a bite ? Victor, uncork the bottle. You ought to know how."

" Know how ; I know how !" muttered Sitnikof between his teeth with his little shrill laugh.

"Have you any pretty ladies ,here?" asked Bazarof, after emptying his third glass.

" Yes," replied Eudoxia; "but they are so insignificant. *Mon amie* Odintsof, for example, is not bad. Only she has the reputation of being a little ... Any way the harm wouldn't be great; but she has no elevation in her ideas, no breadth, absolutely nothing .. of all that .. we should have to change our system of education. I have often thought of it; our women are very badly educated."

" You will do no good," said Sitnikof. " You ought to

despise them, and I despise them sovereignly and completely! (Sitnikof loved to despise and to express this
feeling; it fell principally on what he called *the sex*, without
thinking that it was reserved for him to cringe some months
after before his wife, only because she was born a princess.)
There is not a single one that can rise to the height of our
conversation; there is not a single one that is worth the
trouble of occupying serious men like us!"

"I don't see that it is necessary for them to understand
our conversation," said Bazarof.

"Whom do you speak of?" said Eudoxia.

"Pretty women."

"How! you share then perhaps the ideas of Proudhon?"

Bazarof drew himself up with a disdainful air. "I share
no one's ideas; I have my own way of seeing."

"Down with authorities!" cried Sitnikoff, happy to have
an occasion of expressing himself energetically in presence
of a man before whom he grovelled.

"But Macaulay himself," said Madame Kukshin . . .

"Down with Macaulay!" cried Sitnikof in a thundering
voice. "Do you take the part of these silly girls?"

"I do not sustain silly girls, but the rights of women,
that I have sworn to defend to the last drop of my blood."

"Down! . . ." Sitnikof did not finish his phrase. "But
I don't attack them," he added.

"Yes; I see that you are a Slavophile!"

"Not at all; I am not a Slavophile, though assuredly .. "

"Yes! yes! you are a Slavophile! You are a disciple
of the *Domostroï.** You only need to take a whip in
your hand."

"A whip is a good thing," replied Bazarof; "but we
have arrived at the last drop . . ."

* A manuscript of the Seventeenth century attributed to the
Monk Sylvester, and giving very curious details on the domestic
manners of that time.

4*

"Of what?" eagerly asked Eudoxia.

"Of champagne, worthy Eudoxia Nikitishna; of champagne and not of your blood."

"I cannot remain indifferent when women are attacked," continued Eudoxia; "it is frightful! frightful! Instead of attacking them, read Michelet's book *De l'Amour;* it is admirable! Gentlemen, let us talk of love," she added, languishingly letting her hand fall on the shapeless cushion of the divan.

A sudden silence followed this appeal.

"No; why speak of love?" said Bazarof; "let us rather talk of Madame Odintsof. That is her name, is it not? Who is this lady?"

"She is divine! divine!" cried Sitnikof. "I will present you to her. She is spiritual, rich, and a widow. Unhappily she is not yet sufficiently developed; she ought to approach our Eudoxia a little closer. I drink your health, *Eudoxie!* Touch glasses! 'Et toc, et toc, et tin, tin, tin! et toc, et toc, et tin, tin, tin!!'"

"Victor, you are a spoiled child."

The lunch lasted some time longer. The first bottle of champagne was followed by a second, by a third, and even by a fourth. . . . Eudoxia talked without interruption; Sitnikof kept pace with her. They discussed for some time what marriage was, whether a prejudice or a crime; they examined the question whether men were born with the same dispositions, and in what, properly speaking, individuality consisted. Things came to that point that Eudoxia, her cheeks inflamed with wine, striking with her flattened nails the keys of her discordant piano, began to sing in a hoarse voice first gypsy songs; then the romance of Seymour Shiff. "Sleeping Grenada dreams." Sitnikof, his head turbaned with a scarf, tried to represent the reconciled lover, when the singer pronounced these words:

> " And my lips with thine,
> Join in burning kisses."

Arcadi could no longer restrain himself, " Gentlemen," he said aloud, " this begins to remind one somewhat of Bedlam." Bazarof, who had confined himself to occasionally throwing a jest into the conversation, busied himself principally with the champagne ; he let a long yawn escape him, rose and went out with Arcadi, without taking leave. Sitnikof darted out after them.

" Well ! well ! " he asked them, running from one to the other with an obsequious air, " I told you that she was a very remarkable person ! These are the women we ought to have ; she is, in her way, a phenomenon of high morality."

" Is this establishment of *thy* father also of a high morality ? " replied Bazarof, pointing with his finger to a dram shop, which they were at that moment passing.

Sitnikof gave the forced laugh that was habitual to him. He blushed at his extraction, and did not know whether to appear flattered or offended at Bazarof's unexpected use of the second person singular.

XIV.

The ball of the governor took place a few days after. Matveï Ilitch was truly the hero of the festival. The marshal of the nobility declared to every comer that he had only come in his honor. As to the governor, he continued, even in the midst of the ball, and without budging from his place, to attend answering to the cases of the administration. The affability of Matveï Ilitch did no injury to the majesty of his manners. He flattered everybody, some with a shade of disdain, others with a slight degree of consideration ; he loaded the women with polite attentions, *en vrai chevalier*

français, and laughed continually—a loud, echoless laugh—
as suits a great personage. He tapped Arcadi on the shoulder, calling him in a loud voice his dear nephew, and honored
Bazarof, who had put on a rather old-fashioned coat, with a
distracted but benevolent look from the corner of his eye,
and with an amiable grumbling, in the midst of which one
could only distinguish the word "I," and the termination
"'tremely;" he extended a finger to Sitnikof and smiled,
though turning his head away; he even threw an "*enchanté*"
to Madame Kukshin, who came to the ball without crinoline
and in soiled gloves, but with a bird of paradise in her hair.
The reunion was large, and gentlemen were not lacking;
the men in civil dress, for the most part, stood up against
the wall, but the military men danced eagerly, especially
one of them, who, having lived in Paris nearly six weeks,
had brought back certain characteristic expressions, like
"*Zut!*" "*ah! fichtrre,*" "*pst, pst, mon bibi,*" &c. He
pronounced them perfectly, with the true Parisian ring,
which did not hinder him from saying "*si j'aurais,*" instead of "*si j'avais,*" and "*absolument,*" in the sense of
certainly; in a word, he spoke this Russian-French, that
the French laugh at so much when they do not consider it
necessary to tell us that we speak French like angels,
"*comme des anges.*"

Arcadi, as we have already said, hardly danced, and Bazarof did not dance at all; they drew back into a corner of
the hall with Sitnikof. He, a smile of disdain on his lips,
made remarks that he believed to be very wicked, looked
about him with a provoking air, and seemed to feel a lively
satisfaction. Suddenly, the expression of his features
changed, and leaning towards Arcadi, he said, with a kind
of troubled look:

"There is Madame Odintsof."

Arcadi turned and perceived a tall lady in a black

dress standing at the door of the hall. The distinction of her whole person struck him. Her naked arms fell gracefully over her slim waist; light stems of fuchsia also hung gracefully from her brilliant hair over her beautiful shoulders; her limpid eyes, above which rose a white and slightly convex forehead, were tranquil and intelligent rather than pensive. An almost imperceptible smile played about her lips. A certain caressing and friendly air was spread over her whole face.

"You know her?" Arcadi asked of Sitnikof.

"Very intimately. Would you like me to present you?"

"Very gladly . . . after this quadrille."

Bazarof also remarked Madame Odintsof.

"Who is that figure?" he said; "she does not seem like the other girls."

When the quadrille had ended, Sitnikof conducted Arcadi towards Madame Odintsof; but he appeared to know her much less than he had said; he soon got confused in his words, and she looked at him with a kind of astonishment. Yet a kind expression was painted on her face, when he pronounced the family name of Arcadi. She asked him if he was a son of Nicholas Petrovitch.

"Yes," he answered.

"I have seen your father twice, and I have heard him much spoken of," she replied; "I am charmed to make your acquaintance."

At this moment there came up a young aid-de-camp and invited her for a quadrille. She accepted.

"You dance then?" Arcadi said respectfully.

"Yes; but why do you ask that question? Do I seem to you too old to dance?"

"How can you suppose such a thought in me? Allow me to engage you for a mazurka."

Madame Odintsof smiled. "With great pleasure," she

answered, looking at Arcadi, not with a patronizing air, but as married sisters look at their young brothers. Madame Odintsof was a little older than Arcadi. She was full twenty-nine; but in her presence he felt himself a little student, a school-boy, as if the difference of age between them were much greater. Matveï Ilitch came up to her with a majestic air and addressed her some compliments. Arcadi drew back a few steps, but he continued to observe her; he did not take his eyes off from her even during the quadrille. She conversed as simply with her dancer as with Matveï Ilitch, gently turning her head and eyes from one side to the other. Arcadi heard her laugh two or three times almost silently. Her nose was perhaps a little large, like the noses of nearly all Russian women, and her complexion was not absolutely alabaster; but Arcadi did not the less decide that he had never yet met more perfect beauty. The sound of her voice did not go out of his ears; it seemed to him that the folds of her dress fell differently on her than on the women by whom she was surrounded, with more symmetry and breadth, and that all her movements were at once full of nobility and naturalness.

When the first chords of the mazurka were heard, Arcadi felt a sort of commotion in his heart; he sat down by the side of his partner, and not knowing how to begin the conversation, confined himself to passing his hand through his hair. But this trouble was not of long duration; the calm of Madame Odintsof quickly gained on him; a quarter of an hour had not passed before he conversed without embarrassment of his father, his uncle, his mode of life at St. Petersburg and in the country. Madame Odintsof listened to him with an attentive politeness, opening and shutting her fan; the talk of Arcadi did not stop except when his partner was engaged; Sitnikof among others asked her twice. She returned to her place, sat down, took up her fan again;

the movements of her breast were no more hurried than before; and Arcadi began his stories again, full of pleasure at feeling himself near her, at speaking to her, at looking into her eyes, at her beautiful forehead, her face almost grave but so gracious. She spoke little, yet her words revealed a certain experience of life; Arcadi was led to conclude from some of her remarks that, notwithstanding her youth, she had already passed through many emotions and reflected on many things.

"Whom were you with, when Mr. Sitnikof introduced you," she asked him.

"Then you have noticed him?" replied Arcadi; "has he not a striking physiognomy? He is named Bazarof, and is my friend."

Arcadi began to talk to her about "his friend." He entered into so many details and expressed himself with so much fire that Madame Odintsof turned toward Bazarof and looked curiously at him. Meanwhile the mazurka was drawing near its close. Arcadi regretted to be obliged to separate from his partner; he had passed an hour so agreeably with her! Not that during all this time he had not always felt that she treated him, so to speak, with a kind of condescension; but he did not feel hurt, for young hearts are never humiliated by the patronage of a pretty woman.

The music ceased.

"*Merci*," said Madame Odintsof rising. "You have promised to call on me; I hope that you will bring your friend. I am very curious to know a man who has the audacity to believe nothing."

The governor coming up to Madame Odintsof announced that supper was ready, and gave her his arm with his busy air. In going away, she turned and made Arcadi a slight bow accompanied by a half-smile. He made a low bow, and while following her with his eyes (how elegant her form, surrounded by the brilliant waves of her black dress, appeared to him !) he said to himself: " She has doubtless already completely forgotten that I exist." And he felt almost immediately a certain beautiful resignation.

" Well ! " Bazarof asked his friend as soon as he had re-joined him in his corner, " you have been lucky ! I have just now been told that this lady is . . . hum, hum ! To be sure the gentleman who assured me of it could indeed be a fool. But what do you think about it ?. Is she truly . . . hum, hum ? "

" I do not understand the meaning of this interjection, answered Arcadi."

" Come now, what an innocent ! "

" If it is that, I do not understand your gentleman. Madame Odintsof is very amiable, I admit, but she has such cold and severe manners that . . . "

" Still waters *. . . you know ! " replied Bazarof. " You say she is cold, that is what makes her merit. Do you not like ices ? "

" That is all possible," replied Arcadi, " I don't pretend to judge of it. But she wishes to make your acquaintance, and asked me to bring you to see her."

" I imagine that you must have made a fine portrait of me ! Well, it's indifferent to me. Let her be what will, a simple country belle, or an 'emancipated' woman in the style of Madame Kukshin, she nevertheless has such shoul-ders as I have seldom seen."

The cynicism of these words affected Arcadi painfully, but he hastened, as one often does, to answer his friend on subjects foreign to this impression.

" Why do you refuse women the liberty of thinking ? " he asked him in a low voice.

---

* A Russian proverb says : " The devil lies hid where the water is most still."

" Because I have noticed, my dear boy, that all women who use this liberty are real old hags."

The conversation stopped there. The two young men went away immediately after supper. Madame Kukshin gave a stifled laugh, but full of anger ; neither of them had shown her the slightest attention, and her feelings had been hurt by it. She remained till the last, and even at four o'clock in the morning danced a polka-mazurka with Sitnikof with the Parisian graces. This edifying representation terminated the governor's ball.

XV.

" Let us see to what class of mammiferæ your new acquaintance belongs ? " said Bazarof the next day to Arcadi, while ascending the stairs of the hotel at which Madame Odintsof was staying ; " I somehow feel that there is something equivocal there."

"You astonish me ! " cried Arcadi ; " how can you, Bazarof, set yourself up as a defender of the strict morality. . . . You who . . ."

" What a dull fellow you are ! " Bazarof negligently answered. " Do you not know that in our peculiar language, 'equivocal' signifies quite the contrary ? It means that there is no doubt. Did you not tell' me yourself that she had made a strange marriage ; although in my opinion to marry a rich old man is by no means a strange act, but to the contrary, a very rational proceeding. The talk of the town does not inspire me with great confidence ; but I like to believe, as our learned governor says, that it has some foundation."

Arcadi did not reply, and knocked at the door of the room that Madame Odintsof occupied. A young servant in livery ushered the two friends into a large room, poorly furnished, as are all rooms in furnished hotels in Russia, but ornamented with flowers. Madame Odintsof soon appeared herself, in morning dress. She seemed still younger in the light of a spring sun. Arcadi presented Bazarof to her, and noticed, to his great astonishment, that he seemed intimidated, while Madame Odintsof was as calm as the evening before. Bazarof himself felt that his face betrayed some embarrassment, and was vexed at it.

"Here is a new thing! This girl makes me afraid!" thought he, and sitting down in an arm-chair, just as Sitnikof himself would have done, he began to chat with an exaggerated assurance, under the steady gaze of Madame Odintsof, who observed him carefully with her limpid eyes.

Anna Serghéïevna Odintsof was the daughter of Serghéï Nikolaïtch Loktef, a gentleman celebrated for his beauty, his passion for play, his skill in money affairs, and who, after having shone a dozen of years at Moscow and St. Petersburg, living by expedients, at last ruined himself entirely, and took refuge in the country, where he soon died, leaving a very scanty estate to his two daughters, Anna and Katerina, one twenty and the other twelve years old. Their mother, belonging to the family of the princes N——, much fallen from their ancient greatness, had died at St. Petersburg, while her husband was still in full prosperity. The position of Anna Loktef when she became an orphan, was very painful. The brilliant education that she had received at St. Petersburg had in no way prepared her to endure the domestic cares and the annoyances of every kind that awaited her without resources in the country. She did not know any of her country neighbors, and had no one of whom to ask advice. Her father had always abstained from visiting the country proprietors ; he despised them, and they returned him the like coin, each in his way. Notwithstanding she did not lose her head, and wrote immediately to her mother's sister, the princess Avdotia Stepanovna N——, an ugly and proud old maid, to come and live with her. The princess came to her niece's, installed herself in one of the finest chambers of the house, grumbling and scolding from morning to night, and never going out to walk, even in the garden, unless followed by her only servant, a taciturn serf lackey, dressed in an old-fashioned yellowish livery, with blue trimming and a cocked hat. Anna patiently endured all the whims of her aunt, busied herself meanwhile with the education of her sister, and appeared resigned to end her days in this isolation. . . . But fate disposed otherwise of her. A certain Odintsof, a very rich man, odd, hypochondriacal, fat and heavy, but not lacking mind, an honorable man besides, made her acquaintance, fell in love with her and asked her hand. She consented to this marriage ; and six years after he died, leaving her all his fortune. Anna Sergheïevna remained a year without leaving the country ; then she went with her sister for a tour of Europe, but she contented herself with visiting Germany ; soon wearied with travelling, she returned to her dear village of Nikolskoia, situated near the city of X——. Her country house was spacious, richly furnished, and surrounded by a magnificent garden and orangery ; her late husband liked to live in grand style. Anna Sergheïevna went to town rarely and only on business, and did not stay there long. She was not much liked in the government ; her marriage had excited much talk. There circulated about her stories of other days, as for example, that she had aided her father in some of his gambling tricks, that her journey abroad was to conceal sad consequences.

"You understand what," added the good souls. "She has passed through fire and water," said other persons ; and a wit of the town who thought he had the privilege of good sayings, usually added; "That is to say, through all the elements." All these rumors were not unknown to her; but they went in at one ear and out at the other; she had a great freedom of mind and did not lack firmness.

Seated in an arm-chair, her hands placed on each other, Mme. Odintsof listened to Bazarof. Contrary to his habit, he spoke willingly enough, and evidently sought to interest Anna Sergheiëvna. That was very surprising to Arcadi; but it would have been impossible for him to decide whether Bazarof had succeeded or not. The emotions that Madame Odintsof could experience were not distinctly painted on her face; she always preserved the same expression. Amiable and pleasant, her beautiful, intelligent eyes were always attentive, but her attention never grew animated. The strange manners of Bazarof in the first moments of their interview had caused her a disagreeable impression, like a bad odor or a harsh sound; but she soon understood that he was embarrassed, and this discovery flattered her. Trivialness alone was insupportable to her, and Bazarof had certainly nothing trivial about him. It was fated that this day Arcadi should go from surprise to surprise. He thought that Bazarof would speak to Madame Odintsof, an intelligent and spiritual woman, of his convictions and his views; she had expressed in advance the desire of talking with "a man who dared believe nothing;" instead of that Bazarof discoursed to her of medicine, homœopathy and botany. Madame Odintsof had put to profit the leisure of her solitude; she had read some good books and spoke Russian very correctly. Having said a few words on music, she perceived that Bazarof did not esteem the arts, and she returned gradually to botany, though Arcadi had launched out into a dissertation on national melodies. Madame Odintsof continued to treat him like a young brother ; she seemed to appreciate in him the goodness and the frankness of youth ; nothing more.

This calm conversation, varied and lively, lasted nearly three hours.

The two friends rose at last and prepared to go. Madame Odintsof, with the best grace in the world, extended to each her beautiful white hand; and having reflected a little, said to them with an undecided but kind smile: " If you do not fear *ennui*, gentlemen, come and see me at Nikolskoia."

" Can you suppose Anna Serghei͏̈evna," cried Arcadi, " that I don't consider myself too happy to . . ."

" And you, Mr. Bazarof ? "

Bazarof only bowed; and Arcadi made a last observation which surprised him still more; he noticed that his friend blushed.

" Well," he asked him in the street ; " do you still think that she is . . . hum, hum ? "

" Who knows ? She is prettily dressed ! " Bazarof answered; and after a moment of silence, he added ; " A true duchess, a sovereign ! She only lacks a crown on her head and a train to her dress."

" Our duchesses do not speak Russian as she does," said Arcadi.

" She has been in distress, my dear fellow ; she has eaten the same bread that we have."

" But she is nevertheless ravishing," added Arcadi.

" A magnificent body," replied Bazarof; " how fine it would be on a dissecting table."

" Be still, in Heaven's name, Eugene ! You are abominable."

" Come, don't be angry, girl ! She is of the first quality ; that is agreed. We must go and see her."

" When ? "

" Day after to-morrow, if you wish. What have we to do

here ? Drink champagne with Madame Kukshin ? Admire
the eloquence of your relation, the liberal dignitary ? . . .
Let us start day after to-morrow. Especially since my
father's hamlet is quite near there. Is not Nikolskoia on
the road to D——? "

" Yes."

" *Optime!* We must not lose time. Only imbeciles lose
time . . . and embarrassed people. A magnificent body ! I
tell you."

Three days after, the two friends rode along on the high
road to Nikolskoia. The day was beautiful, the heat
moderate ; the well-fed horses of their driver moved lightly
their little braided and knotted tails. Arcadi looked at the
road and smiled without knowing why.

" Give me your compliments," cried Bazarof all at once,
"to-day is the 22d of June, the festival of my patron angel.
We are going to see if he is interested in me. They expect
me at home to-day," he added, lowering his voice . . . " So
much the worse for them, they will only have their expecta-
tion'! A fine business this ! "

XVI.

The house in which Madame Odintsof lived was situated
on a bare and low hill, in the vicinity of a stone church, with
a green roof and white pillars, the front being ornamented
with a fresco painting in the Italian style representing the
Resurrection. A great swarthy warrior in a coat of mail,
lying on the first story especially excited the admiration of
the peasants. Behind the church extended the two rows of
the village houses, whose chimneys rose here and there over
the turf roofs. The manor-house was built in the same
style as the church; in the style known under the name of

Alexandrine; * it also was painted yellow; it likewise had a green roof, white pillars, and a front decorated with an escutcheon. A country architect had constructed these two classic edifices to the great satisfaction of Mr. Odintsof, who could not endure futile, and, as he used to say, arbitrary novelties. The house was surrounded by the trees of the old garden; an alley of cedars, cut like yew trees, led to the portico.

The young people found in the antechamber two grand liveried lackeys; one of them ran immediately to seek the major-domo. He, a fat man in a black coat, came at once, and conducted the guests by a carpeted staircase into a large room where were already two beds and all the objects necessary to the toilet. The house was evidently kept on a good footing; propriety reigned everywhere, and a certain official perfume was inhaled there as in the reception rooms of ministers.

"Anna Serghe ïevna asks you to come down in half an hour," said the major-domo; " have you any orders to give in the meantime ? "

" None, worthy servitor;" replied Bazarof, " unless you would deign to have a glass of brandy brought us."

" Very well," said the major-domo, not without surprise, and he went away, his boots creaking as he walked.

 "What high life ! " said Bazarof; " I believe that the thing is called thus with you ? She is a great duchess, I always come back to that."

" A famous duchess ! " said Arcadi; "she invites two aristocrats of our standing to visit her without other preliminary."

" An aristocrat like me especially; a future physician, son of a physician and grandson of a sexton ! for I don't

* From Alexander I.

know as I have told you, I am grandson of a sexton . . .
like Speranski*;" Bazarof added between his teeth after a
moment of silence: "The dear lady is a spoiled child of
fortune; yes, and happily spoiled. Shall we be obliged to
put on our dress coats?"

Arcadi contented himself with shrugging his shoulders,
but at heart he felt himself also a little intimidated.

Half an hour after, Bazarof and Arcadi went down to the
parlor. It was a spacious and lofty room, rather richly decorated, but without much taste. The massive and costly furniture, ranged in accustomed regularity along the walls, was covered with a brown stuff brocaded with gold. Mr. Odintsof had
had it brought from Moscow, by means of one of his friends,
a Frenchman dealing in wines. Above the middle sofa
hung the portrait of a blond man with swollen features,
which seemed to look at the visitors with an evil eye. "That
must be the dear departed," whispered Bazarof in his friend's
ear, and turning up his nose he added "let us clear out."
But at that instant the mistress of the house came in. She
wore a light barege dress; her smooth hair was brought
behind her ears, and this kind of head-dress joined to the
purity and freshness of her figure gave her the air of a young
girl.

"I thank you for having kept your word with me," she
said; "I hope that you will not go away soon; you see
we are not uncomfortable here. I will present you to my
sister; she plays very well on the piano. That will hardly
please you, Mr. Bazarof; but you, Mr. Kirsanof, I believe you
like music. Besides my sister we have also an old aunt, and
one of my neighbors comes sometimes to make a card-
party; we are not numerous, as you see. Now let us sit
down if you will."

* A celebrated statesman in the reign of Alexander I.

This little *speech* was pronounced with a perfect ease, Mme. Odintsof seemed to have learned it by heart. She immediately engaged in conversation with Arcadi; she said her mother had known the mother of Arcadi very well, and that she while still a young girl had made her a confidante of the love that she felt for Nicholas Petrovitch. Arcadi spoke with animation of his mother; while he chatted there, Bazarof turned over the leaves of an album.

" How tame I have become ;" he said to himself.

A pretty greyhound with a clean blue collar ran into the room, making a pattering noise on the floor with his claws ; soon after appeared a young girl of about eighteen, a brunette with little bright eyes and black hair ; her face though not regular was not unpleasing. She held in her hand a basket full of flowers.

" That is my Katia ; " said Madame Odintsof, designating her sister by a sign of the head.

The young girl sat down lightly at her side and began to arrange the flowers. The greyhound, which was called Fifi, approached successively the two guests, wagging its tail, and pushing its cold nose against their hands.

" Did you pick all those yourself ? " asked Madame Odintsof.

" Yes ; " replied Katia.

" Will my aunt come to tea ? "

" She is coming."

When speaking, Katia smiled with a timid and frank air, looking up with a sort of graceful wildness. All about her had the freshness of youth; her voice, the bloom of her face, her pink hands, whose palms were covered with whitish circles, her rather narrow shoulders. She blushed continually, and gave little abrupt sighs.

Madame Odintsof turned towards Bazarof.

'You examine that album merely from politeness,

5

Eugene Vasilitch," she began; "that cannot interest you. Draw up nearer to us and let us discuss some subject, no matter what."

Bazarof drew up his chair.

"With much pleasure; but what do you wish to discuss?"

"That is indifferent to me. I warn you that I love to contradict."

"You?"

"Yes. That seems to astonish you. Why?"

"Because you are, as far as I can judge, of a cold and calm character; a certain enthusiasm is necessary for discussion."

"How could you learn to know me in such a little time? Be assured, first, that I am impatient and obstinate; ask Katia rather. In the second place I can very easily become enthusiastic."

Bazarof looked at Anna Serghéïevna in silence.

"Perhaps," he replied; "you ought to know better than I. You really wish then to discuss? With pleasure. I just saw in your album views of the Saxon Switzerland, and you told me that they could not interest me. You said so because you suppose that I do not have the artistic sense, and you are not mistaken; but these views can yet interest me very much in a geological way, in the formation of mountains, for example."

"I do not admit it; in your quality of geologist, you ought rather to have recourse to a book, to a special work, and not to drawings."

"A drawing represents to my eyes what demands ten pages of description in a book."

Anna Serghéïevna did not reply.

"You do not then have the artistic sense," she said, resting her elbow on the table so that her face was brought nearer to that of Bazarof. "How do you get along without it?"

" Of what use is it ? allow me to ask you."

" If it were only to know and study men ? "

Bazarof smiled.

"In the first place," he continued, "you reach that by the experience of life ; and, in the second place, I will allow myself to say to you, that I do not believe it at all necessary to know each individual in particular. All men resemble each other as well in body as in soul ; each of us has a brain, a heart, spleen, lungs, constructed in the same way. The qualities that are called 'moral' are likewise identical in all men ; they present only insignificant differences. A single human example is enough to judge all the rest by. Men are like beeches of the forests ; no botanist would think of studying each specimen separately."

Katia, who was slowly selecting her flowers one by one, raised her eyes to Bazarof with an astonished air, but, meeting his careless and bold look, she blushed up to her ears. Anna Serghefevna shook her head.

" The beeches of the forests," she repeated ; "so then, according to you, there is no difference between a fool and a wise man, between the good and the wicked ? "

"Yes ; as between the healthy and the sick man. The lungs of a consumptive are not in the same state as yours or mine, although their structure is the same. We know approximately the cause of certain physical maladies ; as to the moral maladies, they spring from a bad education, from follies of all kinds that are stuffed into our heads, in a word, from the absurd condition of our social law. Reform society and you will have no more maladies."

Bazarof pronounced these words with an expression that seemed to say : "Believe me or not, it is exactly the same to me." He slowly passed his long fingers through his moustaches, and his glance moved from one side of the room to the other.

"And you believe," said Anna Serghéïevna, "that when society is reformed there will be no more fools or wicked men?"

"What is certain is that, society once well organized, it will be all the same whether a man is stupid or intelligent, bad or good."

"Yes, I understand; all will have the same position."

"Precisely, madame."

Madame Odintsof turned toward Arcadi.

"What do you think about it?" she asked him.

"I agree with Eugene," he replied.

Katia looked up askance.

"You astonish me, gentlemen," replied Madame Odintsof; "but we shall come back to all this. I hear my aunt coming to tea; we have to manage with old people."

The aunt of Anna Serghéïevna, the princess N——, a little old woman, fleshless, with a face of the size of one's fist, with hard and moveless eyes, surmounted by a grey tower, entered the room, bowed very slightly to the two young men, and sank down into a large velvet armchair that was exclusively reserved for her. Katia put a footstool under her feet; the old woman did not thank her, even with a look; she moved her hands a little under her yellow shawl which almost entirely hid her body. The princess loved yellow; she had also ribbons of a lively yellow in her cap.

"How have you passed the night, aunt?" asked Madame Odintsof, elevating her voice.

"This dog is here again," replied the old lady grumbling, and having noticed that Fifi made two undecided steps towards her, she cried out: "Go away! go away!"

Katia called Fifi and opened the door.

The dog ran joyously at her voice, believing that a walk was in question; but seeing itself alone on the other side of the door, it began to scratch and whine. The princess frowned. Katia started to go out. . . .

"Tea must be ready?" said Madame Odintsof. "Come gentlemen. Aunt, will you come take some tea?"

The princess rose in silence, and passed first into the dining room. A little Cossack, dressed in livery, noisily pushed a cushioned armchair to the table, and the princess sat down in it; Katia, who poured the tea, served her first, in a cup ornamented with her arms. The old lady sweetened her tea with honey (she would have believed that she had committed a mortal sin by using sugar,* and besides, according to her, sugar was too dear; yet enough for her would not have cost a kopeck). An instant after she asked in a hoarse voice :

"What does Prince Ivan say in his letter?"

Nobody replied to her, and the young men soon understood that, while showing her much respect, they did not trouble themselves much about her. "She is kept here for a clock . . . a princess . . . that is very well in a parlor," thought Bazarof. . . . After tea Madame Odintsof proposed taking a walk; but some drops of rain began to fall, and all the company, with the exception of the Princess, returned to the parlor. The card-playing neighbor came in; his name was Porphyry Platonitch. He was a fat, bald man, whose feet seemed made in a lathe, amiable besides, and of a gay disposition. Anna Serghe'evna, who talked almost constantly with Bazarof, asked him if he did not wish to match himself with them at the old game of *preference.* Bazarof consented to it, saying that he ought to prepare himself for his duties of country physician.

"Take care," said Madame Odintsof to him, "we are going to beat you. You, Katia," she added; "play some-

* Because it is clarified with blood.

thing to Arcadi Nikolaïevitch. He loves music, and we will
listen to you too."

Katia went with little eargerness to the piano, and Arcadi,
although he really loved music, followed her against his
will ; he said to himself that Madame Odintsof seemed to wish
to get rid of him, and like all young people of his age, he
felt himself already animated with that confused and almost
painful feeling that precedes love. Katia opened the piano,
and asked Arcadi, without looking at him :

"What shall I play you ?"

"What you like," replied Arcadi in an indifferent tone.

"What kind of music do you prefer ?" answered Katia
without changing her position.

"Classical music," said Arcadi in the same tone.

"Do you like Mozart ?"

"Yes."

Katia took the sonata fantasia in C minor of this master.
She played very well, though her execution was severe and
even a little hard. She held herself immoveable and erect,
her eyes fixed on the notes, and her lips closed ; yet, towards
the end of the sonata her face colored, and a little tress of
hair became undone and fell over her black eyebrow.

Arcadi listened with pleasure to the last part of the sonata,
where in the midst of the charming gayety of a happy
melody are all at once heard the transports of a bitter, almost
tragic grief . . . But the ideas that Mozart's music inspired
did not relate to Katia. In looking at her only a single
thought came into his mind :

"This young girl," he said to himself, "plays well, and is
not bad looking."

The sonata ended, Katia asked him without taking her
hand from the keys :

"Is that enough ?"

Arcadi replied that he did not wish to abuse her kindness,

and began to speak of Mozart; he asked her if she had chosen that sonata herself, or if some one had recommended it to her. But Katia replied only in monosyllables; she had hidden herself; she had, so to speak, drawn back into her shell. When she had fallen into this state, it was a long time before she dared to raise her eyes, and her features took an expression of obstinacy; one would have taken her for an insignificant little girl. It is not that she was timid; she was rather a little frightened, so to speak, by her sister, who, as we have seen, watched over her education, and did not suspect what was passing within her. Arcadi was reduced, in order to give himself countenance, to call Fifi, who had come back, and he began to caress her head, smiling kindly the while. Katia returned to her flowers.

As to Bazarof, he made mistake after mistake. Madame Odintsof played wonderfully, and Porphyry Platonitch was also a very good player. Bazarof was beaten, and though his loss was small, it was nevertheless unpleasant.

During the supper Madame Odintsof turned the conversation again to botany.

" Let us go walk to-morrow morning," she said to him; " I will ask you to tell me the Latin names of the field plants and their properties."

" Why do you wish to know the Latin names ? " Bazarof asked.

" Order is necessary in everything," she answered.

" What an admirable woman Anna Serghéïevna is ! " cried Arcadi when he was alone with his friend in the room that had been given them.

" Yes, replied Bazarof, the gossip does not lack brains, and she ought to know how to manage."

" In what sense do you say that ? "

" In a good sense, my dear fellow ; I am sure she ought

to manage her estate well. If there is anything admirable
here, it is her sister."

"What ? that little brunette ?"

"Yes, that little brunette; she is fresh, untouched and
fearful and silent; she deserves attention. You could still
make of this nature what you wished, while the other ! ... "

Arcadi did not reply to Bazarof, and each of them went
to sleep with ideas of his own in his head.

Anna Serghe\u00efevna also thought that evening about her
guests. Bazarof pleased her by the complete absence of
pretence, even by the severity of his judgments. He was
something quite new for her, and she was curious. Anna
Serghe\u00efevna was a rather strange person. Having no prejudices, nor even any strong beliefs, she recoiled before
nothing and hardly advanced. She saw many things clearly,
many things interested her, and nothing could content her. I
do not even know whether she desired an entire satisfaction.
Her mind was at once curious and indifferent; her doubts
were never effaced so as to leave no traces, and never became strong enough to trouble her. If she had not been rich
and independent perhaps she would have thrown herself
into the *mêlée* and learned to know passions ... But her
existence was calm, although she sometimes felt ennui, and
she continued to live from day to day, without agitation and
without haste. Too seductive images sometimes involuntarily arose before her eyes ; but when the image had disappeared, she fell into her quietude and regretted nothing.
Her imagination often passed the limits that the ordinary rules
of morals allow; but even then her blood flowed as calmly
as usual in her fair body always fresh and peaceful. Often
in the morning on coming warm and languid out of her perfumed bath, she had dreamed on the vanities of life, on its
sadness, on its pains and its labors ... A sudden boldness
animated her heart ; she felt noble aspirations awake in her ;

but a half-open window has let a light breath of wind into
the room, and Anna Serghenïevna has shivered and complained ; she has even had trouble in keeping down a movement of anger, and only asked one thing at that moment ;
that this ugly wind would stop blowing. Like all women to
whom it has not been given to love, she constantly desired
something, without knowing exactly what she desired. The
fact is that she desired nothing, though she thought she
wanted the whole world. She had hardly been able to
endure her husband. She had married from calculation ;
she would probably not have consented to marry Mr. Odintsof, if she had not supposed him an honorable man ; but
there had remained to her a secret aversion for all men in
general, whom she imagined to herself as careless in person,
heavy, indolent, perpetually disgusted, and without energy.
Yet she had met in her travels a young and handsome
Swede, with a chivalric face, eyes blue and honest, a brow
lofty and uncovered; he had made on her a strong impression, but that had not kept her from returning to Russia.

"This physician is a strange man," she said to herself,
lying in her magnificent bed on lace pillows, under a light
silk coverlet... Anna Serghenïevna had inherited some
part of her father's taste for luxury. She had loved her father
very much, vicious as he was ; and he adored his daughter,
jested with her as with a friend, showed her an unbounded
confidence and often consulted her. She had kept only a
confused recollection of her mother.

"This physician is a strange man !" she repeated as she
thought about him. She stretched herself out in her bed,
smiled, passed her arms under her head ; then having read
through two or three pages of a poor French novel, she let
the book fall, and went to sleep, white, pure and cold in her
perfumed bed.

The next morning, after breakfast, Madame Odintsof
5*

went to botanize with Bazarof, and only returned in time
for dinner. Arcadi, who had not gone out, had passed
nearly an hour with Katia. He had not got wearied.
She had proposed to play him the sonata of the evening
before; but when Madame Odintsof had at last returned,
when he had seen her again—his heart closed immediately... She advanced through the garden with a tired
look; her cheeks were red, and her eyes had more than
usual brilliancy under her round straw hat. She was twirling
the slender stem of a field flower between her fingers; her
light mantilla had slipped down from her shoulders on her
arms, and the large ribbons of her hat clung together under
her chin. Bazarof walked behind her with an assured step,
with carelessness as always; but the expression of his face,
though gay and even affectionate, did not please Arcadi.
After having thrown him a "good day" pronounced between
his teeth, Bazarof went to his room; Madame Odintsof
clasped Arcadi's hand in a distracted way and also passed
before him.

"Good-day?" thought Arcadi... "Have we not already
seen each other to-day?"

XVII.

Time (an acknowledged fact) often flies like a bird, and
often crawls like a tortoise; but it never seems more agreeable than when one does not know whether it goes quickly
or slowly. It was precisely thus that Bazarof and Arcadi
passed nearly a fortnight with Madame Odintsof. The
order that she had established in her house and in her mode
of life doubtless contributed much to that. She rigorously
observed it as far as she was concerned, and to oblige the
rest to do so, she used despotism at need. Everything was

done at stated hours in the house. In the morning at eight o'clock precisely everybody met to take tea; each was then free in his actions till breakfast, and the mistress of the house passed the time in working with her overseer, her steward and chief butler. Before dinner the family met again to chat or read; the evening was consecrated to walking, play and music; Madame Odintsof retired at half past ten, gave her orders for the next day, and went to bed. This regular and, in a way, somewhat solemn life, hardly pleased Bazarof; he said that it seemed to roll on rails; the liveried lackeys, the majestic butlers clashed with his democratic feelings. He found that to be consistent he should also have to dine in the English style in dress coat and white cravat. He had an explanation one day on this point with Anna Serghe\u00efevna, who allowed each one to express his opinion freely. She heard him to the end and said to him: " From your point of view the observation is just; and it is true that I play the despot a little. But in the country it is impossible to live without order; you would be consumed with ennui." She continued to act in her own way; Bazarof grumbled; but it was precisely because the life rolled "as on rails," that it appeared so agreeable to him, as well as to Arcadi. Besides, since their arrival a change worth noting had taken place in them. Bazarof, for whom Madame Odintsof had a marked preference, although she was rarely of his opinion, began to show an agitation that had not been known in him; he easily got excited, spoke what he did not believe, often had a sad air, and could not remain in one place, as if something continually impelled him to change his position. As to Arcadi, who had immediately decided that he was in love with Madame Odintsof, he did not delay giving himself up to a calm melancholy. But that did not prevent him at all from drawing near to Katia, it even contributed in some way to dispose him to it. "*She* does not appreciate me! Eh! Well, let it be so . . . But here is a good creature who does not repulse me," he said to himself, and his heart tasted anew the sweetness of feeling himself generous, as before in the case of his father. Katia confusedly understood that he sought some consolation in her society; she did not refuse him the sweet satisfaction that is afforded by a friend-ship at once timid and confiding, and she gave herself up to it. They did not talk to each other in the presence of Madame Odintsof. Katia drew herself in in some way under the clairvoyant look of her sister; and Arcadi, as suited a lover, could not grant the least attention to anybody whatever in the presence of the object of his flame; but he was at his ease only with Katia. He had the modesty of not believing himself worthy of occupying Madame Odintsof's attention; he lost countenance when he found himself alone with her, and he did not know what to say to her; Arcadi was too young for her. With Katia, on the contrary, he was perfectly at his ease; he treated her with indulgence, did not hinder her from telling him the impres-sions that she got from music, novels, verses and other "trifles," without remarking or being willing to confess that he himself was occupied with these "trifles." Katia, on her part, did not prevent him from being melancholy. Arcadi found himself at his ease with Katia, Madame Odintsof with Bazarof ;—and therefore when they were all together, the two pairs usually separated at the end of a few instants, and went each their own way, especially during the walks. Katia adored nature; Arcadi loved it also, although he did not dare avow it; Madame Odintsof was rather indifferent to it, as well as Bazarof. The two friends finding themselves almost constantly separated, the result was that their old relations began to be modified. Bazarof ceased to talk with Arcadi about Madadme Odintsof, or

even to criticise her "aristocratic manners;" he continued
to praise Katia, and he only suggested to Arcadi to moderate the sentimental tendencies that he noticed in her ; but
his praises were short, his advice a little dry ; he conversed with Arcadi much less than before ; he even avoided
him ; he almost seemed ashamed before him.   Arcadi noticed all this very plainly ;·but he did not confide it to any
one.

The true cause of this new state of things was the feeling with which Madame Odintsof had inspired Bazarof;
a feeling that tormented him and enraged him, and against
which he would have exclaimed with a scornful laugh and
cynical language if any one had made the slightest allusion
to it.   Bazarof was fond of women and appreciated beauty,
but he treated as unpardonable nonsense, as folly, love
in its ideal or *romantic* sense, as he called it, and put chivalric feelings nearly in the same rank as maladies and physical monstrosities.   He expressed more than once his
astonishment that Toggenburg with all the Minnesingers
and Troubadours had not been shut up in a lunatic asylum.
"If a woman pleases you," he used to say, "try to attain
your end ; if she refuses you, leave her in peace and turn
another way ; the earth is large enough." Madame Odintsof
pleased him ; the rumors that were afloat concerning her,
the frankness and independence of her character, the kindness that she manifested to him, all seemed to encourage
him ; but he soon understood that with her he would not
attain his end, and yet he did not feel, to his great surprise,
the courage to turn another way.   As soon as he thought
of her, his whole blood was on fire ; he could easily have
got to the end of his blood, but he felt another thing besides,
a thing that he would never have admitted, that he had
always laughed at, and that offended his pride.   In his conversations with Madame Odintsof, he showed more strongly

than ever his disdainful indifference for any kind of romanticism ; and, when alone, he recognized with a sombre indignation that romanticism had gained on him himself.   He
would take refuge in the woods and walk with large strides,
breaking the branches in his passage, murmuring impreca-
tions against himself and against her; at other times he
would go to a barn of hay, and obstinately keeping his eyes
closed, he would try to compel himself to sleep, and did not
always succeed, as was natural.   It was enough to imagine
that those chaste arms would one day encircle his neck,
that those proud lips would reply to his kisses, that those
intelligent eyes would look with tenderness, yes, with tenderness into his ; and he felt himself seized with a vertigo,
he forgot himself for some instants, until indignation burst
out anew in his whole being.   He surprised himself *in fla-
grante delicto* in effeminate thoughts, as if the devil tempted
him.   It sometimes seemed to him that a change had taken
place in Madame Odintsof, that her face had another expression, that perhaps . . . But then, he almost always stamped
his foot, or gnashed his teeth, striking his heart with his fist.

Yet Bazarof was not completely wrong.   He had struck the
imagination of Madame Odintsof ; he occupied her much.
Not that she was weary of herself when away from him, or
that she waited for him with impatience ; but his coming
animated her suddenly, she liked to be *tête-à-tête* with him,
and gladly talked with him, even when he opposed her and
shocked her elegant tastes and habits.   She seemed to wish
to make a study of putting him to the proof.

One day when he was walking with her in the garden, he
announced without preamble and in an abrupt tone that he
must soon go to his father's place.   She grew pale, as if
something had pricked her to the heart, and her emotion
was so lively that she was astonished at it ; she became lost
in reflections on what it could mean.   Bazarof had not

spoken to her of his departure to try her, to see how she would take it; he was never a man to have recourse to such means, to deceptions. The overseer of his father and his old servant Timofeïtch had come to find him that morning. This Timofeïtch, an active and old man, with yellowish hair, his face lightened up by the fresh air, and with little tearful eyes, had suddenly presented himself before him, in a coat of coarse bluish cloth, with a girder of leather, and tarred boots.

"Ah! good day, old man!" cried Bazarof.

"Good day, little father Eugene Vasilitch," said the old man with a joyful smile, which covered his whole face with wrinkles.

"What brings you here? Have you come to find me?"

"How can you believe it?" stammered Timofeïtch (Bazarof's father had expressly commanded him not to let it be suspected that he had been sent). "I have been to the town with errands of the master, and as they told me you had come, I stopped to see Your Honor . . . ; I did not come to disturb you!'

"Come! don't lie," replied Bazarof; "this village is not at all on your way."

Timofeïtch turned away with an embarrassed air without replying.

"Is my father well?"

"God be praised! he is very well."

"And my mother?"

"Arina Vlassievna also, God be praised."

"They are expecting me? are they not?"

The old man nodded his little head sideway.

"Ah, Eugene Vasilitch, why shouldn't they expect you? Believe me, my heart bleeds to see your parents . . . "

"Come, that's all right! all right! no descriptions. Tell them I'll come soon."

" I shall not fail," answered Timofeïtch with a sigh. When out of the house, he pulled his cap with both hands over his ears, got into a little droshky that he had left at the door, and went off at a jog-trot, but not in the direction of the town.

The evening of the same. day Madame Odintsof was seated in the parlor with Bazarof, while Arcadi was walking to and fro listening to Katia who was playing on the piano. The Princess had retired ; she could not endure visitors, and particularly these tatterdemalions of fresh date, as she called them. While she was in the parlor, her humor was endurable : but before her maid she abandoned herself to such fits of passion that her cap and her false front flew from her head. Madame Odintsof knew it all.

" How can you think of going away," she said to Bazarof ; "and your promise ? "

Bazarof started.

" What promise ? "

" You have forgotten it ? You were going to give me some lessons in chemistry."

" Unfortunately my father is expecting me ; it is impossible to wait longer. Besides, you have only to read Pelouze and Fremy, ' *Notions générales de chimie ;* ' it is a good book and easy to understand. You will find there all that you want to know."

" Yet you told me yourself, a few days ago, that a book can never replace. . . . I don't remember the term you used, but you know what I mean . . . ; don't you ? "

" What shall I do ? " replied Bazarof.

" Why go ? " said Madame Odintsof, lowering her voice.

He looked at her. She had her head leaning on the back of the chair, and her arms, bare to the elbow, crossed over her breast. She appeared paler in the glimmer of the lamp, which was covered with a light shade of cut paper. A long white dress enveloped her with its soft folds; you hardly saw the ends of her feet that were also crossed.

"And why should I remain?" answered Bazarof.

Madame Odintsof turned her head a little.

"How why? Do you not enjoy it here? Do you think you will not be regretted?"

"I doubt it."

"You are wrong to think so;" replied Madame Odintsof, after a moment of silence.—"Besides I do not believe you. It is impossible that you have said that seriously.—" Bazarof remained still without moving.—"Eugene Vasilitch, why are you silent?"

"What do you want me to say to you? Nobody is worthy of regret, and I less than any other."

"Why so?"

"I am a positive man, little interesting. I don't know how to converse."

"You would like compliments."

"That is not one of my habits. Do you not know yourself that the elegant side of life is foreign to me, precisely that which you appreciate so much?"

Madame Odintsof bit the corner of her pocket-handkerchief.

"Think what you please, but I shall have ennui when you are gone."

"Arcadi will stay," said Bazarof.

Madame Odintsof slightly shrugged her shoulders.

"I shall be *ennuyée*," she repeated.

"Indeed? Well you will not be so long."

"What makes you think so?"

"You yourself told me, that to give you ennui, your rules must be deranged. Your existence is so perfectly regulated, that it can leave no place for ennui or chagrin, or any painful feeling."

"You find that I am perfectly—or at least that my existence is arranged with great regularity?"

"Without a doubt! Hold; ten o'clock will strike in a few minutes, and I know in advance that you will drive me away."

"No, I shall not drive you away. You can stay. Open this window,—it is stifling here."

Bazarof rose and pushed up the window. It opened suddenly and noisily. He was not expecting it to open so easily; his hands trembled. The soft and warm night appeared with its almost black sky, accompanied by the feeble murmur of the trees and the healthy odor of a free and pure air.

"Pull down the shade and sit down," continued Madame Odintsof; "I should like to chat with you before you go. Tell me something of yourself; you never speak of yourself."

"I try to talk with you about useful things."

"You are modest ... notwithstanding, I should have liked to know something about you, about your family, about your father, for whom you abandon us."

"Why does she say all that to me?" Bazarof asked himself.

"All that would interest you very little," he added aloud; "you particularly; we are obscure people."

"I am then, in your opinion, an aristocrat?"

Bazarof raised his eyes to Madame Odintsof.

"Yes," he said, accenting the word strongly.

She smiled.

"I see that you know me badly," she replied, "although you assert that all natures are the same, and that it is not worth while to study them separately. Some day perhaps I will tell you my life ... ; but you will first tell me yours."

"You say that I know you badly," replied Bazarof, "it is

probable ; perhaps each individual is really an enigma. Let us speak of you for example ; you shun society, it fatigues you, and here you invite to you two students. Why, beautiful and intelligent as you are, do you live in the country ? "

"What ? What did you say then ? " quickly answered Madame Odintsof ; " I am . . . beautiful . . . "

Bazarof frowned.

" That is of little consequence," he continued with embarrassment, " I meant that I did not understand why you had fixed yourself in the country."

" You do not understand it ? . . . yet you explain it to yourself in some way ? "

" Yes, I suppose that you remain in the same place, because you are spoiled, because you love comfort, and are very indifferent to everything else."

Madame Odintsof smiled again.

" You decidedly do not wish to admit that I am susceptible of giving myself up to my imagination ? "

" From curiosity perhaps," Bazarof answered, looking down at her, " but not otherwise."

" Indeed ! Oh ! now I comprehend why we understand each other so well ; you are quite like me in this respect."

" We understand each other . . . ? " Bazarof hoarsely repeated.

" In fact ! I had forgotten that you wish to go."

Bazarof rose. The lamp burned feebly in the middle of the perfumed and darkened room, the window shade swung from time to time and let in the voluptuous freshness and the mysterious noises of the night. Madame Odintsof was completely motionless, but a secret emotion got possession of her little by little—and gained Bazarof. He understood all at once that he was tête-à-tête with a young and beautiful woman.

" Where are you going ? " she slowly said.

. He did not answer and fell back into his chair.

"So, you suppose me happy, spoiled by fortune," she continued in the same voice, holding her eyes fixed on the window, "and I, on the contrary, know that I have the right to consider myself very unhappy."

"You unhappy? How so? Are you, perchance, sensitive to foolish reports?"

Madame Odintsof let a kind of discontent appear on her face. She felt piqued at being so badly understood.

"These idle rumors have not even the power to make me laugh, Eugene Vasilitch, and I am too proud to be wounded at them. I am unhappy because life ... has nothing that charms me, that attracts. You look at me with an air of doubt, you say to yourself: 'Is it an aristocrat covered with lace and sitting in a velvet armchair that talks so?' I do not hide it from myself, I love what you call comfort, and in spite of that I hardly care to live. Reconcile these contradictions as you will. But, you must consider all this romanticism."

"You are in good health, free in your actions, rich," answered Bazarof, shaking his head; "what besides? What do you want more?"

"What do I want," said Madame Odintsof, and she sighed; "I feel very weary, I am old, I seem to have lived a very long time. Yes, I am old," she repeated, slowly drawing the ends of her mantilla over her bare arms. Her eyes met those of Bazarof and she blushed a little. "I have already behind me so many recollections: an opulent existence at St. Petersburg, then poverty, then the death of my father, my marriage, my travels in Germany ... and all that follows ... How many recollections! and none on which I care to dwell! and in future, before me, a long road, and no end ... So I have no wish to walk on."

"You are disenchanted?" asked Bazarof.

"No," answered Madame Odintsof after a pause, "but I am not satisfied. It seems to me that if I could attach myself strongly to something . . ."

"You would like to love;" Bazarof answered, "and you cannot. That is all your misfortune."

Madame Odintsof began to examine the trimming of her mantilla.

"Is it that I cannot love?" she said.

"I doubt it! only, I am wrong to call that a misfortune. On the contrary he to whom such mischance comes is the one to be pitied."

"What mischance?"

"To love."

"How do you know it?"

"By hearsay," Bazarof answered with humor. "You play the coquette," he thought; "you are *ennuyée*, and to pass time you make me angry; but I . . ."

His heart did in fact beat violently.

"Besides, you are perhaps too difficult," he added, and leaning over he began to play with the fringe of her armchair.

"Perhaps. All or nothing, that is what I wish. A complete exchange of feelings; if I give, it is to receive, and that without regret and without return. Otherwise, rather nothing."

"After all," answered Bazarof, "the conditions seem to me reasonable, and I am astonished that you have not found before now the one you look for."

"You believe then that it is easy to find one that will make this fair exchange?"

"Easy? no, if you set about reflecting coldly on it, if you calculate, inquire what you want, estimate yourself; but it is very easy to give yourself away without reflection."

"But how help valuing oneself a little dear? If one were

not worth something, what would be the good of giving oneself away ? "

" That does concern the one who gives herself, it is for the other to calculate how much the gift is worth. The essential thing is to be able to give oneself."

Madame Odintsof raised her shoulders a little, which were supported by the armchair.

" You speak exactly as if you had experienced all that," she said to Bazarof.

" Pure chance, Anna Serghefevna ; for affairs of this kind, as you know, are not in my line."

" But could you give yourself ? "

" I do not know that ; I do not wish to boast."

Madame Odintsof did not reply, and Bazarof was silent. The sound of the piano struck their ears.

" How late Katia plays this evening," said Madame Odintsof.

Bazarof rose.

" It is in fact very late," he replied ; " you ought to retire."

" Wait, why hurry . . . I have one word to say to you."

" What ? "

" Wait," repeated Madame Odintsof in a low voice, and her eyes rested on Bazarof ; she seemed to examine him attentively. Bazarof made some steps in the room, then he suddenly drew near Madame Odintsof, said to her abruptly : " Adieu ! " and went out of the room after having pressed her hand with so much force that she almost screamed. She put her fingers still pressed together to her mouth, blew on them ; then, rising hurriedly, she went with a rapid step to the door, as if to recall Bazarof. A maid came in with a carafe on a silver salver. Madame Odintsof stopped, told her to go out, threw herself again into the armchair and began to reflect again. Her hair became loosened and rolled down on her shoulders like a black serpent.

The lamp continued to burn a long while yet in the parlor, and Madame Odintsof remained still motionless: sometimes only she passed her fingers over her arms that the freshness of the night began to chill.

Nearly two hours after Bazarof went back to his room with a fierce air, his hair in disorder, and his shoes damp with dew.

Arcadi was still at his table, a book in his hand, and his overcoat buttoned up to his chin.

"You are not in bed?" said Bazarof to him almost with spite.

"You remained very long this evening with Madame Odintsof," said Arcadi, without replying to this question.

"Yes, I stayed with her all the time that you played on the piano with Katerina Serghelevna."

"I did not play;—" answered Arcadi, and he did not say more. He felt that tears were going to come into his eyes, and he did not wish to weep before his friend, whose mocking humor he dreaded.

XVIII.

The next day, when Madame Odintsof appeared for tea, Bazarof remained a long while leaning over his cup; then, he all at once fixed his eyes on her. She turned towards him as if he had just touched her, and he thought he noticed that she was paler than the evening before. She soon went back to her room and did not show herself again till breakfast. The morning was rainy. The whole party came together in the parlor. Arcadi took up the last number of a review, and began to read aloud. The princess, as her

habit was, appeared at first much surprised, as if he had
committed some great impropriety, then she coughed with
an ugly air; but he paid no attention to her.

" Eugene Vasilitch," said Madame Odintsof, "come into
my room ... I should like to ask you ... You mentioned to
me yesterday a manual ... "

She rose and went towards the door. The princess threw
a glance around her and her looks seemed to say : "See I
see I how astonished I am I" She looked at Arcadi again,
but he raised his voice, exchanged a rapid glance with
Katia who sat near him, and continued to read.

Madame Odintsof went to her room at a rapid pace.
Bazarof followed her without raising his eyes, and listening
to the light rustling of the silk dress that glided before him.
Madame Odintsof sat down in the same chair as on the
previous evening, and Bazarof also took the same place.

" How did you call that book?" she said to him after
a moment of silence.

"Pelouze and Fremy, *Notions Générales*," replied Bazarof.
"In addition I can also recommend to you Ganot, *Traité
élémentaire de physique expérimentale.* The cuts in it are
more detailed, and this manual is in general ... "

"Pardon me, Eugene Vasilitch," said Madame Odintsof
holding out her hand ; " I did not invite you here to speak
of manuals. I should like to take up our yesterday's conversation. You left me so abruptly ... This will not be displeasing to you?"

" I am at your service, Anna Serghéïevna. But what
were we talking about yesterday evening?"

Madame Odintsof gave a little side glance at Bazarof.

" I believe," she said to him, " that we were speaking of
happiness. I was talking to you about myself. But since I
have just pronounced this word happiness, I must ask you
a question. Why, even when we enjoy music, for example,

a fine evening, or a conversation with one who sympathizes
with us, why does the enjoyment appear to us an allusion
to some unknown happiness to be found somewhere else,
much rather than real happiness, a happiness that we are
ourselves enjoying? Answer me ... but it is possible that
you feel nothing of that kind."

"You know the proverb: 'One is well off only when
one is not present,'" replied Bazarof; "besides, you yourself
told me yesterday that you were not satisfied. But, it is
very true that such ideas never come into my mind."

"Perhaps they seem ridiculous to you?"

"No, but they have never come into my head."

"Indeed? I should like to know what *you* think about."

"How? I don't understand you."

"Listen to me; I have desired to have an explanation
with you for a long time. I have no need to tell you that
you are not an ordinary man, you know it very well. At your
age there is yet a long path before you. What are you preparing for? What is the future that awaits you? What is
the end that you look for? Where are you going? What
have you in mind? In a word, who are you, what are you?"

"You astonish me, Anna Serghëievna. You know very
well that I am studying the natural sciences; and as to my
person ... "

"Yes, who are you?"

"I have already had the honor of telling you I am a
future country physician."

Madame Odintsof made a sign of impatience.

"Why do you speak to me thus?" she answered; "you
do not yourself believe what you say. Arcadi would have
replied to me in this way, but you?"

"But in what is Arcadi—"

"Well then! Is it possible that so modest a sphere of
activity could content you? Do you not yourself assert that

6

you do not believe in medicine? A country physician?
You! with your self-esteem! You do not reply to me so,
except to get rid of my question. I do not inspire you with
any confidence. Yet, Eugene Vasilitch, I can assure you
that I could have comprehended you; I have been poor
myself, and as full of self-esteem as you; I have perhaps gone
through the same trials as you."

"That is all very well, Anna Sergheïevna, but you will
excuse me—I am not in the habit of making confidences,
and besides there is such a distance between us—"

"What distance? · Are you going to tell me once again
that I am an aristocrat. I thought I had proved to you—"

"Besides," said Bazarof, "I do not understand the pleasure that one can find in speaking of the future, which
generally does not depend upon us. If an occasion of doing
something presents itself, nothing better; in the contrary
case, one should consider oneself at least very happy not to
have given oneself up to useless chatter."

"You call a friendly conversation chatter—After all,
perhaps, in my quality of woman, you do not believe me
worthy of your confidence? You have so small an opinion
of us!"

"I have not a small opinion of you, Anna Sergheïevna,
and you know it very well."

"No, I know nothing;—but, admit it. I understand
that you do not wish to speak of your future; but that which
is produced in you to-day—"

"*Is produced!*" repeated Bazarof; "am I by chance an
empire or a society! The fact is that seems to me very un-
interesting; and besides, can each of us thus proclaim
aloud what *is produced* in us?"

"I really do not know why one should not confide all that
one has in mind."

"*You* can do it?" asked Bazarof.

"Yes," replied Anna Serghefevna, after a moment of hesitation.

Bazarof bowed.

"You are more fortunate than I," he said.

Anna Serghefevna looked at him as if to ask him to explain himself.

"Say what you will," she answered, "but I am no less brought to believe that we have not met each other in vain, that we shall be good friends. I am sure that you—how shall I call it? your stiffness, your reserve will disappear after a while."

"You find in me then a great reserve—or what else did you say—? stiffness?"

"Yes."

Bazarof got up and went to the window.

"And you would like to know the motives of this reserve, you would like to know what goes on in me?"

"Yes," answered Madame Odintsof, with an apprehension that she could not yet account for.

"And you will not be angry?"

"No."

"No?" Bazarof turned his back to her. "Well then, I love you foolishly, even to madness—That is what you force me to tell you."

Madame Odintsof stretched out her hands, and Bazarof rested his forehead against one of the window-panes. He was choking, a convulsive shudder ran through his members. But it was not emotion caused by the timidity of youth, nor the sweet fear springing from a first declaration, it was the passion that was struggling in him, a strong and violent passion, resembling wickedness, and perhaps not far from it.

Madame Odintsof felt at once fear and pity.

"Eugene Vasilitch," she said, and an involuntary tenderness betrayed itself in her voice.

He turned quickly, threw a devouring glance at her, and, forcibly seizing her two hands, drew her to his breast.

She could not disengage herself at once—Some seconds after she had taken refuge in a distant corner of the room.

He darted towards her—

"You did not understand me," she said hurriedly in a low voice, and quite cold with terror. One step more and she probably would have cried out; her whole attitude showed it. Bazarof bit his lips and went out.

Half an hour afterwards a maid brought Anna Serghelevna a note from Bazarof. This note contained only one line: "Ought I to go to-day, or can I stay till to-morrow?" Madame Odintsof replied: "Why go? I did not understand you, and you did not understand me." While writing these words, she said to herself: "In fact I did not understand myself."

She did not appear till dinner, and passed all the morning in walking up and down the room, her arms folded over her breast, stopping at intervals, sometimes before the glass, sometimes before the window, and continually passing a handkerchief over her neck; she seemed to feel a burning spot there. She asked herself why she had "forced" Bazarof, as he himself had said, to declare himself, and if she had not already suspected it herself. . . . "I am culpable," she said aloud, "but I could not foresee all that." She became thoughtful and blushed, recalling the almost fierce expression that the face of Bazarof had taken when he had sprung toward her.

"Or indeed," she said all at once—And stopping herself suddenly, she shook the knots of her hair. Seeing herself in the glass, her head half turned upside down, a mysterious smile in her half shut eyes and on her half open lips, it seemed to her that this image said something to her, that deeply moved her.

" No, no," she said at last, " God knows where that will end ; these things are not to be jested with ; tranquillity is still the best thing in this world."

Her tranquillity was not troubled ; but she grew sad and even shed some tears without well knowing why. It was not the shame of having been humiliated that made her weep. She did not feel herself humiliated ; she felt herself culpable rather, under the influence of different confused feelings, of the consciousness that her life was passing away, of a desire for novelty. She had by degrees advanced to a certain limit, and having glanced beyond, she had perceived there not an abyss, but emptiness or ugliness.

XIX.

Although Madame Odintsof had a great mastery over herself and was above prejudices, she nevertheless did not feel at her ease when it was necessary for her to appear in the dining room. However, the meal passed without any incident. Porphyry Platonitch arrived and told various anecdotes. He had just returned from town. Among other news he had learned there that the governor had ordered the clerks attached to his person to wear spurs, for greater speed in case he sent them anywhere on horseback. Arcadi chatted with Katia in a low voice, and like a skilful diplomat rendered little services to the princess. Bazarof was obstinately silent and sombre. Madame Odintsof, when he lowered his eyes, cast two or three times a furtive glance on his severe and bilious face, imprinted with a contemptuous firmness, and said to herself : " No, no, no." After dinner, she went into the garden with the rest, and seeing that Bazarof wished to speak to her, she went on some steps and stopped.

He drew near her, always with his eyes cast down, and said to her in a hoarse voice:

"I owe you an apology, Anna Seigheïevna, you cannot help being angry with me."

"No, I am not angry with you," replied Madame Odintsof, "but I am sorry."

"So much the worse; in any case I am punished enough. My position, you will admit, is sufficiently foolish. You wrote to me: 'Why go?' and I cannot and do not wish to stay. To-morrow I shall be gone."

"Eugene Vasilitch, why—"

"Why do I go?"

"No; that is not what I meant."

"The past does not return, Anna Sergheïevna—and sooner or later that must have happened. You see, it is absolutely necessary for me to go. I could stay on only one condition. That condition will never be realized. Pardon my boldness; but is it not so? You do not love me, and you never will love me?"

The eyes of Bazarof sparkled for a moment under their black lashes.

Anna Serghéïevna did not answer him. "This man frightens me," she said to herself.

"Good-bye;" Bazarof said to her, as if he had divined her thought, and turned toward the house.

Anna Serghéïevna slowly followed him. She called Katia, took her arm, and did not leave her until evening. She would not play cards, smiled slightly at every proposition for amusement, and the smile did not become her pale and exhausted face. Arcadi did not understand it at all, and observed it like all young people, that is, he continually asked himself: " What does this mean ? " Bazarof was shut up in his room. He appeared however for tea. Madame Odintsof would have been glad to address some kind words to him; but she did not know what to say to him. An unforeseen circumstance came to her relief; the butler announced Sitnikof.

It would be hard to describe exactly the strange entry that the young *progressive* made. Having decided, with his peculiar impudence, to visit a lady whom he hardly knew, and who had never invited him, but with whom he knew that cultivated acquaintances of his were staying, he was no less terribly frightened; and, instead of saying the excuses and compliments that he had prepared in advance, he stammered some nonsense, saying that Eudoxia Kukshin had sent him to learn some news of Anna Serghéïevna, and that Arcadi Nicolaïevitch had always expressed himself about her in terms of the greatest praise. He stopped short in the midst of his stupidities, and lost his head so completely that he sat down on his own hat. Notwithstanding, as no one drove him away, and as Anna Serghéïevna even presented him to her aunt and sister, he soon began to chatter in his usual style. The apparition of human folly often has its use in this world; it relaxes nerves too tightly strung, and calms feelings too presumptuous, or too vain, by reminding them that folly and wit have a common origin and almost an analogy. The arrival of Sitnikof gave everything in the house a more common —and more simple—turn; every one eat supper even with more appetite, and retired in the evening a half hour earlier than usual.

" Now," said Arcadi, already in bed, to Bazarof, who was also preparing to retire, " I can repeat what you once said to me: 'Why are you so sad?' Doubtless because you have performed some sacred duty?"

For some time the two young men had taken the habit of teasing each other in a somewhat bitter way, a sure sign of a secret discontent, and of suspicions that they wished to hide.

"I am going to my father's to-morrow," said Bazarof. Arcadi raised himself up and leaned on his elbow. This news surprised him and rejoiced him at the same time.

"Oh !" he replied, "and that is why you are sad ?"

" He who wants to know too much, grows old soon," * said Bazarof yawning.

"And Anna Serghe'ievna ? " replied Arcadi.

"Well, what of Anna Serghe'ievna ?"

"I mean : will she let you go ?"

" I am not in her employment."

Arcadi became thoughtful, and Bazarof turned his face to the wall.

The two friends kept silence for several minutes.

"Eugene !" cried Arcadi all at once.

"What ?"

" I will go with you to-morrow."

Bazarof made no answer.

" But I shall return home," continued Arcadi. " We will go together as far as the village of Khoklov, where you can arrange with Fedoti to continue your journey. I should have liked to get acquainted with your parents, but I should be afraid of troubling them, and of troubling you. I hope that after that you will come back to us for a while ?"

"I left my luggage with you," answered Bazarof without turning over.

" Why don't he ask me why I go ? and so unexpectedly too ?" said Arcadi to himself. "In fact, why do we go ; either of us ?"

---

* Russian proverb.

These questions remained unanswered in the mind of Arcadi, and his heart became filled with a secret bitterness. He felt that it would be hard to abandon a mode of life to which he had become so pleasantly accustomed; but to stay alone after the departure of Bazarof seemed to him harder yet. "Something has doubtless happened between them," he thought; "what good would it do for me to stay rooted before her after his departure? I should decidedly displease her, and should entirely ruin my prospects." He pictured to himself vividly Anna Serghefevna, then, other features by degrees replaced the face of the young widow.

"Katia also troubles me!" he whispered to his pillow, on which he had just let fall a tear. But all at once pushing back his hair, he cried:

"Why in the devil did that fool of a Sitnikof come here?"

Bazarof moved in his bed.

"I perceive, my dear fellow, that you are still stupid," he said at last. "The Sitnikofs are indispensable to us. Idiots of his kind are absolutely necessary to me. Do you understand? It is not for the gods to make pots." *

"Eh! eh!" Arcadi said to himself; and for the first time the conceit of Bazarof presented itself to him in all its greatness. "We are then gods, you and I? I mean, you, for I am perhaps only an idiot?"

"Yes," answered Bazarof, "you are still stupid."

Madame Odintsof did not show any great surprise when Arcadi told her the next morning that he was going with Bazarof; she appeared *distraite* and tired. Katia looked at him with a serious air and said nothing; the princess crossed herself under her shawl, in a way that he could not

---

* Russian proverb.

6*

help noticing. As to Sitnikof, this news undid him completely. He had just put on for breakfast a new coat,
which this time had nothing of the Slavophile ; the evening
before, the domestic who served him had seemed much
surprised at the quantity of linen that the new guest had
brought ; and now his companions abandon him ! He
struggled a little with mortification ; a hare when pursued
hesitates thus on the edge of the wood ; then he announced
all at once, with a frightened air, almost with a cry, that he
also proposed to go. Madame Odintsof did not press him
to stay.

"My calash is very comfortable," said the unfortunate
young man to Arcadi. "I can take you home. Eugene
Vasilitch has only to take your tarantass ; it will be much
more convenient."

"I am obliged to you, but our place is not at all in your
way ; you will have to make a great *détour*."

"That is nothing, I have plenty of time, and besides my
business calls me that way."

"Brandy business ?" Arcadi answered with an air which
was a little too contemptuous.

But Sitnikof was so overwhelmed that he did not begin
to laugh as he usually did.

"I assure you that my calash is very comfortable," he continued, "and there will be more room then for everybody."

"Do not chagrin Mr. Sitnikof by a refusal," said Anna
Sergheïevna.

Arcadi looked at her and bowed low.

They departed after breakfast. At the moment of parting
Madame Odintsof held out her hand to Bazarof and said to
him :

"We shall meet again, shall we not ?"

"As you wish."

" In that case, we shall see each other again."

Arcadi went down the steps first ; he took his seat in the calash with Sitnikof. The butler respectfully aided him to get in, but he himself felt quite disposed either to beat him, or to weep. Bazarof got into the tarantass. When they reached the village of Khoklov, Arcadi waited till Fedoti, the inn-keeper, had harnessed his horses to the tarantass, he then approached the carriage and said to Bazarof with his old cordiality :

" Eugene, take me with you, I want to accompany you."

" Get in," Bazarof answered between his teeth.

When Sitnikof, who was whistling and walking about the wheels of the calash, heard these words, he opened his mouth wide with surprise ; Arcadi quietly took his luggage, sat down by the side of Bazarof, politely saluted Sitnikof and cried :

" Go on ! off !"

The horses started and the tarantass was soon out of sight.

Sitnikof, thoroughly confused, cast an angry look at the coachman, who was busy giving little taps with his whip to the leading horse, jumped into the calash, cried to two peasants who passed : " Put on your hats, fools ! " and took again the road to town, where he arrived very late. The next day in the parlor of Madame Kukshin, he treated as their conduct deserved " the two proud and rude persons " that he had just left.

As he took his place by Bazarof's side, Arcadi clasped his hand warmly, and remained a long time without speaking. Bazarof appeared to understand this hand-clasp and this silence. He had neither slept nor smoked the night before ; he had hardly eaten anything for several days. His sombre and thin face was clearly marked out under the protruding visor of his travelling cap.

"Come, my friend," he said at last, "give me a cigar—I ought to have a yellow tongue? Look."

"Yes," answered Arcadi.

"I was sure of it—Well this cigar does not seem good—The machine is dislocated."

"In fact you have been changed for some time past," said Arcadi.

"That is nothing: I shall get right. A single thing troubles me, my mother's tenderness. If one does not stuff one's stomach ten times a day, you should see how she worries! My father is not like that, happily; he has seen the world; he has been through the mill, as they say. It is impossible to smoke!" he cried throwing his cigar into the midst of the dusty road.

"Your property is about twenty-five versts from here?" asked Arcadi.

"Yes. But here is a philosopher who can tell us exactly," and he showed the peasant sitting on the box to whom Fedoti had given the charge of the horses.

The peasant merely answered:

"Who knows? The versts are not measured here?" He began to grumble in a low voice at the leader who was shaking his head and pulling on the reins.

"Yes, yes," replied Bazarof, "that ought to serve you for a lesson, my friend. I really believe that the devil is mixed up with it! Each man hangs on the end of a thread; an abyss can open any moment under his feet. Eh, well, this perspective is not enough for him, and he imagines some folly or other that makes his life still more wretched."

"What do you allude to?" asked Arcadi.

"To nothing; just as I say without any allusions that we have both acted like fools. Besides, I have already noticed, in our climate, that sick people who worried over their condition always got well."

"I don't understand you very well," answered Arcadi; "it seems to me that you have had nothing to complain of."

"Since you don't understand me, I am going to tell you, as follows: My opinion is that it is better to break stones on the highway, than to let a woman get power over you, were it only with the end of her little finger. All that is—" Bazarof was going to pronounce his favorite term " romanticism," but he stopped himself and said "folly." "You won't believe me now, but I tell you the truth; we fell into the society of women, and it was pleasant to us; but it is as pleasant to leave this life as to bathe in cool water on a hot summer day. A man has something better to do than busy himself with such follies ; a man ought to be fierce, says an excellent Spanish proverb."

"Look here, you," he added, addressing the driver on the box, "have you a wife?"

The peasant turned round and showed to the two friends his flat face and weak eyes.

"A wife? Certainly. How not have a wife?"

"Do you beat her?"

"The wife? It sometimes happens. We do not beat without reason."

"Of course, and does she beat you?"

The peasant jerked the horses' reins. "What do you say, master? You like to joke." He evidently felt hurt.

"You understand, Arcadi Nicolaïevitch! But we have been beaten—See what it is to be civilized people."

Arcadi smiled with a constrained air, and Bazarof turned around, and did not open his mouth again during the rest of the journey.

The twenty-five versts seemed to Arcadi as long as fifty; but at last the little village in which the parents of Bazarof lived showed itself on the slope of a moderate hill. Near it in a grove of young birches was seen the turf-roofed manor-house. At the first hovel stood two peasants, with their hats on their head, quarrelling. "You are a big hog," said one to the other. "And your wife is a witch," replied the other.

"This graceful familiarity," said Bazarof to Arcadi, "and the warm tone of their discussion, ought to convince you that my father's peasants are not under very strict discipline. But there he comes himself, out of his house. He probably heard the bells. Yes, that is he, I recognize his face. Eh! eh! how gray he has grown, poor man!"

XX.

Bazarof was leaning out of the tarantass; Arcadi raised his head over his friend's shoulders, and perceived, on the steps of the manor-house, a tall, thin man, with bristling hair, a thin and curved nose, dressed in an old military cloak. He stood with his legs apart, a long pipe in his hand, and winked to defend himself from the sun.

The horses stopped.

"Here you are at last!" said Bazarof's father, without leaving off smoking, though the stem of his pipe seemed to dance between his fingers. "Come! descend! descend! let's have a good kiss!"

He began to embrace his son.

"Eniousha! Eniousha!"* cried a trembling voice within the house. The hall door opened, and a little old woman, in a white cap and short dress of a large-flowered pattern, appeared. She uttered a cry, staggered, and would certainly have fallen, had not Bazarof held her up. Her little plump hands were immediately clasped around his neck,

* Eniousha, Enioushenka, diminutives of Evgheni, Eugene.

and she laid her face on his breast. There was a long silence. One could hear only stifled sighs, panting sobs. The father of Bazarof winked even harder than before.

"Come! come! Arisha! enough of this," said he at last to his wife, at the same time exchanging a glance with Arcadi, who stood motionless near the tarantass, while the peasant on the box had turned away, very much moved. "This is quite useless! put an end to it, I entreat."

"Ah! Vasili Ivanovitch—" replied the old woman in the midst of her sobs. "To think that he is here. Our Enioushenka, our dear pigeon!" And still holding him in her arms, she lifted her face, all wet with tears, looked at him with a comically happy air, then hugged him anew.

"Oh, yes, all that is in the nature of things," replied Vasili Ivanovitch, "only it would be better to go into the house. Eugene has brought us a visitor. Excuse us," he added, turning to Arcadi with a slight bow. "You understand, the feebleness of woman—besides the heart of a mother—"

While he spoke thus, he was so moved himself that his lips, his eye-brows and his beard trembled . . . ; but he evidently forced himself to keep up his *sang-froid* and even to give himself an air of indifference.

Arcadi bowed.

"Come, my mother," said Bazarof, "let us go in," and he led the good old woman, who was all in tears, into the parlor. Having seated her in a convenient arm-chair, he rapidly embraced his father once more, and presented Arcadi to him.

"Enchanted to make your acquaintance," said Vasili Ivanovitch, "but don't expect too much; everything here is unpretentious, in military style. Arina Vlassievna, calm yourself for Heaven's sake; do me this favor; what a want of spirit! Our honorable guest will have a poor idea of you."

"My young friend," said the old lady in a lachrymose tone! "I have not the honor of knowing your baptismal name, nor that of your father."

"Arcadi Nikolaïtch," replied Vasili Ivanovitch in a low tone, with a dignified air.

"Pardon me, stupid woman that I am." She wiped her nose, and turning her head, first towards the right, then towards the left, she carefully wiped her eyes, one after the other. "Pardon me, but I thought that I was going to die without having again seen my—my p . . . p . . . pigeon."

"And now you have seen him, Madame," replied Vasili Ivanovitch quickly. "Tanioushka," he added, addressing a girl of twelve or thirteen, who, with bare feet, in a bright red calico dress, stood with a timid air near the door. "Bring your mistress a glass of water,—on a tray, do you hear? And you, gentlemen," he continued with a certain sprightliness which savored of the old style, "permit me to invite you to walk into the veteran's cabinet."

"Let me give you one more little kiss, Enioushenka," said Arina Vlassievna, in a plaintive voice.

Bazarof leaned towards her. "What a handsome boy you have grown to be!"

"As for that, no," said Vasili Ivanovitch, "but he has become, as the French say, an *hommefé*. But by this time, Arina Vlassievna, I hope that having satisfied your maternal heart, you are going to occupy yourself with getting our dear guests something to eat, for you ought to know that a nightingale does not live on songs."

The old mother arose.

"The table will be served immediately, Vasili Ivanovitch, I am going to run into the kitchen myself to make them put on the plates. All will be ready immediately. It is three years since I have seen him, since I have given him anything to eat or drink. That is something."

"Come then, housekeeper, make haste, try to get through with honor. And you, gentlemen, please follow me. Timofeitch here has just saluted you, Eugene. He too ought to be content, the old dog. Is it not so, old dog? Gentlemen, have the kindness to follow me." And Vasili Ivanovitch opened the march with an important air, dragging his old slippers over the floor.

His whole house consisted of six little rooms. That to which he conducted our young friends was called the cabinet. A table of heavy wood, covered with papers so black with dust that they looked as if smoked, occupied the space between two windows; on the walls hung Turkish guns, nagaïkas,* a sabre, two large maps, anatomical drawings, the portrait of Hufeland, a crown made of hair, placed in a black frame, and a diploma, likewise under glass; between two enormous closet bookcases of birch root was a leathern divan, well rubbed and torn in several places; books, little boxes, stuffed birds, vials and retorts were placed pell-mell on the shelves; finally, in one corner of the room was a worn-out electrical machine.

"I have forewarned you, my dear visitors," said Vasili Ivanovitch, "that we are lodged here, so to speak, as on a bivouac—"

"Cease your excuses!" replied Bazarof; "Kirsanof knows very well that we have not the wealth of Crœsus and that our house is not a palace? Where shall we lodge him? That is the question."

"Rest easy, Eugene. I have an excellent room in the wing; your friend will do very well there."

"You have built a wing then in my absence?"

"What! there where the bath is," said Timofeitch.

"That is, at the side of the bath room," Vassili Ivanovitch hastened to add; "besides in summer—I will run

* Cossack whips.

there and give my orders. Timofeitch, you would do well, meanwhile, to go and look after the baggage of these gentlemen. As for you, Eugene, it is well understood that I shall stow you away in my cabinet; *suum cuique.*"

" The droll old fellow ! " said Bazarof when his father had gone. " He is as odd as yours, only in another way. He talks a little too much."

" Your mother appears to me also an excellent woman," replied Arcadi.

" Yes, she is not bad. You will see what kind of a dinner she will give us."

" They did not expect you to-day, little father; we have no meat," said Timofeitch, who had just brought in Bazarof's valise.

" We will let the meat pass ; where there is nothing the king can have nothing. Poverty is not a vice, they say."

" How many peasants has your father ? " asked Arcadi.

" The estate is not his, it belongs to my mother, and I think that there are at the most, about fifteen souls."

" Twenty-two, if you please," said Timofeitch with a wounded air.

The sound of slippers was again heard, and Vasili Ivanovitch reappeared in the cabinet.

" A few minutes yet," he cried triumphantly, " and your room will be ready for you Arcadi .. Nikolaïvtch ...? that is your honorable name if I am not mistaken? And here is some one who will wait on you," he added, designating a servant who had just entered with him, a young boy with closely cropped hair, clothed in a blue coat torn at the elbows, and wearing boots which were not made for him. " His name is Fedka. Show yourself indulgent to us ; I must again ask it, although my son has forbidden me.

However, this boy knows very well how to fill a pipe. You smoke of course ? ”

“ I generally smoke cigars,” replied Arcadi.

“ And you do wisely. I prefer cigars too, but it is extraordinarily difficult to procure good ones in the country here, so far from the capital ? ”

“ Finish singing *miserere*,” said Bazarof to him ; “ rather sit down on this divan and let me look at you.”

Vasili Ivanovitch seated himself laughing. He strongly resembled his son ; only his forehead was lower and narrower, his mouth a little larger, and he had a habit of continually moving his shoulders, as if the armholes of his coat pinched him ; he winked his eyes, coughed and moved his fingers ; his son, on the contrary was remarkable for a sort of listless immobility.

“ Sing *miserere*,” repeated Vasili Ivanovitch. “ Don't imagine, Eugene, that I wish to excite the pity of our guest. I particularly desire that he should not think us reduced to living in a desert. On the contrary, I even think that to a reflecting man there is no desert. In any case, I shall do my utmost not to let myself gather moss, as the saying is ; not to remain behind the age.”

Vasili Ivanovitch drew from his pocket a yellow silk handkerchief, quite new, which he managed to get when he went into Arcadi's room ; and he continued moving it in the air :

“ I do not speak for instance, of my having put a yearly tax on peasants, and giving them up half of my land, though that causes me considerable loss. I consider it a duty ; simple good sense commands me to act thus ; I am astonished that all the landed proprietors do not . comprehend it. It is of the sciences, of education in general that I speak.”

“ In fact, I see that you have the *Friend of Health* * for 1855,” said Bazarof.

* A worthless little Medical Journal.

" One of my old friends sends it to me as a remembrancer,"
replied Vasili Ivanovitch hastily. " But we have also some
ideas of phrenology, for instance," he added, addressing the
rest of his remarks principally to Arcadi, and showing in
the closet a little plaster head, the upper part of which was
divided into a multitude of compartments; " the names
of Schönlein and of Rademacher are not unknown to us."

" They still believe in Rademacher in the government of
X—?" asked Bazarof.

Vasili Ivanovitch began to cough.

" In the government of X—" he replied. " Doubtless,
gentlemen, you must know more than we; we must not
dream of catching up with you, who are destined to replace
us. In my time, I remember that the *humoralist* Hoffmann,
or Brown with his *vitalism*, appeared very ridiculous to us,
and yet they had made some noise in their day. Some
new man has replaced Rademacher with you and you adopt
him, but it is possible that in twenty years he will be laughed
at in his turn."

" I will tell you to console you," added Bazarof, " that at
present we laugh at medicine in general and recognize no
master."

" How so? Yet you are going to be a doctor ?"

" Yes, but the one does not prevent the other."

Vasili Ivanovitch thrust his fingers into his pipe, which
still contained a few warm ashes.

" Perhaps, perhaps," said he, " I will not dispute. After
all, what am I ? A staff-surgeon on the retired list, *volatou.*
Now I have become an agriculturist. I served in your
grandfather's brigade," he added, turning again to Arcadi.
" Yes, yes, I have seen many things in my life. What society have I not frequented; whom have I not met ! I myself, the individual who is now before you. I have felt the
pulse of prince Witgenstein and of Zhukovski! I have

likewise known, in the army of the South, the men of the Fourteenth * ; you understand me."

Vasili Ivanovitch pronounced these last words pinching his lips in a very significant way.

" I had them all on my finger ends. As for the rest, I did not mix myself up in what did not concern me ; I knew my lancet and nothing more. I ought to tell you that your grandfather was a very worthy man, a true soldier."

" He was a true blockhead, acknowledge it," said Bazarof negligently.

" Ah ! Eugene ! how can you employ such terms ! it is unpardonable—Doubtless General Kirsanof was not of the number—"

" Come ! let him rest ! " replied Bazarof. " As we arrived I noticed with great pleasure that your birch grove has grown very nicely."

Vasili Ivanovitch became suddenly animated.

" That is nothing ; you must see the garden. I planted it with my own hand ! We have fruit trees, all sorts of shrubs and medicinal plants. You may laugh as you please, young people, but old Paracelsus did not the less proclaim a great truth : *In herbis, verbis et lapidibus.* . . . As for me, you know very well that I have given up practice ; however, it happens two or three times a week that I take up my old trade again. They come to ask my advice ; it is impossible to drive people away. Often the poor come ; besides, there is no physician in the country. I have a neighbor, an old major, who also tries to cure sick people. I asked him one day if he had studied medicine. He said : ' No, he had not studied medicine, but it was from philanthropy !' Ha ! ha ! how do you like that ? Ha ! ha ! ha !"

" Fedka ! fill me a pipe," cried Bazarof in an undertone.

" We have still another doctor," continued Vasili Ivan-

* An allusion to the conspiracy of the 14th of December, 1825.

ovitch in a voice which expressed a sort of anguish. "Imagine him coming to an invalid who is already *ad patres*. The
servant does not wish to let him enter, and says, 'you are
not needed any more.' The doctor, who did not expect
this reply, is troubled and asks the servant: 'Did the sick
man have the hiccoughs before he died?'—'Yes.'—'And
very hard?'—'Yes.'—'Ah? that is good!' And he goes
away, ha! ha! ha!"

The old man laughed alone; Arcadi smiled from politeness. Bazarof contented himself with inhaling a whiff of
tobacco smoke. The conversation lasted thus for nearly an
hour. Arcadi went into his room, which served as a sort
of ante-room to the bath, but was nevertheless very comfortable. At length Tanioushka appeared, and announced
that dinner was ready.

Vasili Ivanovitch rose first.

"Come gentlemen, pardon me generously if I have fa-
tigued you. I hope that my housekeeper will please you
better than I."

The dinner, though hastily prepared, was very good, even
abundant; the wine alone left something to be desired; the
sherry, in color almost black, which Timofeitch had bought
in the city of a merchant of his acquaintance, had an after
taste of resin and copper. They were also much incon-
venienced by flies; usually a little servant drove them away
with a branch of a tree, but Vasili Ivanovitch had dis-
pensed with this care in order not to expose himself to the
criticisms of the young progressives. Arina Vlassievna had
found time to make her toilet; she wore a large cap trimmed
with ribbons and a blue flowered shawl. She began to cry
again as soon as she saw her Eniousha, but it was not
necessary for her husband to interfere to calm her; she
herself dried her eyes as soon as possible, for fear of spoil-
ing her shawl. The young men did honor to the repast;

the hosts, having already dined, did not eat anything. The waiting was done by Fedka, who was much incommoded by his boots, and by a woman, blind in one eye, with masculine features, named Anfisushka, uniting the functions of butler, laundress and poultry-keeper. All through dinner Vasili Ivanovitch walked the floor with a happy and even ecstatic air, while he told of the cruel anxiety which the policy of the emperor Napoleon and the obscurity of the Italian question caused him. Arina Vlassievna did not seem to see Arcadi; her chin supported on her hand, one had a full view of her round face, to which the little swollen lips, red as cherries, and the moles scattered over her cheeks and above her eyebrows, gave a remarkable expression of simple good nature. With her eyes fixed on her son she sighed continually; she was dying to know how long he was going to stay, but she did not dare ask him. "If he should tell me only two days?" she said to herself, and her heart throbbed with fear. After the roast, Vasili Ivanovitch disappeared for a moment and returned soon, bringing half a bottle of champagne which he had uncorked.

"Although we live in a savage country," said he, "we have something to enliven us on great occasions."

He filled three large glasses and a small one, drank to the health of the "dear visitors," emptied his glass at one draught, and obliged Arina Vlassievna to drain the little glass to the last drop. When they came to the dessert, Arcadi, who could not endure sweetmeats, felt obliged to taste three different kinds, newly prepared, all the more since Bazarof refused them flatly, and began to smoke a cigar. After the dessert came tea, crackers and butter; then Vasili Ivanovitch led them all into the garden, in order to enjoy the evening, which was magnificent. As they passed a bench, he whispered in the ear of Arcadi—"It is in these places that I love to become a philosopher, as I contemplate the sunset; that suits a solitary man.   A little farther on **I** have planted the trees dear to Horace."

" What trees ?" asked Bazarof brusquely.

" But—— acacias, I think ——" Bazarof began to yawn.

" I think that the travellers would do well to abandon themselves to the arms of Morpheus," said Vasili Ivano-vitch.

" That means that it is time to go to bed," said Bazarof. " I approve of the proposition.   Come !"

And saying good night to his mother, he kissed her on the forehead ; as she embraced him she made the sign of the cross three times behind his back.   Vasili Ivanovitch conducted Arcadi to his room, and left him after having wished him " the sweet repose which he himself enjoyed at that happy age."   In truth Arcadi slept very well in his little room which exhaled an odor of fresh shavings, and where two crickets behind the stove sang sleepily.   Vasili Ivanovitch went from Arcadi's room into his own cabinet, and seating himself on the foot of his son's bed, that is, on the divan, he disposed himself to talk a little ; but Bazarof sent him away immediately, telling him that he was sleepy ; however, he did not close his eyes that night.   His sullen glance went out into the darkness; the recollections of infancy had no power over him, and the sad impressions of the day before still agitated his mind.   Arina Vlassievna prayed earnestly before her images ; then she remained for a long time with Anfisushka, who, standing like a statue before her mistress and looking at her with one eye, confided to her mysteriously, in a low voice, a host of remarks and conjectures relative to Eugene Vasilievitch.   The joy, the wine, and the tobacco smoke, had so unsettled the brain of the old lady, that her head turned ; her husband began to talk with her, but he soon gave it up, and departed with a resigned wave of the hand.

Arina Vlassievna was a true type of the lesser Russian nobility of the old *régime;* she ought to have come into the world two hundred years earlier, in the time of the grand dukes of Moscow. Very impressible and of great piety, she believed in every possible omen, in divinations, in witchcraft, in dreams ; she believed in the "Yourodivi,"* in familiar spirits, in wood spirits, in evil conjunctions, in the evil eye, in popular remedies, in the virtues of salt placed on the altar on Holy Thursday, in the approaching end of the world; she believed that if the tapers of the midnight mass at Easter were not extinguished, the buck- wheat harvest would be good, and that the mushrooms do not grow after a human eye has looked on them; she be- lieved that the devil likes places where there is water, and that all Jews have a blood stain on their breasts ; she was afraid of mice, of adders, of frogs, of sparrows, leeches, thunder, of cold water, draughts of air, horses, gnats, red- haired men, and black cats, and considered crickets and dogs impure creatures ; she eat neither veal, nor pigeons, nor crabs, nor cheese, nor asparagus, nor artichokes, nor hares, nor water-melons (because a cut melon recalls the cut head of St. John the Baptist); and the mere thought of oysters, which she did not even know by sight, made her shudder; she liked to eat, and fasted rigorously ; she slept ten hours a day and did not go to bed at all if Vasili Ivan- ovitch complained of a headache. The only book which she had read was entitled : *Alexis, or the Cottage in the Forest;* she wrote, at the most, but one or two letters a year, and was admirably skilled in sweetmeats and pre- serves, although she did not put her hand to anything, and did not usually like to stir from her place.

Arina Vlassievna was besides very good, and not wanting

* The Russian Yourodivi resemble the "Innocents" of the mid- dle ages.

7

in a certain common sense.   She knew that there existed
in the world masters to command and men of the people to
obey, and that was why she found no fault with the obse-
quiousness of inferiors, and with their grovelling salutations ;
but she treated them with great gentleness, never let a beg-
gar pass without giving him alms, and criticised nobody,
although she was not an enemy to gossip.   In her youth she
had an agreeable face, played on the harpsichord and spoke
French a little.   But during the long journeys of her husband, whom she had married against her will, she had grown
fat and forgotten the music and French.   While she adored
her son, she was very much afraid of him ; it was Vasili
Ivanovitch who administered her estate, and in that respect
she left him full liberty ; she sighed, fanned herself with her
handkerchief, and lifted her eyebrows with fear, when her
old husband began to talk to her of reforms in process of
execution and of his own plans.   She was distrustful, continually on the watch for some great misfortune, and began
to weep as soon as she happened to remember anything
sad.   Women of this sort are beginning to become rare ;
God knows whether we ought to rejoice at it !

XXI.

As soon as he arose the next morning Arcadi opened the
window, and the first object that met his eyes was Vasili
Ivanovitch in a Tartar dressing gown, with a pocket handkerchief for a girdle, working in the kitchen garden.   Noticing his young guest he leaned on his spade and called to
him :—

"Good morning ! how have you passed the night ?"

"Very well," replied Arcadi.

"You see before you a sort of Cincinnatus," replied the

old man: "I am preparing a bed for the autumn radishes. We live now in a time, God be praised for it, when every one is obliged to support himself with his own hands; one cannot depend on others; we must work for ourselves. Whatever may have been said to the contrary, Jean Jacques Rousseau was right. Half an hour ago, my dear sir, you would have surprised me in a very different position from that in which you see me. A peasant came to consult me about a case of dysentery; I—how shall I say it? I gave him an injection of opium; I drew a tooth for another. I proposed to the latter to take ether, but she would not consent to it. All this I do gratis—*as amater*. For the rest, I have nothing to blush for; I am a plebeian, *homa novus;* I have no coat of arms, like my beloved wife—But would it not be agreeable to you to come here in the shade, to breathe the morning freshness before breakfast?"

Arcadi went out to join him.

"Welcome," continued Vasili Ivanovitch, raising his hand in military style to the greasy cap which covered his head; "I know that you are accustomed to all the refinements of luxury, but even the great men of this world do not disdain to pass some time under the roof of a cottage."

"How can you call me a great man of this world?" exclaimed Arcadi; "and I am not at all accustomed to luxury."

"Permit me, permit me," replied Vasili Ivanoitch with a gracious air; "although I find myself at present laid on the shelf, in former days I came in contact with the world, and I recognize a bird by its flight. I am also something of a psychologist and physiognomist. If I had not had this gift, as I shall permit myself to call it, I should have been lost long ago; I should have been crushed, poor little worm of the dust that I am. I will say to you without a compliment, the friendship which exists, according to what

I see, between you and my son delights me very much. I have just left him; he has risen very early, according to his habit, which you ought to know, and is walking about the neighborhood. Permit me to ask a question : Have you been long acquainted with my son ? "

" We became acquainted last winter."

" Indeed ?   Let me ask one more question.—But we. might sit down.   Permit me to ask you as a father, with all frankness, what you think of my Eugene ? "

" Your son is one of the most remarkable men I have ever met," responded Arcadi with animation.

The eyes of Vasili Ivanovitch opened suddenly, and a slight flush colored his cheeks.   He dropped the spade which he had been holding.

" You think so ? "—he began.

" I am certain," continued Arcadi, " that a great future awaits your son ; he will make your name illustrious.   I was convinced of it at our first meeting."

" How—how so ? "—said Vasili Ivanovitch with an effort. An ecstatic smile played upon his large lips, and did not leave them.

" Would you like to know how we became acquainted ? "

" Yes—and generally—" ·

Arcadi began to speak of Bazarof with even more animation than on the evening when he danced a mazurka with Madame Odintsof.   Vasili Ivanovitch listened to him, blew his nose, gathered his handkerchief up into both hands, coughed, tossed back his hair, and at last, no longer able to contain himself, he leaned towards Arcadi, and kissed his shoulder.

" You have made me the happiest of men," said he without ceasing to smile.   " I must confide to you that I—that I idolize my son !   I do not speak of my poor wife ; she is a mother, and she has the feelings of one.   But for myself,

I dare not let my son know how much I love him, it would displease him. He cannot endure effusions of that kind : many persons even reproach him for this firmness of character, and attribute it to pride or insensibility ; but men like him ought not to be measured by the same standard with common mortals, don't you agree with me ? For instance, any one else in his place would have made demands on the paternal purse. Well, he has never asked us for a kopeck too much, God knows."

"He is a disinterested, honorable man," said Arcadi.

"A model of disinterestedness. As for me, Arcadi Nikolaïtch, I am not contented with idolizing him, I am proud of him, and what flatters my pride the most is the thought that some day the following lines will be read in his biography : 'The son of a simple regimental surgeon, who, however, early understood him, and neglected nothing for his instruction. . . ' " The old man's voice was choked.

Arcadi pressed his hand.

"What do you think ? " asked Vasili Ivanovitch after a moment of silence ; "it is not in the medical career that he will arrive at the celebrity which you predict for him ? "

"No, but, doubtless, even in that he may be destined to take his place among the most learned."

"What then is the career which—"

"That is hard to tell now,—but he will be celebrated."

"He will be celebrated," repeated the old man, and fell into a profound revery.

"Arina Vlassievna asks you to come to tea," said Anfisushka, who was passing by with a dish of raspberries.

Vasili Ivanovitch started and straightened himself up.

"Will there be cream for the raspberries ? " said he.

"Yes, there will be some."

"Let it be very cold ; do you hear ! Do not stand on

ceremony, Arcadi Nikolaïtch, take more. Why does not Eugene return?"

"I am here," said Bazarof from Arcadi's room.

Vasili Ivanovitch turned quickly.

"Ah! you thought to surprise our guest, but you are late, *amice*, for we have been talking for an hour. Now come and take some tea, your mother is waiting for us. By the way, I have something to ask you."

"What?"

"There is a peasant here who is suffering from an icterus."

"That is, he has the jaundice?"

"Yes, he is attacked with a chronic and very obstinate icterus. I have prescribed centaury and St. Johnswort; I have also told him to eat carrots and to drink soda water. But those are only palliatives; something more energetic ought to be adminstered. Although you ridicule medicines, I am sure you can give me good advice. But we will speak of that later. Come and take tea."

Vasili Ivanovitch jumped lightly from the bench, and sang these lines of *Robert le Diable*:

> "Le vin, le vin, le vin, le jeu, les belles,
> Voilà, voilà, voilà mes seuls amours."

"What vitality!" said Bazarof leaving the window.

It was mid-day. The heat was stifling, in spite of the fine curtain of white clouds which veiled the sun. Everything was silent; the cocks alone crowed in the village, and their languid voices gave all who heard them a singular sensation of laziness and *ennui*. From time to time the piercing cry of a young sparrow-hawk came like a plaintive appeal from the top of a tree. Arcadi and Bazarof were lying under the shade of a little hay-mow, on some armfuls of a plant which made a dry sound at the least friction, although it was still green and odorous.

"That aspen, "said Bazarof, "recalls to me my childhood ; it grows on the edge of a hollow, formed on the site of some brick-works. I used to believe that this tree and hollow had the power of a talisman : I was never weary in their neighborhood. I did not then comprehend that if I did not suffer from ennui it was because I was a child, now that I have grown up, the talisman has lost its power."

"How many years in all have you passed here ?" asked Arcadi.

"Two years in succession ; then we came here from time to time. We had a wandering life, we almost always roved from one city to another."

"Has this house been built long ?"

"Yes . . . it was my grandfather—my mother's father—who built it."

"Who was your grandfather ?"

"The devil take me if I know! A second major, I believe. He had served under Suvorof and used perpetually to be telling how they had crossed the Alps. He probably bragged."

"That then is why you have a portrait of Suvorof ? I like little houses like yours very much, old and warm ; they have too a peculiar smell."

"They smell of lamp oil* and lye," replied Bazarof. "And the flies in these pretty houses ! Phew ! "

"In your childhood," replied Arcadi, after a moment's silence, "they did not treat you severely ? "

"You know my parents ; they are not stern people."

"You love them very much, Eugene ? "

"Well—yes, Arcadi."

"They have so much affection for you ! "

Bazarof did not reply.

* Used for the lamps that burn before the images.

" Do you know what I am thinking of?" said he at last, putting his arms under his head.

" No ; tell me."

" I think that life is very pleasant for my parents! my father is interested in everything, although he is sixty years old ; he talks of *polliative* means, treats invalids, is generous with the peasants ; in a word, he follows the instincts of his heart ; my mother has no more to complain of ; her day is so filled with all sorts of occupations, with 'ohs!' and 'ahs!' that she has no time to reflect ; and I—"

" And you ? "

" And I say to myself : here am I, lying near this mow —the space which I occupy is so infinitely small compared with the rest of the space where I am not, and where one has nothing to do with me, and the duration of the time which will be given me to live is so short compared with the eternity in which I have not existed, and in which I shall never exist—and yet, in this atom, in this mathematical point, the blood circulates, the brain works, and also wants something—What nonsense ! What absurdity ! "

" Permit me to make an observation : what you say applies generally to all men—"

" It is true," replied Bazarof ; " I meant to say that these good people—I am speaking of my parents—busy themselves and do not think of their nothingness, it does not disgust them, it is not offensive to them, while I—I can only feel ennui and hatred ! "

" Hatred ? Why so ? "

" Why? What a question ! You have forgotten then ? "

" I remember everything, but I do not think that that gives you a right to hate. You are unfortunate, I admit, but—"

"Yes! yes! Arcadi Nikolaïtch. I see that you understand love like all the young people of the day; you say: chick, chick, chick! to the hen, and as soon as the hen comes near you, you take to your legs! That is not my way of doing. But let us drop this subject. When one cannot remedy a thing, it is foolish to occupy one's self with it." He turned over on his side and continued. "Ah! here is an ant merrily dragging a half-dead fly. Drag away; my old friend, drag away! Don't be troubled by its resistance; you can, in your quality of animal, despise all feeling of pity. It is not like us who are voluntarily crushed and broken."

"You should not speak in that way, Eugene! When have you been broken, as you call it?"

Bazarof raised his head.

"I think I have a right to be proud of it. I am not broken myself, and there is no woman that will ever break me. Amen! it is finished! You will not hear another word from me on the subject."

The two friends lay for some minutes without speaking.

"Yes," said Bazarof, "man is a strange creature. When one casts his eyes from one side and from a distance, over the obscure existence which the *fathers* lead here, it seems to be all very good. Eat, drink, and know that you conduct yourself in the most regular and wisest manner. Well, no; ennui soon overtakes you. You feel a desire to mingle among men, were it only to dispute with them; but in short you *must* mix with them."

"It would seem that one must arrange his life so that each instant should have a significance," said Arcadi, thoughtfully.

"Doubtless! it is always pleasant to make something significant, even when one does it wrongly. One could accommodate himself even to the hardships of insignificant

7*

things . . . but the little things, the petty troubles, there is the sore spot ! "

" There are no petty troubles to him who will not recognize them."

" Hum ! you have just said the reverse of a commonplace."

" How ! What do you mean by that ? "

" I mean this : To affirm, for example, that civilization is useful, is to utter a common-place ; but to declare that civilization is injurious, is to say the reverse of a common-place. It seems a little more *distingué*, but at the bottom it is absolutely the same thing."

" But where then can one seek the truth ? "

" Where ? I reply like an echo; where ? "

" You are melancholy to-day, Eugene."

" Indeed ? The sun must have affected my head; and then we have eaten too many raspberries."

" Then it would be well to take a nap," said Arcadi.

" Very well ; only don't look at me—People always look stupid when they are asleep."

" Then you are not indifferent to what people think of you ? "

" I do not know how to answer you. A man truly worthy of the name ought not to trouble himself with what people think about him ; the true man is he of whom there is nothing to be thought, but who makes himself obeyed or detested."

" It is strange ! I don't detest anybody," said Arcadi, after a moment of reflection.

" And I detest a great many people ! You have a gentle soul, mere water-gruel, how could you detest ? . . . You are timid, you lack confidence in yourself."

" And you," replied Arcadi, " have you a great deal of confidence in yourself ? Do you esteem yourself highly ? "

Bazarof did not reply immediately.

"When I have met a man who does not yield in my presence," he said slowly, "then I shall change my opinion of myself. Detest?" he pursued; "but for instance, you said one day when passing before the large and neat hut of your *starosta* Philip: Russia will never attain perfection till the last of the peasants has a dwelling like that, and each of us ought to contribute to it—Well. I immediately began to detest this peasant, whether Philip or Sidor, for whose well-being I should be obliged to trouble myself, and who would not have the slightest liking for me. However, what have I to do with his gratitude? When he shall inhabit a good hut I will do to cultivate nettles. Well, after that?"

"Be silent, Eugene,—listening to you to-day, one would be almost tempted to think those are right who accuse me of not having any principles."

"You talk like your worthy uncle. There are no principles in existence. You have not doubted that till now? There are only sensations. All depends on sensations."

"How so?"

"Yes. Take me for example. If I have a negative, skeptical mind, that depends on my sensations. It is pleasant to me to deny, my brain is thus constructed, and that is all! Why does chemistry please me? Why do you like apples? Always by virtue of sensations. The truth is there, and men will dig no further; not every one says this to you, and even I will not again repeat it to you."

"But, according to that, virtue itself would be but a sensation?"

"Undoubtedly!"

"Eugene!" said Arcadi, in a distressed tone.

"Ah! indeed? the morsel is not to your taste?" said Bazarof. "No, my dear, when one has decided to cut away

everything, one must not spare his own limbs. But we
have philosophized in this way enough. Nature inspires
the silence of sleep, says Pushkin."

" He never said anything of the kind," replied Arcadi.

" If he didn't, he could and should have done it in his
quality of poet. By the way, he was a soldier then ? "

" Pushkin never was a soldier."

" Come now! there is not a page where he does not exclaim : ' To arms ! to arms ! for the honor of Russia ! ' "

" How far are you going to carry all these fabrications ?
I call that a calumny."

" A calumny ? that's a good thing! Do you think to
frighten me by that word ? However much one may calum-
niate an individual, he deserves twenty times as much as he
gets."

" Let us try to go to sleep," said Arcadi with an offended air.

"With the greatest pleasure," replied Bazarof.

But neither of them could get to sleep. A sentiment
which resembled hostility crept into their hearts. After
several minutes they opened their eyes and looked at one
another in silence.

" See," said Arcadi suddenly, " see that dead leaf which
has just detached itself from a plane tree, and which is falling to the ground ; it flutters in the air exactly as a butter-
fly would do ? Is it not strange ? That which is most sad
and dead is like that which is gayest and fullest of life."

" O my dear Arcadi Nikolaïvitch ! " exclaimed Bazarof.
" I ask you as a favor not to talk poetically."

" I speak as I feel—But, really, this is despotism. A
thought comes to me. Why should I not express it ? "

" True ; but why should I not likewise say what I think ?
I think that it is indecent to talk poetically."

" It is doubtless more proper, according to you, to say
rude things."

"Ah! I see that you have decided to walk in the steps of your uncle. How happy that idiot would be if he could hear you!"

"What did you call Paul Petrovitch?"

"As he deserves; an idiot."

"This is becoming unbearable!" exclaimed Arcadi.

"Ah! the family feeling is awakened," said Bazarof tranquilly. "I have noticed that it is strongly implanted in all men. They are capable of renouncing everything, of stripping themselves of all prejudices; but to acknowledge, for instance, that a brother who has stolen pocket handkerchiefs is a thief,—that is beyond their strength. Indeed, when a person is so near to me, my brother, may it not be that he is a genius?"

"I have only obeyed the feeling of justice, and not that of family," replied Arcadi with vivacity. "But as you do not comprehend this feeling, as this *sensation* is lacking in you, you ought not to speak of it."

"That means that Arcadi Kirsanof is too superior to me for me to be able to comprehend him. I yield, and condemn myself to silence."

"Cease, Eugene, I entreat. We shall end by quarrelling."

"Ah! Arcadi, let us quarrel, I beg, let us beat one another even to the extinction of animal heat!"

"That might in fact end in—"

"In blows of the fist?" replied Bazarof; "Why not? here, on this hay, with all these idyllic surroundings, far from the world and from human eyes, nothing could be better. But you have not strength to measure yourself with me. I shall seize you by the throat."

Bazarof opened his bony fingers—Arcadi turned laughing, and took an attitude of defence—But the face of his friend, the sneer which contracted his lips, and the sombre fire with which his eyes shone, seemed to express a threat so real that Arcadi experienced a feeling of involuntary fear.

"Ah! I find you at last," cried at that instant Vasili Ivanovitch, appearing before the young men in a homespun white linen jacket, and on his head a straw hat, also home-made.

"I have been looking for you everywhere—but you have chosen an admirable spot and given yourselves up to a very pleasant pastime, lying on the ground, looking at the sky.— Do you know that this attitude has a peculiar signification?"

"I only look at the sky when I want to sneeze," said Bazarof peevishly, and approaching Arcadi he added in a low tone; "I regret that he has prevented us."

"Come, enough of that," replied Arcadi, and he pressed his hand furtively.

"I am looking at you, my young friends," continued Vas-ili Ivanovitch, shaking his head and supporting his joined hands on a stick which he had twisted, even artistically, into a spiral, and whose upper end was surmounted with a Turk's head; "I am looking at you, and I cannot weary of it. How much strength, youth in its bloom, ability, talent! —Castor and Pollux!"

"Good!" exclaimed Bazarof. "See how he launches off into mythology! You can see at once that he was strong in Latin in his time. Were you not honored with a silver medal for your themes?"

"Dioscuri! Dioscuri!" repeated Vasili Ivanovitch.

"Come, father, be reasonable; a little less tenderness."

"Once in a while does not make a custom," stammered the old man. "But I did not come to find you, gentlemen, to address compliments to you, but in the first place to an-nounce to you that we shall dine soon, and secondly to in-form you, Eugene—You are a talented boy, you know

men and women, and consequently you will pardon—
your mother was anxious to have prayers and thanksgivings
said on account of your arrival. Don't imagine that I am
going to ask you to be present at them, the ceremony is already over. But father Alexis——"

"The priest?"

"Yes, the priest is at the house—and will remain to
dinner—I did not expect that, and even discouraged it—
but, I don't know how it has been·done—he has misunder-
stood me—besides Arina Vlassievna—But he is a man who
is very sensible, and very well in all respects."

"I suppose that he will not eat my portion at the table?"
asked Bazarof.

Vasili Ivanovitch began to laugh.

"No, certainly not!" he replied.

"That is all that I ask. I am ready to sit down at table
with any one, no matter who."

Vasili Ivanovitch straightened his hat.

"I knew very well," he replied, "that you were above all
prejudices as to that. I, who have just entered my sixty-
third year, am free ·from them." (Vasili Ivanovitch did
not dare to confess that he had desired the prayers quite
as much as his wife; for he was no less religious than she.)
"But father Alexis was very desirous of making your acquaintance. He will please you, I am sure. He likes well
enough to take a hand at cards, and he even,—but that is
between us—smokes his pipe quite like the rest of us."

"Well! after dinner we will have a game of yeralash,*
and I shall beat you."

"Aha! we'll see about that."

"What? Perhaps you will bring certain talents into
play?" said Bazarof with a very peculiar intonation.

* A sort of whist.

A slight color flushed the bronzed cheeks of Vasili Ivan-ovitch.

" Are you not ashamed, Eugene—what is past is past. Well, yes, I am ready to acknowledge before our young friend that I had this passion in my youth, but I have paid dearly for it ! How warm it is to-day ! Allow me to sit down beside you, unless I shall disturb you ? "

" Not at all," replied Arcadi.

Vasili Ivanovitch seated himself on the hay, sighing.

" This couch," said he, " recalls to me, my dear sirs, my military life, the bivouacs, the field hospitals, often behind just such a haystack, now all over, praise be to God,—" He sighed.—" Ah ! I have seen cruel things in my life ! If you will permit me I will relate to you an interesting episode of the plague in Bessarabia."

" And which gave you the cross of St. Vladimir," said Basarof; " I know it, I know it.—By the way, why don't you wear it ? "

" I have just told you that I have no prejudices," replied Vasili Ivanovitch with embarrassment. (He had taken the red ribbon out of his button-hole only the evening be-fore.) And he began to relate the episode.

" Look at him, he is asleep ! " he whispered suddenly to Arcadi, pointing to Bazarof, and winking amicably.

" Eugene, get up ! " he added aloud. " Let us go to din-ner ! "

Father Alexis, a tall, robust man, with thick hair care-fully combed, and wearing over his lilac silk robe a large embroidered sash, conducted himself with much cleverness and tact. He was the first to shake hands with the young men, as if comprehending beforehand that they did not care to receive his benediction, and altogether acted with-out forced restraint. He preserved his own character, yet did not attack others. He was not afraid to introduce some

pleasantries on the Latin taught in seminaries, and under-
took, on another occasion, the defence of his archbishop;
after drinking two glasses of wine he refused a third; he
accepted the cigar which Arcadi gave him, but did not
smoke it, saying that he would take it home. He had,
however, a rather disagreeable habit of every now and then
raising his hand slowly and prudently to his face and crush-
ing the flies which settled there. He took his place at the
card-table without showing too much satisfaction, and
ended by winning from Bazarof two roubles and fifty kopecks in notes. (They had no idea of a *silver* rouble in the
house of Arina Vlassievna.) She, seated by the side of her
son (she never played), her chin resting on her hand according to her habit, only rose to order some new dainty to
be brought. She feared to be too attentive to Bazarof, and
he did not encourage her in any way; besides, Vasili Ivanovitch had enjoined upon her not to torment him: "Young
men do not like that," he repeated to her. (Do not let us
forget to say that nothing was spared for the dinner. Timofeitch in person went at day-break to the town to get
meat of the best quality; the starosta went to another point
to procure *nalimes,** perch and crabs; they gave as much
as forty kopecks to the peasants for mushrooms.) But the
eyes of Arina Vlassievna constantly fixed on Bazarof, expressed not only devotion and tenderness; one could also
read in them a sadness mingled with curiosity and fear, and
also an indescribable humble reproach. However, Bazarof
occupied himself very little with what his mother's eyes
might express; he scarcely spoke to her, and, when he did
so, confined himself to very brief questions. Nevertheless
he asked for her hand in the hope that it would bring him

* Fish of an exquisite flavor: of which is made *ukha,* a sort of
soup.

luck. Arina Vlassievna put her little soft hand into the
large, rough one of her son.

"Well!" she asked him after an instant, "has that had
its effect?"

"It is worse yet," he replied with a careless smile.

"You play entirely too boldly," said father Alexis com-
passionately, stroking his handsome beard.

"It is in the style of Napoleon;" replied Vasili Ivanovitch as he played an ace.

"And it is to that style that Napoleon owed his death on
St. Helena," replied father Alexis taking the ace with a
trump.

"Enioushenka, would you like a glass of currant water?"
asked Arina Vlassievna of her son.

Bazarof contented himself with shrugging his shoulders.

"No," he said the next day to Arcadi, "I shall leave here,
I am bored here, I want to work and it is impossible for me
to do anything. I am going to return to your home where
I have left all my preparations. One can at least be alone
when one wants to in your house. But here my father continually says to me: 'You can have the use of my cabinet, no one will disturb you;' and he himself does not leave
me for a moment. Besides it would somehow go against
my conscience to shut my door on him. My mother is not
less troublesome; I hear her constantly sighing in her
room, and when I go and stay with her I don't know what
to say to her."

"She will be very much grieved, and your father too,"
replied Arcadi.

"I shall return."

"When?"

"As I return to St. Petersburg."

"I especially pity your mother."

"Why? Because she makes you eat good fruit?"

Arcadi lowered his eyes.

"You do not know your mother," said he to Bazarof. " Not only has she an excellent heart, but she is also very intelligent. We talked together for more than half an hour this morning, and her conversation is very sensible and interesting."

"I was doubtless the subject of it?"

"We talked of other things also."

" It is possible that you are right. One often sees these things best from the gallery, as at billiards. When a woman can carry on a conversation for half an hour, it is a good sign. But all that will not prevent me from going."

" I don't know how you will tell them. They seem to think that we shall be here for two weeks yet."

" It is rather embarassing. Besides I had to-day the absurd idea of teasing my father, on account of a peasant whom he had whipped lately, and rightly. Yes, yes, rightly; don't make such eyes at me ; he did well to punish him, because he is an incorrigible thief and drunkard ; only my father did not think that I should be so well informed, as they say. He was very much confused about it ; and now that I am obliged to grieve him—as for the rest, it doesn't matter! Between here and marriage it will be all right! * "

Although Bazarof had pronounced these last words with a tolerably resolute air, he decided to defer the announcement of his departure until his father should be in his cabinet. At the moment of bidding him good night, he said to him with a forced yawn :

"Wait—I nearly forgot to tell you— Our horses will have to be taken to Fedoti to-morrow for the relay."

Vasili Ivanovitch was struck dumb.

* A Russian proverb.

" Is M. Kirsanof going to leave us," he asked at length.

" Yes, and I am going with him."

Vasili Ivanovitch started back dismayed.

" You are going to leave us ? "

"Yes—I have business. Be so obliging as to send the horses."

" It is very well," stammered the old man, " as far as the relay is concerned—it is very well—only—why—is it possible ? "

" It is necessary that I should go home with him for some days. I shall come back here again afterwards."

" Yes ? for some days—very well."

Vasili Ivanovitch took out his handkerchief and blew his nose, bending nearly to the ground.

" Well ! be it so ! —it shall be done. But I was thinking that you—longer. Three days after three years of absence, it is very—it is very little, Eugene ! "

" I have just told you that I shall come back soon. This is indispensable to me—"

" Indispensable—Well ! one must fulfil his duty before all—You want me to send the horses ? It is all right, but we did not expect it, Arina and I ! She has just asked some flowers from a neighbor to ornament your room."

Vasili Ivanovitch did not add that every morning in naked slippered feet he went to find Timofeitch and gave him a torn note which he sought at the bottom of his purse with his trembling fingers. This note was for the purchase of various provisions, principally eatables and the red wine of which the young men consumed so much.

" There is nothing more precious than liberty ; that is my principle—one must not restrain people—one must not—"

Vasili Ivanovitch was suddenly silent, and turned toward the door.

"We shall see one another again soon, father, I promise you."

But Vasili Ivanovitch did not turn back, he went out making a gesture with his hand. On entering his bed-chamber he found his wife already asleep, and began to pray in a low voice in order not to disturb her slumber; however, she awoke.

"Is it you Vasili Ivanovitch?" she asked.

"Yes, my dear."

"You have just left Eniousha? I am afraid that he will not find the sofa comfortable. I have, however, told Anfisushka to give him your camp mattress and the new pillows; I would also have given him our feather bed, but I think that I remember that he does not like a soft bed."

"That is nothing, my dear; do not disturb yourself. He gets along very well. Lord have mercy on us sinners!" he added, continuing his prayer. Vasili Ivanovitch said no more; he did not wish to tell his poor wife a piece of news which would have disturbed her repose.

Bazarof and Arcadi departed on the morrow. From early morning, everything assumed an aspect of sadness; Anfisushka dropped the dishes she was carrying; Fedka himself was quite disconcerted, and ended by leaving off his boots. Vasili Ivanovitch was more restless than ever; he forced himself to conceal his grief, talking very loud and walking noisily; but his face was furrowed, and his eyes seemed always to avoid his son. Arina Vlassievna wept silently; she would have quite lost her head if her husband had not lectured her lengthily in the morning. When Bazarof, after having repeated several times that he would return in less than a month, tore himself at last from the arms that detained him, and seated himself in the tarantass, when the horses started, and the sound of the bell mingled with the rolling of the wheels. when it became useless to look longer;

when the dust was entirely quieted, and Timofeitch, bent double and staggering, had got home again; when at last the two old people once more found themselves alone in the house which seemed to them also to have become narrower and older—Vasili Ivanovitch, who a few minutes before was so proudly waving his handkerchief from the top of the steps, threw himself on a chair and let his head fall on his breast. "He has abandoned us!" said he in a trembling voice: "Abandoned us! he became weary of us. Here I am a lone man, alone!" he repeated several times, each time holding up the forefinger of his right hand.* Arina Vlassievna approached him, and laying her whitened head against the whitened head of the old man, she said to him: "What is to be done, Vasili? a son is like a piece cut off from one. He is like a young falcon; it pleases him to come and he comes; it pleases him to go and he flies away; and we two, you and I, are like two puff-balls in the hollow of a tree; placed side by side we stay there forever, only I shall not change for you, as you will not change for me!"

Vasili Ivanovitch uncovered the face which he had hidden in his hands, and embraced his wife, his companion, more fervently than he had ever done, even in his youth; she had consoled him even in his grief.

XXII.

The two friends scarcely exchanged a word until they arrived at Fedoti's house; Bazarof was not satisfied with himself, and Arcadi was displeased with his friend. He felt besides that causeless sadness which is known only to young people on their first entrance into life. The coachman

* A Russian proverb says: "Alone like a finger."

having changed the horses remounted the box and asked if he must take the right or the left.

Arcadi started. The road on their right led to the city, and thence to his father's estate ; that on their left to the house of Madame Odintsof.

He looked at Bazarof.

" Eugene," said he, " to the left ? "

Bazarof averted his eyes.

" What folly ! " he replied between his teeth.

" I know very well that it is folly," answered Arcadi. " But what does that matter ? it will not be the first foolish thing that we have done."

Bazarof pulled down the visor of his cap.

He ended by saying, " Do as you choose ! "

" Turn to the left ! " cried Arcadi to the coachman.

The tarantass rolled from the side of Nikolskoia. But the two friends, having decided to commit a piece of folly, were more obstinately silent than before ; they seemed almost angry.

From the way in which Madame Odintsof's butler received them at the steps of the house, the young men speedily perceived that they had acted inconsiderately in yielding to this caprice. They were not at all expected, it was easy to perceive. Invited to walk into the drawing-room, they remained there for some time cutting a sorry figure. Madame Odintsof appeared at last ; she greeted them with her usual amiability, but seemed surprised at their prompt return ; she was scarcely charmed to see them again, judging by the slowness of her words and of all her movements. They hastened to tell her that they had stopped in passing, and that they should set out for the city in two or three hours. She confined herself to making a little exclamation, requested Arcadi to salute his father for her, and sent word of their arrival to her aunt. The princess came in looking very sleepy, which added to the habitually disagreeable expression of her yellow and withered old face. Katia was indisposed and did not leave her room. Arcadi comprehended at this moment that he wanted to see Katia quite as much as Anna Serghe*ï*evna herself. Four-hours passed in talking on indifferent subjects; Anna Serghe*ï*evna talked and listened without smiling. It was only at the moment of their departure that her old affability seemed to reanimate her.

"You must have found me very bad-humored," she said to them, "but do not mind that, and be sure and come and see me again, both of you, after a while."

Bazarof and Arcadi only replied by bowing, got into the carriage again, and went directly to Marino, where they arrived without hindrance, the next evening. On the road neither of them pronounced the name of Madame Odintsof. Bazarof especially maintained an almost constant silence, and kept his eyes obstinately fixed on the landscape far in the distance.

They were very glad to see them again at Marino. The long absence of his son was beginning to trouble Nicholas Petrovitch; he uttered a cry, leaped up on his sofa, and began to move his feet, when Fenitchka, entering his room with her eyes animated with joy, announced the "young gentlemen." Paul Petrovitch himself was agreeably surprised, and smiled with a patronizing air as he pressed the hands of the new-comers. They began to tell about their journey; Arcadi was the one who talked most, especially at supper, and the repast was prolonged until long after midnight. Nicholas Petrovitch opened several bottles of porter which came from Moscow, and he found it so to his taste that his cheeks became purple, and he laughed without cessation at once childishly and nervously. This general good humor extended even to the servants.

Duniasha did nothing but come and go like a madwoman, slamming the doors behind her; and at two o'clock in the morning Peter was still trying vainly to play a Cossack waltz on the guitar. The cords of the instrument had plaintive and agreeable vibrations in the calm of the country and the night. But the accomplished *valet de chambre* could never get beyond the preliminary flourishes; nature had denied him musical talent, as well as every other kind.

However, the inhabitants of Marino were not entirely free from care, and poor Nicholas Petrovitch had his good share of it. The farm gave him every day more trouble, miserable and paltry annoyances. The hired workmen caused difficulties which were really insupportable. Some demanded accounts and required an increase of pay, others left after having received an advance on their pay; the horses fell sick; the harness was constantly giving out; the work was badly done. A threshing-machine which had been brought from Moscow proved too heavy to be used; a bolting-mill was broken the first time it was tried; half of the cattle-sheds burned down, thanks to an old purblind servant, who went, in a high wind, to exorcise her cow with a pan of lighted charcoal; and this very old woman afterwards declared that the misfortune had happened because the master had taken it upon himself to have cheese and other novelties of the same nature made. The steward was suddenly attacked with laziness, and began to grow fat, as every Russian does who is fed on "free bread." His activity was confined to throwing a stone at a little pig which was passing, or threatening a half naked child as soon as he saw Nicholas Petrovitch; he slept almost all the rest of the time. The tenantry paid nothing and stole wood: often at night the guard drove away, not without a lively resistance, horses belonging to peasants, pasturing in the meadows of the "farm." Nicholas Petrovitch had appointed a penalty for this offence,

8

but generally the captured animals were returned to their
owners, after having spent some days in the master's stables. To crown all these annoyances, the peasants began
to quarrel among themselves ; brothers asked a distribution,
their wives being no longer able to live under the same roof ;
battles were continually taking place in the village ; a crowd
of peasants assembled suddenly, as if in obedience to an
order, in front of the overseer's office, repairing thence to
the master's house, their faces bruised with fist blows, often
in a state of intoxication, and loudly calling for justice ; in
the midst of the tumult the sobs and shrill lamentations of
the women mingled with the vociferations and abusive
words of the men. It was necessary to judge the quarrel,
to raise one's voice until one got hoarse, although knowing
beforehand that these efforts would be useless. They were
in want of hands for the harvest; an *odnovóiets* * of the
neighborhood, whose honest features inspired the greatest
confidence, and who had promised to furnish workmen for
two roubles a *desiatine*, broke his word in the most scan-
dalous way ; the peasants of the village demanded an un-
heard of price, and meanwhile the grain began to shell ;
there was the same trouble about the hay crop ; and as if
these vexations were not enough, the Board of Guardians
demanded with threats the immediate payment of the interest due.

"I am at my wit's end ! " exclaimed Nicholas Petrovitch
more than once. "It is impossible to correct these people
myself, and my principles do not permit me to have recourse to the police ; but yet they will do nothing without
the fear of punishment."

"*Du calme ! du calme !*" Paul Petrovitch would reply ;
and even in giving the advice he appeared very dissatisfied
himself, and pulled his moustache.

* A free peasant of noble origin.

Bazarof remained a stranger to these "miseries," and, besides, his position in the house scarcely permitted him to act otherwise. The day after his return to Marino, he had recommenced his experiments on frogs, infusoria and certain chemical combinations, and was entirely absorbed in this work. As for Arcadi, he thought it his duty, even if he did not come to the aid of his father, at least to appear disposed to do so. He listened patiently and ventured one day to give his father some advice, not with the hope of seeing it adopted, but in order to manifest his good will.

Domestic affairs inspired him with no aversion; he promised himself even with pleasure to devote himself at some day to agriculture; but for the moment he had other ideas in his head. To his great astonishment he thought continually of Nikolskoia; formerly he would have shrugged his shoulders if any one had told him that he could feel bored under the same roof with Bazarof, and moreover under what roof! under the paternal roof: but he really did suffer from ennuí, and he would have liked to be far away from there. He continued to take long walks, but that did not do him any good. Talking one day with his father he found that the latter had kept several rather interesting letters addressed to his wife by the mother of Madame Odintsof, and he begged so hard for them, that Nicholas Petrovitch hunted them up, not without pain, among his old papers, and gave them to him. Having come into possession of these half-effaced letters, he felt calmer, as if he had at last found the end to which he had been tending. "I say it to both of you," she had herself added. This thought did not leave his head.

"I will go, I will go! yes, the devil may take me!" But he recalled his last visit to Nikolskoia, the coldness of their reception, and his timidity got the upper hand. However, the "Perhaps" of youth, the secret desire to put fortune to the proof, to try his strength without a witness, without patronage, ended by taking him off. Ten days had not passed since the return of the young men to Marino, when, under the pretext of studying the organization of Sunday schools, he set out again for the city, and thence for Nikolskoia. Continually urging the coachman to go faster, he seemed a young officer rushing to the combat; joy, fear and impatience divided his heart.

" Above all, I must not reflect," he repeated to himself unceasingly. The coachman who drove him was an ugly peasant, who stopped before every tavern and asked :
" Shan't we kill the worm ? "

But the worm killed he remounted his box, and did not manage his horses. The high roof of the well-known house showed itself at last to Arcadi's eyes.

" What am I going to do there ? " he said to himself suddenly, but he had no longer any means of return.

The horses were pushing along, the coachman cried and whistled to keep up their ardor. Already the little wooden bridge resounds under the iron-shod feet of the horses and the wheels : here is the long alley of pines trimmed into a wall. A pink dress is visible in the midst of the dark foliage; a young face shows itself under the light fringe of a parasol. Arcadi has recognized Katia, and she has also recognized him.

He orders the coachman to stop the horses, which were still galloping, leaps to the ground, and runs to her.

" Is it you ! " exclaimed Katia, and blushed slightly. " Let us go and find my sister ; she is there in the garden; she will be very glad to see you again."

Katia led Arcadi into the garden. The way in which he had met her seemed to him a good omen; he saw her again with as much joy as if she had been one of his near relatives. All was as pleasant as possible ; no butler with his solemn gestures, no waiting in the salon. At the end of an alley he saw Anna Serghe*i*evna ; she had her back to him, and turned quietly at the sound of their steps. Arcadi was on the point of losing countenance again, but the first words which she pronounced completely reassured him.

"Good day, runaway !" she said with her even and caressing voice, and she advanced towards him, smiling and shutting her eyes on account of the wind and sun.

"Where did you find him, Katia ?"

"I bring you," began Arcadi, "something which you scarcely expect."

"You have brought yourself, that is the best of all."

XXIII.

After having conducted Arcadi to his carriage, with ironical regrets and certain words which gave to understand that he divined the true object of his journey, Bazarof began to live quite by himself; he seemed a prey to a fever of work. He disputed no more with Paul Petrovitch, the latter putting on airs which were quite too aristocratic under the circumstances, and expressing himself less by words than by sounds. Once only Paul Petrovitch entered into a discussion with the *nihilist* concerning the rights of the nobility of the Baltic provinces, a subject on the carpet at that time, but he checked himself all at once, and said with a cold politeness :

"Well, we shall never understand each other. I, at least, have not the honor of comprehending you."

"I do not doubt it," exclaimed Bazarof. "Man can comprehend everything; the undulations of ether and the changes which operate on the sun, but he will never comprehend that any one can wipe his face in a different way from his."

"You think that witty?" replied Paul Petrovitch with an inquiring accent, and moved to the other end of the room.

Notwithstanding, he sometimes asked Bazarof's permission to be present at his experiments, and once even put his carefully washed face, perfumed with the rarest essences, to the microscope, in order to see a transparent infusory swallow a greenish atom which it turned over and over very quickly with the *ciliæ* fixed in its throat. Nicholas Petrovitch visited Bazarof's room much oftener than his brother; he would have gone every day to "take his lesson" there, as he said, if domestic affairs had not called him elsewhere. He did not in the least incommode the young naturalist; he seated himself in a corner of the room, followed the experiments attentively, and permitted himself but rarely to ask a discreet question. During dinner and supper he sought to lead the conversation to the subject of physics, geology, or chemistry, since all other subjects, even questions of agriculture, not to speak of politics, could start, if not disputes, at least disagreeable discussions. Nicholas Petrovitch very much doubted whether his brother's aversion for Bazarof had at all diminished. A circumstance, otherwise of little importance, had just confirmed him in this opinion. The cholera was beginning to show itself in the neighborhood, and had even carried off two inhabitants of Marino itself. Paul Petrovitch was quite severely attacked with it one night; he suffered until morning without having recourse to Bazarof's knowledge. When he saw him in the morning, and when Bazarof asked why he had not had him called, he replied, still very pale, but nevertheless carefully combed and shaven: "I think I have heard you say that you do not believe in medicine." So the days went on. Bazarof still pursued without relaxation his solitary labors. There was however one person in the house with whom he was not entirely unreserved, it is true, but whose society pleased him. That person was Fenitchka.

He generally met her early in the morning, in the garden or in the court; he never went into her room, and she only approached his door once, to ask him if it would be well for her to bathe Mitia. And yet, far from fearing him, she had entire confidence in him, and felt freer and bolder in his presence than before Nicholas Petrovitch himself. It would be difficult to give a reason for it; perhaps it was because she understood instinctively that there was in Bazarof absolutely nothing of the gentleman, of the lord, nothing of that sort of superiority which attracts and frightens at the same time. He was in her eyes an excellent doctor and an honest man. His presence did not prevent her from busying herself about her child, and one day, when she was suddenly·taken with giddiness and headache, she accepted a spoonful of medicine from his hand. Before Nicholas Petrovitch, she was less familiar with Bazarof, not at all from calculation, but from a certain feeling of propriety. Paul Petrovitch inspired her with fear more than ever; for some time he had seemed to spy upon her conduct, and would appear suddenly, as if he had come out of the ground, behind Fenitchka, in his English costume, with his immovable face, his penetrating look, and his hands in his pockets. " It makes you shiver," Fenitchka would say to Duniasha, and the latter would reply by a sigh wrung from her by the recollection of another stony-hearted man. It was Bazarof, who, without knowing it, had become the cruel tyrant of her soul.

If Fenitchka was pleased with Bazarof, the feeling was returned. In talking with the young girl, Bazarof's face took a new expression; it became more serene, almost gentle, and at the same time a sort of mocking kindness mingled with his ordinary nonchalance. Fenitchka grew more beautiful from day to day. There comes a time for young women when they begin suddenly to develop and bloom like summer roses; this time had come for Fenitchka. Everything disposed her to it, even the July heats which had just come on. Clothed in a light white dress she seemed still lighter and whiter herself; the sun did not tan her, and the heat, from which it was impossible for her to protect herself, slightly flushed her cheeks and ears, spread over her whole being a soft indolence, and, giving to her pretty eyes the languor of a half sleep, added as it were an involuntary tenderness to her glances. She could scarcely work, her hands slid, so to speak, from her knees. She felt scarcely able to walk, and did not cease to complain of herself with a comical depression.

"You ought to bathe oftener," said Nicholas Petrovitch to her. He had had a large tent erected for that use on one of his ponds, which was not yet quite dried up.

"Oh! Nicholas Petrovitch! But I should be dead before reaching the pond, or I should die returning. You know very well that there is no shade in the garden."

"That is true," replied Nicholas Petrovitch, rubbing his forehead.

One morning about seven o'clock Bazarof, who was returning from his walk, found Fenitchka in the lilac grove, the blossoms of which had long since dropped off, but which was still fresh and green. She was seated on the bench, her head covered with a white handkerchief; by her side was a heap of red and white roses all covered with dew. He wished her good morning.

"Ah! Eugene Vasilitch!" she said to him, slightly raising the corner of her handkerchief to look at him, and in the movement uncovering her arm to the elbow.

"What are you making there?" replied Bazarof, seating himself near her; "bouquets?"

"Yes; to put on the table for breakfast. Nicholas Petrovitch is very fond of them."

"But we do not breakfast so soon. What a quantity of flowers!"

"I picked them now, before the heat prevents my going out. One can breathe only at this hour. I cannot stand any more heat; I am afraid of falling ill."

"What an idea! Let me feel your pulse."

Bazarof took her hand, placed his finger on the artery so well hidden under a soft and moist skin, and did not even give himself the trouble of counting its calm pulsations.

"You will live a hundred years," he said, dropping her hand.

"Ah! God keep me from it!" she exclaimed.

"Why? Do you not care then to live long?"

"A hundred years! My grandmother lived eighty years, and she was a real martyr! All black, deaf, deformed, always coughing; only a burden to herself. Is that living?"

"It is better to be young, then?"

"I think it is!"

"And why? Tell me that?"

"How? but here am I for instance; I am still young, and I can do everything; I go, I come, I wait on myself and need no one. What is better?"

"But to me it is all the same whether I am young or old."

"How can you say that it is the same to you? It is impossble for you to think so."

"I will make you a judge of it, Fedossia Nikolaïevna. What good does youth do me? I live alone, like an orphan."

"That depends on yourself."

8*

"But it does not depend on anybody. No one wishes to take pity on me."

Fenitchka stole a glance at him, but did not reply to him.

"What book have you there?" she asked, after some instants.

"That? It is a learned work, difficult to understand."

"You are always studying! Do you never weary of it? You ought to know everything by this time, it seems to me."

"It seems not. But try to read a little in this book."

"But I shall not understand any of it. Is it Russian?" asked Fenitchka, taking in both hands the thickly bound book which Bazarof held:—"How large it is!"

"It is all in Russian."

"That doesn't matter; I shall not understand it."

"I know it; but I should like to see you read. When you read the end of your nose moves very prettily."

Fenitchka, who was trying in a low voice to decipher a paragraph treating "Of creosote," began to laugh, and pushed away the book, which slid to the ground.

"I like your laugh also," said Bazarof.

"Have done!"

"I like to hear you talk. One might call it the murmur of a little brook."

Fenitchka turned away her head.

"How odd you are!" she said, drawing her fingers over the flowers. "Why should you listen to me? You must have talked with such accomplished ladies!"

"Ah! Fedossia Nikolaïevna, believe me, all the accomplished ladies in the world are not worth even your elbow."

"You are at a loss what to invent!" said Fenitchka in a low tone, pressing her arms against her body.

Bazarof picked up the book.

"It is a medical book," said he; "why did you throw it down?"

"A medical book?" repeated Fenitchka, turning towards him. "You remember giving me some drops? Well, since then Mitia sleeps like a charm. How grateful I am to you! you are so good! truly!"

"Strictly, every physician ought to be paid," replied Bazarof, smiling; "physicians, you must know, are selfish people."

Fenitchka looked at Bazarof; the white reflection which brightened the upper part of her face gave her eyes a still deeper tint. She did not know whether he was speaking seriously or in jest.

"With pleasure," she replied; "but Nicholas Petrovitch must be spoken to about it."

"You think that I want money?" replied Bazarof; "no, it is not money that I ask of you."

"What then?"

"What?" repeated Bazarof; "guess!"

"Do I know?"

"In this case I will tell you; I should like to have—one of those roses."

Fenitchka began to laugh again, and even clapped her hands, so singular did Bazarof's request appear to her. She felt very much flattered at the same time.

Bazarof looked at her fixedly.

"Willingly! willingly!" she said at last; and leaning over the bench she began to choose a rose. "Do you wish a red or a white one?"

"A red one, and not too large."

Fenitchka raised herself again.

"Take it," she said, but immediately withdrew the hand which she had just held out, bit her lips, glanced at the entrance of the grove, and listened.

"What is the matter?" asked Bazarof; is it Nicholas Petrovitch?"

"No ; he is in the fields—and besides I am not afraid of him. But Paul Petrovitch—I thought—"

"What ? "

"I thought that he was coming. No, not at all. Take it ; " and Fenitchka gave Bazarof the rose.

"Why are you afraid of Paul Petrovitch ? "

"He makes me afraid. It is not that he talks to me. Oh, no ! but he looks at me with such a singular air ! You don't like him any better, either. I remember that you used to be always disputing with him. I didn't know what it was about, but understood that you were turning him back nicely—like that—like that."

Fenitchka showed with her hands how, according to her, Bazarof *turned back* Paul Petrovitch.

Bazarof smiled.

"And if he had appeared to overpower me," said he, "would you have undertaken my defence ? "

"Would I have been able to defend you ? But you are not so easily conquered as that."

"You think so ? Well, I know a hand which would over-turn me with one finger."

"What hand is it ? "

"As if you didn't know ! Smell the rose which you have given me ; it smells very good."

Fenitchka bent her neck and put her face near the flower. The handkerchief slid from her head to her shoulders and left uncovered her thick brilliant black hair, a little in dis-order.

"Wait ; I want to smell it with you," said Bazarof, and leaning down he forcibly kissed the half-open lips of the young girl.

She started and put her two hands against Bazarof's breast ; but she held them there feebly, and he was able to give her a second kiss. A dry cough was heard behind the foliage. Fenitchka threw herself precipitately to the other end of the bench. Paul Petrovitch appeared, made a slight bow, said slowly but with an expression of bitter sadness : "You are here ? " and departed. Fenitchka immediately gathered up her roses and left the grove.

"It is very wrong in you, Eugene Vasilitch," she murmured in a low voice as she left him.

Bazarof remembered a scene of the same kind, and still recent; this recollection awakened in his heart a sort of shame, and almost self-contempt. But he immediately shook his head, congratulated himself ironically in "walking in the steps of Celadon," and regained his room.

As for Paul Petrovitch, he left the garden and walked slowly towards the woods. He was absent for some time, and when he returned to breakfast Nicholas Petrovitch asked him anxiously "if he were well," his face was so darkened.

"You know that I am subject to bilious attacks," Paul Petrovitch quietly replied.

XXIV.

Two hours after he knocked at Bazarof's door.

"Pardon me for disturbing you in your learned occupations," he said, seating himself on a chair near the window, and supporting himself with both hands on an elegant cane with an ivory head, (he generally went out without a cane,) "but I am forced to ask you to grant me five minutes of your time ; no more."

"All my time is at your service," replied Bazarof, who felt his face contract slightly as soon as Paul stepped over the door-sill.

"Five minutes will suffice me ; I have come to ask you a question."

"A question ? about what ? "

"Please listen to me. At the beginning of your sojourn here, when I did not deprive myself of the pleasure of talking with you, I had the honor of learning your opinion on many subjects; but as far as I can recollect, you have never, in my presence, said what you thought of duelling in general. Permit me to ask you?"

Bazarof, who had risen to meet Paul Petrovitch, seated himself on the edge of the table and crossed his arms.

"This is my opinion," he said: "the duel, from the theoretic point of view, is an absurdity; but from the practical point of view only—another thing."

"You mean, if I understand you, that laying aside your theoretic opinion of the duel, you would not allow yourself, in practice, to be insulted, without asking satisfaction?"

"You have seized my thought perfectly."

"It is well. I am charmed to know that that is your way of looking at it. That puts an end to my ignorance—"

"To your uncertainty, you mean."

"That matters little, sir; I only wish to make myself understood: I am not—a seminary rat. Your words impose on me a certain duty—a sad enough one. I have decided to fight with you."

Bazarof opened his eyes.

"With me?"

"Yes, with you in person."

"And for what cause? I do not at all comprehend."

"I could explain it to you," replied Paul Petrovitch; "but I prefer not to do so. I find that you are not wanted here; I cannot endure you. I despise you, and if that does not seem to you to be sufficient—"

The eyes of Paul Petrovitch sparkled with anger; those of Bazarof also shone suddenly.

"Very well," cried he; "any other explanation would be superfluous. You have taken a fancy to exercise your chivalric ardor on me. I could refuse to grant you that pleasure, but what good would that do ? "

" I am greatly obliged to you," replied Paul. " I may hope that· you will accept my challenge without driving me to coercion."

" Which means, metaphor aside, to that cane," replied Bazarof coldly. " You are perfectly right. You can dispense with the trouble of insulting me; the more, since it would not be absolutely without danger to yourself. Continue to act like a gentleman; it is as a gentleman that on my side I accept your challenge."

" Very well," replied Paul, and he placed his cane in a corner of the room. " It remains for us to arrange the conditions of our meeting; but I should like to know first, if it appears necessary to you to feign a quarrel, which might serve as a pretext for the affair ? "

" No ; that seems to me quite useless."

" That is also my opinion ; I likewise think that it is useless to search into the true motives of our meeting. We cannot endure one another. What more is needed ? "

" What more is needed, truly," repeated Bazarof ironically.

" As for the conditions of our affair, as we shall have no witnesses—for where should we find them ? "

" It is true, where should we find them ? "

" I shall have the honor to make you the following proposition : We will fight to-morrow, at six o'clock, behind the forest, with pistols ; the distance shall be ten paces."

" Let it be ten paces. We detest one another enough to fight at that distance."

" Eight paces, if you wish ? "

" Why not ? willingly."

" We will fire two shots ; and for greater safety, each one of us will have in his pocket a letter declaring himself the author of his death."

"That last clause seems unnecessary," replied Bazarof. "That would appear improbable; it would be a little too much like French romance."

"Perhaps. But you will agree that it is unpleasant to pass for a murderer?"

"Doubtless. But there are means of preserving oneself from that painful imputation. We will have no witnesses, properly so-called, but there is nothing to prevent some one from being present at the combat."

"Whom will you choose for that, permit me to ask you?"

"Peter, for instance."

"What Peter?"

"Your brother's *valet de chambre*. He is a man quite up to the civilization of the present day, and he will play his part quite certainly with all the *comme il faut* necessary on such an occasion."

"I think that you are jesting, my dear sir?"

"Not at all, sir; reflect on my proposition and you will see that it is full of good sense and very natural. An awl cannot be hidden in a sack,* and then I charge myself with preparing Peter for the affair and conducting him to the field of battle."

"You continue to jest," said Paul Petrovitch, rising. "But after the amiable alacrity you have just shown, I have no right to find fault with you. Then everything is arranged.—Have you any pistols?"

"How should I have them, Paul Petrovitch? I am not a soldier."

"In that case, let me offer you mine. It is more than five years since I have used them, and you can believe my word."

"That is a very tranquillizing assertion."

* A Russian proverb, meaning that one cannot long dissimulate.

Paul Petrovitch went to get his cane.

"Now, my dear sir," he continued, "I can do no more than to reiterate my thanks and leave you to your occupations. I have the honor to salute you."

"With the pleasure of seeing you again, sir," replied Bazarof, conducting his guest to the door.

Paul Petrovitch went out, and Bazarof, who had stopped near the door, exclaimed :

"The devil take me ! it is very fine, but it is very stupid. What a farce we have been playing ! Like learned dogs that dance on their hind legs. It was impossible to refuse; he would have struck me, and then—" Bazarof grew pale at the thought; it roused all his pride. "I should have had no resource but to strangle him like a chicken."

He returned to his microscope, but his heart was disturbed, and the tranquillity indispensable for the observations he was making had vanished.

"He saw us to-day," he said to himself; "but is it possible that he has taken the thing so to heart for his brother? Besides, a kiss ! such a little thing ! There is something deeper. Can he be in love with her himself? It must be ; I have put my hand into the fire ! What a mess it is ! "

"An ugly business !" he said to himself again, after reflection. "An ugly business ! In the first place I have got to punish him, and perhaps fly. Then—Arcadi—and that stupid, good old fellow, Nicholas Petrovitch ! An ugly, ugly business ! "

The day passed even more tranquilly than usual. One would have said that Fenitchka had taken her departure from the world; she kept herself in her room like a mouse in its hole. Nicholas Petrovitch had an anxious air ; he had just learned that the blight had begun to touch his wheat, on which he was building great hopes. Paul Petrovitch weighed every one down with his icy politeness, even Prokofitch. Bazarof began a letter to his father; but he tore it up and threw it under the table. "If I die," he thought, "they will know it; but I shall not die. Yes, I shall drag out some time yet in this world."

He ordered Peter to come to him the next morning at day-break, on important business; Peter imagined that he wanted to take him to St. Petersburg. Bazarof went to bed late, and odd dreams tormented him all night. Madame Odintsof passed before his eyes; she was at the same time his mother; a little cat with black moustaches followed her, and this little cat was Fenitchka. He saw Paul Petrovitch under the form of a great forest, and was not less decided to fight with him. Peter awoke him at four o'clock in the morning; he dressed himself and they went out immediately.

The morning was magnificent, and fresher than the preceding days. Little mottled clouds passed in flakes over the pale azure of the sky; a fine dew covered the leaves of the trees, and the spiders' webs shone like silver on the grass; the damp, dark ground seemed still to keep some traces of the first flush of the day; the song of the larks came down from all parts of the sky. Bazarof went on to the wood, seated himself in the shade, and informed Peter of the service which he expected from him. The accomplished servant was seized with a mortal terror; but Bazarof soothed him by assuring him that he would have nothing to do but to look on from a distance, without incurring the least responsibility.

"Meanwhile," he added, "consider the important part you are going to play."

Peter moved his arms, dropped his head, and supported himself, his face quite green with fear, against a tree.

The road which led to Marino followed a little wood; the light dust with which it was covered had not been disturbed

since the evening before, either by wheel or foot. Bazarof
involuntarily cast his eyes on the side of the road, picked
and chewed a blade of grass, and continually repeated to
himself: "What folly?" The morning freshness made
him shiver two or three times. Peter looked at him mournfully, but Bazarof only smiled ; he had not the least fear.

Horses' hoofs sounded on the road.—A peasant appeared
soon after ; he came from the village and was driving two
horses with clogs on their feet. As he passed Bazarof he
looked at him strangely, without touching his cap, which
seemed to Peter a bad omen and visibly moved him.

"That man," thought Bazarof, "has also risen early ; but
he at least is going to do something useful, while we—"

"I think he is coming,' said Peter suddenly in a low
voice.

Bazarof raised his head and distinguished Paul Petrovitch, who was coming rapidly along the road, dressed in a
colored jacket and pantaloons as white as snow ; he had
under his arm a box in a green case.

"Excuse me, I fear I have kept you waiting," he said,
saluting first Bazarof and then Peter, whom he considered
for the moment as a sort of second ; "I did not like to wake
my servant."

"It is nothing, " replied Bazarof, "we have only just arrived."

"Ah ! so much the better ! " Paul Petrovitch glanced
around him.—"Nobody sees us ; we shall not be disturbed.
Shall we begin ? "

"Willingly."

"I suppose you do not desire any further explanations ? "

"Not the least in the world."

"Will you take the trouble of loading them ? " said Paul
Petrovitch, drawing the pistols from the box.

"No: load them yourself. I am going to measure the

distance. I have longer legs," added Bazarof with a malicious smile. "One, two, three—"

"Eugene Vasilievitch," said Peter with an effort, (he trembled as if in an attack of fever,) "do what you choose, but I am going away."

"—Four—five—go away my brave man ; go away; you can get behind a tree and stop up your ears, but do not close your eyes ; if one of us falls, run, fly, hasten to raise him. Six—seven—eight—" Bazarof stopped.—"Enough?" said he, turning to Paul Petrovitch, "or two little steps more?"

"As you choose," replied Paul Petrovitch, forcing in the second ball.

"Well, then, two steps more." Bazarof traced a line on the ground with the end of his boot; "Here is the barrier! By the way, we have not arranged the distance at which we shall place ourselves from the barrier? That also is important. We did not debate this grave question yesterday."

"Ten paces I suppose," replied Paul, presenting the two pistols ; "do me the pleasure of choosing."

"I will do you that pleasure, but allow that our duel is strange, even to absurdity ; look at the face of our second."

"You continue to jest," replied Paul Petrovitch. "I do not deny that our meeting may be odd enough, but I think that I ought to forewarn you that I intend to fight seriously. *A bon entendeur salut.*"

"Oh! I don't doubt that we have decided to exterminate one another ; but why not laugh a little and join *utile dulci?* You see that if you talk French to me I can reply in Latin."

"I shall fight seriously," repeated Paul Petrovitch, placing himself. Bazarof likewise counted ten steps and stopped.

"Are you ready?" asked Paul Petrovitch.

"Yes."

"March."

Bazarof advanced slowly, and Paul Petrovitch did the same ; he held his left hand in his pocket and raised little by little the barrel of his pistol. "He aims right at my nose," said Bazarof to himself; "and how he shuts his eye to make his aim sure,—the brigand. The sensation is not agreeable, it must be confessed. I am going to look at his watch-chain."

Something passed whistling close to Bazarof's ear, and at the same instant there was a report. "I heard it and yet am not hurt," he had time to think. He advanced one more step and pulled the trigger without aiming.

Paul Petrovitch made a slight movement and put his hand to his leg. A streak of blood discolored his white pantaloons.

Bazarof threw down his pistol and ran to him.

"You are wounded ?" he said.

"You have a right to make me advance to the barrier," replied Paul Petrovitch ; "the wound is insignificant. According to our rules, each of us has still another shot."

"As for that, you will permit me to put off my shot until another time," replied Bazarof, and he seized the arm of Paul Petrovitch, who began to grow pale. "At this moment I am no longer a duellist, but a doctor, and first of all I must examine your wound. Peter ! come here, Peter ! Where have you hid ! "

"It is absolutely nothing—I need no one's help," replied Paul Petrovitch, speaking with difficulty ; "and we must— yet once more—" He tried to take hold of his moustache, but his arm fell, his eyes closed, and he fainted.

"That is bad ! He has fainted ! For so little ! " exclaimed Bazarof involuntarily as he laid Paul Petrovitch on the grass. "Let us see what is the matter with him ! " He drew out his handkerchief, staunched the blood, felt the edges of the wound. "The bone is untouched" he said between his teeth, "the ball has not gone deep, and has only

injured a single muscle, the *vastus externus*.   In three
weeks he will be able to dance if he wishes to.—To faint.
How nervous these people are.   How fine his skin is !"

"Is he killed ?" asked Peter behind him, in a trembling
voice.

Bazarof turned around.

"Go and get me some water, comrade, and fear nothing ;
he will live longer than you and I."

But the perfection of a servant did not seem to hear what
was said to him, and remained motionless.   However, Paul
Petrovitch opened his eyes a little.

"He is giving up his soul to God !" replied Peter, cross-
ing himself.

"You are right—What a ridiculous face !" said the
wounded gentleman with a smile of command.

"Go and get some water, idiot !" cried Bazarof.

"It is useless.   The *vertige* is quite gone—help me to
sit up—like that—it will be sufficient to bandage this scratch
with no matter what, and I shall return home on foot ;
though they might send me a droshky.   We will wait for it
then if you choose.   You have conducted yourself like an
honorable man—to-day—to-day, mark it well."

"It is useless to recall the past," replied Bazarof, "and
as for the future, do not trouble yourself further, for I intend
to leave here as soon as possible.   Now, let me bandage
your leg, the wound is slight, but it is always better to stop
the blood.   First of all I must recall that dead fellow to the
feeling of existence."

Bazarof seized Peter by the collar, shook him roughly,
and sent him for a droshky.

"Don't go and frighten my brother," said Paul Petrovitch
to him ; "you need report nothing to him."

Peter departed rapidly, and while he ran to get the
droshky, the two adversaries remained seated side by side

without speaking. Paul Petrovitch avoided looking at Bazarof; he had no desire to become reconciled with him, he reproached himself for his passion, his awkwardness, his whole conduct in the affair, although he felt very well that it had ended in the happiest possible way. "He will at least relieve us from his presence," he said to himself to condole himself, "so much is gained." The silence which the two adversaries continued to maintain was painful and embarrassing. Each was certain that the other thoroughly understood him. This certainty is very pleasant for friends, but very disagreeable for enemies, especially when they can neither explain nor separate.

"Have I not bandaged your foot too tightly?" asked Bazarof at last.

"No, that is nothing. It is all right," replied Paul Petrovitch, and a few instants after he added:—"It will be impossible to deceive my brother; I will tell him that we have had a dispute on a political question."

"Very well," replied Bazarof, "you can say that I attacked all the anglomaniacs in your presence."

"That is it! By the way, what do you suppose that man is thinking about us?" continued Paul Petrovitch, pointing to the same peasant who a few moments before the duel had passed Bazarof driving his horses, and who this time, on seeing the masters, uncovered and turned out of the road.

"Who knows!" replied Bazarof; "probably nothing. The Russian peasant is just that mysterious unknown so much talked about in the romances of Mrs. Anne Radcliffe. Who knows him? He does not know himself."

"Ah! you think so?" replied Paul Petrovitch, but he suddenly exclaimed: "See a little of your Peter's stupidity! here comes my brother himself."

Bazarof turned and saw the pale face of Nicholas Petro-

vitch in the droshky. Leaping to the ground before the
coachman could stop, he ran towards his brother.

"What does this mean?" he asked with emotion; "Eugene Vassilievitch, how is this possible?"

"It is nothing," replied Paul Petrovitch; "it was wrong
to disturb you; we have yielded to impulse, Bazarof and I;
I have been slightly punished for it, that is all."

"But for what cause, good God?"

"How shall I explain that to you? Mr. Bazarof expressed
himself in my presence in an improper manner on the subject
of Sir Robert Peel. But let me hasten to add that I alone
am to blame, and that Mr. Bazarof has behaved very honor-
ably. It was I who provoked him."

"I see blood."

"Do you think then that I have water in my veins? I
assure you that this little bleeding will do me good. Will
it not, doctor? Help me into the droshky, and do not give
up to melancholy. I shall be well to-morrow. There, I am
quite comfortable. Come! drive on, coachman!"

Nicholas Petrovitch followed the droshky on foot; Bazarof had remained behind.

"I must beg you to take care of my brother," said Nicholas Petrovitch to him, "until a physician comes from the
city."

Bazarof bowed without speaking. An hour afterwards
Paul Petrovitch was in bed, and bandages made by a master-
hand were around his leg. The whole house was in a flut-
ter. Fenitchka did not feel well; Nicholas Petrovitch
wrung his hands in silence, and Paul Petrovitch laughed
and jested, especially with Bazarof. He had put on a linen
shirt, an elegant morning jacket and a fez cap; he would
not allow them to draw down the blinds, and complained
jestingly of the spare diet to which he was condemned.

However, a little fever appeared in the evening, and he

had a headache. A physician came from the city. (Nicholas Petrovitch had paid no attention to what his brother recommended, and Bazarof himself had requested that another physician should be called in. He remained in his own room, by himself the whole day, with an irritated face and sallow skin, confining himself to short visits to the wounded man. Two or three times he met Fenitchka, who avoided him with a sort of terror.) The new doctor prescribed refreshing drinks, and confirmed Bazarof's opinion about the slightness of the wound. Nicholas Petrovitch told him that his brother had wounded himself through carelessness, to which the doctor replied: "Hem?" but just then feeling a note of twenty-five roubles slipped into his hand, added: "Indeed! it is a thing that occurs quite often." No one went to bed or closed their eyes that night in the whole house. Nicholas Petrovitch was every instant entering his brother's room on tip-toe, and going out again in the same way. The wounded man dozed by moments, uttered little groans, said occasionally to his brother, "*Couchez-vous,*" and asked for a drink. Nicholas Petrovitch one time made Fenitchka give him a glass of lemonade; Paul Petrovitch looked at her intently, and swallowed the lemonade without leaving a drop. The fever increased towards morning, and the wounded man became a little delirious. At first he pronounced incoherent words, then he suddenly opened his eyes, and seeing his brother, who was leaning over the bed and looking anxiously at him, he said:

"Dont you think, Nicholas, that Fenitchka is a little like Nelly?"

"What Nelly, Paul?"

"How can you ask? The princess R——! Especially in her height. *C'est de la même famille.*"

Nicholas Petrovitch did not reply, and wondered at the

9

persistence of old attachments in the human heart. "See how it is when it mounts to the surface," he said to himself.

"Ah! how I love that creature!" exclaimed Paul Petrovitch mournfully, putting his arms behind his head.—"I shall never suffer an insolent man to touch her—" he murmured a few instants after.

Nicholas Petrovitch merely sighed; he hardly suspected to whom these words referred.

The next morning Bazarof went to him at about eight o'clock. He had had time to pack up his possessions, and to set at liberty all his frogs, his insects, and his birds.

"You are come to say good-bye to me?" said Nicholas Petrovitch, rising.

"Yes, indeed."

"I understand you, and justify you entirely. My poor brother was doubtless wrong, but he is punished for it. I learn from him himself that he made it impossible for you to act otherwise than you have done. I think that it would have been difficult for you to avoid this duel which—which can be explained up to a certain point by the continual antagonism of your reciprocal opinions (Nicholas Petrovitch got entangled in his words and breathed hard). My brother is an irritable, obstinate man, attached to old ideas.—I thank God that it has all passed off thus, without other consequences. However, I have taken all necessary measures to prevent the thing from being noised abroad—"

"I will leave you my address, and in case a story should be made of all this, you can always find me," said Bazarof nonchalantly.

"I hope that the precaution will be useless. Eugene Vasilitch—I deeply regret that your stay in my house has had such an end. That troubles me the more, since Arcadi—"

"I shall probably see him again," replied Bazarof, whom any sort of "explanation" or "declaration" made impatient.—"If it should be otherwise, I shall beg you to greet him for me, and to express to him all the regret that I experience."

"And I also ask—" replied Nicholas Petrovitch, bowing; but Bazarof did not wait for the end of the sentence, and went out.

On learning that Bazarof was going, Paul Petrovitch expressed a desire to see him, and pressed his hand, but Bazarof showed himself, as usual, as cold as ice; he understood very well that Paul Petrovitch wanted to play the magnanimous. He could not take leave of Fenitchka; he merely exchanged a look with her at the window. She seemed to him sad. "She cannot get over it?" he said. —"Why not, after all?" As for Peter, he was so moved as to weep against Bazarof's shoulder until the latter calmed him by asking him "if his eyes were not in a damp spot?" and Duniasha was obliged to run into the woods to hide her emotion. The one who caused all this grief climbed on a *telega*, lighted a cigar; and when, four versts from there, at a turn of the road, he saw for the last time the house of Kirsanof and all its appendages, he spit,* muttering between his teeth: "Accursed lordlings!" and wrapped himself up in his cloak.

Paul Petrovitch soon got better, but he kept his bed for a week. He bore his captivity, as he called it, patiently enough; but he devoted a great part of his time to his toilet, and had *eau de cologne* burned continually. Nicholas Petrovitch read the newspaper to him, and Fenitchka waited on him as usual; she brought him soup, lemonade, eggs in the shell, tea; but a secret terror took possession of her

* A sign of contempt and disdain among the Russians, as among the Orientals.

every time she entered his room. The unexpected prank of Paul Petrovitch had frightened the whole household, and especially Fenitchka; Prokofitch was the only one who spoke of it with *sangfroid;* he said that in his time gentlemen often fought in that way, "but strictly among themselves, and never with ill-bred fellows like that. They flogged those persons at the stables when they were insolent."

Fenitchka's conscience reproached her scarcely at all; but she was tormented when she began to suspect the true cause of the quarrel; the more since Paul Petrovitch looked at her so strangely—since even when her back was turned she felt his eyes. She grew thin under this constant agitation, and like all women of that age, she only became the prettier for it.

Once—it was one morning—Paul Petrovitch, feeling much better, left his bed for his sofa; Nicholas Petrovitch came to inquire about his health, and went out to see the wheat threshed. Fenitchka brought a cup of tea, and having placed it on the table, was about to retire, when Paul Petrovitch detained her.

"Why do you hurry so, Fedossia Nikolaïevna," he began, "have you anything to do?"

"No—yes—I have to pour the tea down stairs."

"Duniasha will do it in your absence; stay a little while with a poor sick man. Besides, I want to speak to you."

Fenitchka seated herself in silence on the edge of a chair.

"Listen," said Paul Petrovitch, pulling his moustache; "I have wanted for a long time to ask you—why you seem to be afraid of me?"

"I?"

"Yes. You—you never look me straight in the eyes; it seems to me that your conscience is not quite clear."

Fenitchka blushed, but she looked at Paul Petrovitch.*
His manner seemed to her so strange that she shuddered
secretly in the bottom of her heart.

"Is your conscience clear?" he asked her.

"Why should it not be?" she said in a low voice.

"How do I know? However, towards whom would you
be guilty? It could not be towards me. Could it be
towards some other person in the house? That seems to
me equally inadmissible. Towards my brother?—No, for
you love him."

"Yes, I love him."

"With all your heart, with all your strength?"

"I love Nicholas Petrovitch with all my heart!"

"Truly? Look at me, Fenitchka (it was the first time he
had called her by that name)—you know that lying is a
great sin."

"I am not lying, Paul Petrovitch. If I did not love Nicholas Petrovitch I should not deserve to live."

"And you would not change him for anybody?"

"For whom then could I change him!"

"For whom? Who knows! Why, for instance, for that
young gentleman who has just left us."

Fenitchka arose.

"For heaven's sake, Paul Petrovitch, why do you torment me thus? What have I done to you? How can any
one say such things?"

"Fenitchka," replied Paul Petrovitch sadly, "I have
seen all—"

"What have you seen?"

"Down there—In the grove—"

Fenitchka blushed suddenly up to her hair.

"Was it my fault?" she said with an effort.

* They say in Russia : " When the conscience is not clear, one
cannot look a person in the face."

Paul Petrovitch raised himself.

" You are not guilty ? No ? In no way ? "

" I do not love and never shall love but one man in the world, and that is Nicholas Petrovitch," replied Fenitchka with sudden energy, while her throat swelled with sobs ready to break out ;—" And as for what you have seen, I will declare at the day of my judgment that I cannot reproach myself with it ; I would rather die now, if it were necessáry, than be suspected of such a frightful thing as to be unfaithful to my benefactor, Nicholas Petrovitch."

Her voice was choked, and she felt at the same moment that Paul Petrovitch seized her hand and pressed it tightly. She looked at him and was petrified. He was even paler than before ; his eyes sparkled ; and, what was still more surprising, a heavy and solitary tear ran slowly down his cheek.

" Fenitchka ! " said he, in a choked and thick voice ; " love, love my brother ! He is so good, so·worthy of affection ! Do not change him for any one in the world, and do not listen to any one's advice ! Nothing is more horrible, mark it well, than a love without return ! Always remain faithful to my poor Nicholas ! "

Fenitchka's tears dried, and her terror vanished, her surprise was so great. But what were her feelings when Paul Petrovitch took her hand and pressed it against his eyes ; then took it again and put it to his mouth, without kissing it, but uttering from time to time a convulsive sigh.

" Good God ! " she said to herself ; " perhaps he is going to have an attack." But at this instant all the past life of Paul Petrovitch was being mournfully retraced in his heart.

The stairs resounded under hasty steps. He pushed Fenitchka far from him, and put his head on one of the sofa cushions. The door opened, and Nicholas Petrovitch entered, joyous, with a fresh and animated face. Mitia, no less fresh and bright than he, was jumping in his arms, and taking hold with his little naked feet of the large buttons on his father's coat.

Fenitchka rushed to Nicholas Petrovitch, and forcibly embracing him together with the child, she rested her head against his shoulder. Nicholas Petrovitch seemed surprised; Fenitchka, timid and reserved, never gave him the least caress in any one's presence.

"What is the matter with you?" he asked her; then, looking at his brother, he gave Mitia to its mother. "You do not feel worse?" he added, approaching Paul Petrovitch.

The latter hid his face in a linen handkerchief.

"No, it is nothing; on the contrary, I am much better."

"You were wrong to leave your bed," said Nicholas Petrovitch to him. "Where are you going?" he added, addressing Fenitchka; but she had already shut the door behind her. "I had come to show you my little fellow; he was restless at not seeing his uncle. Why has she taken him away? But what is the matter with you? Has anything passed between you?"

"Brother!" said Paul Petrovitch solemnly.

Nicholas Petrovitch started. He had a feeling of fear for which he could not account.

"Brother!" repeated Paul Petrovitch, "promise me to grant a request which I am going to make of you."

"What do you wish? Tell me."

"It is a very important thing; all the happiness of your life depends on it. I have reflected a great deal, for some time, on what I propose to say to you—Brother, fulfil your duty, the duty of a man of honor, put an end to a bad example and to the irregular situation in which you are placed, you, the best of men!"

"What do you mean, Paul?"

"Marry Fenitchka—she loves you; she is the mother of your son."

Nicholas Petrovitch drew back a step and clasped his hands.

"It is you who give me this advice, Paul! You, whom I regarded as the most implacable enemy of that kind of marriage! You say this! But if I have not till now fulfilled what you rightly call the holiest of duties, it is only out of regard for you!"

"I regret that your consideration for me should have held you back," replied Paul Petrovitch with a sad smile. "I begin to think that Bazarof was right in calling me an aristocrat. Yes, my dear brother, one must stand, one must act, in the sight of the world; we are already old, and life has made us humble; let us put all this vain disturbance one side. As you have well said, let us fulfil our duty; and it is very probable that we shall yet have more than ordinary happiness!"

Nicholas Petrovitch embraced his brother with emotion.

"You have opened my eyes decidedly!" he exclaimed. "I had always considered you as the best and most intelligent of men; I see now that you are also as wise as generous."

"Softly! softly!" replied Paul Petrovitch. "Take care of the leg of your generous brother, who has just, after living forty-five years, fought a duel like an ensign. So then, the thing is decided. Fenitchka will be my—*belle-sœur.*"

"My dear Paul!—But what will Arcadi say?"

"Arcadi? he will triumph over it, I promise you! Marriage is not, it is true, according to his principles, but this will flatter his love of equality. In fact, what signify all these distinctions, these castes, *au dix-neuvième siècle?*"

"Ah! Paul, Paul! let me embrace you once more! Don't be afraid, I will take care of your leg."

The two brothers embraced one another.

"What do you think? Hadn't you better announce to her your resolution immediately?" asked Paul Petrovitch.

"Why hurry?" replied Nicholas Petrovitch. "Have you been speaking of it?"

"Speak of it? We? *quelle idée!*"

"So much the better! Begin by getting well; the thing will not escape us. It is necessary to reflect maturely—"

"You are decided, however?"

"Perfectly so, and I thank you sincerely for having brought me to it. I am going to leave you; you must rest; emotion is bad for you—but we shall yet return to the subject. Try to sleep a little, my dear brother, and may God soon restore your health!"

"Why does he thank me as he does?" Paul Petrovitch asked himself when he was alone, "as if the thing did not depend on him! And I, as soon as he is married, shall go and settle somewhere, far from here, at Dresden or Florence, and I shall stay there until I die."

Paul Petrovitch moistened his forehead with *eau ae cologne* and closed his eyes. In the daylight, which came full into the room, his handsome, thin head, laid on the white pillow, resembled the face of a dead man. He was indeed a dead man.

XXV.

A few days after, at Nikolskoia, Arcadi and Katia were seated in the garden on a bench, in the shade of a great ash; Fifi was lying on the ground at their side, and she had given her body that graceful curve which the Russian hunters have called the posture of the *russak.** Arcadi

* A gray hare of the Steppes.

9*

and Katia were both silent ; he held in his hand a half-open book ; she was collecting the crumbs of white bread which remained in the bottom of her basket, and throwing them to a little family of sparrows which, with the timid bold-ness which characterizes them, hopped chirping to her feet. A light wind which played through the foliage of the tree made spots of golden light softly come and go on the path and on the yellow back of Fifi ; a uniform shade enveloped Arcadi and Katia ; only at rare intervals a luminous point, bright as a flame, appeared suddenly on the young girl's hair.   Both of them were silent ; but the manner of their silence, as they sat near one another, revealed perfect har-mony ; neither of them seemed to pay any attention to the other, though rejoicing at sitting side by side.   Even their features had changed since we left them ; Arcadi seemed · calmer, Katia bolder and more animated.

"Don't you think," said Arcadi, "that the ash * is well named in Russian ; I do not know any tree whose foliage has so much transparency and lightness."

Katia raised her eyes slowly and replied :

"Yes."

And Arcadi said to himself : " She at least does not re-proach me for expressing myself poetically."

"I do not like Heine—" said Katia, glancing at the book on Arcadi's knees,—"either when he laughs or cries.   I like him when he is sad and dreamy."

"And I like him when he laughs," replied Arcadi.

"It is an old remnant of the satirical turn of your mind."

("An old remnant ! " said Arcadi to himself.   "If Baza-rof had heard that ! ")

"Wait a little, we shall change you."

"Who ? You ? "

* *Yasen,* the name of this tree, in Russian, resembles *Yasnii,* clear, transparent.

"Who? My sister; Porphyry Platonitch, with whom you have already stopped disputing; my aunt, whom you accompanied to church day before yesterday."

"I could not refuse to go! As for Anna Sergheïevna, you know that on many points she agreed with Eugene."

"My sister, as well as you, was under his influence."

"As well as I? Do you then imagine that I have already escaped from that influence?"

Katia did not reply.

"I know," continued Arcadi, "that he always displeased you."

"I cannot judge him."

"Do you know, Katerina Sergheïevna, every time I hear that reply, I disbelieve it. No one that I know is above our judgment. It is simply an evasion."

"Well, I will tell you that he is not positively displeasing to me, but I feel that we belong to two different worlds, and that you also are at bottom perfectly unlike him."

"Why so?"

"How shall I tell you?—He is a bird of prey; he is savage; and you and I are tamed."

"I also, I am tamed?"

Katia nodded.

Arcadi rubbed his ear.

"Do you know, Katerina Sergheïevna, that what you say is a little disagreeable!"

"Would you prefer then to be a bird of prey?"

"No; but I should like to be strong, energetic."

"That does not depend on us—Your friend does not care about being so, and yet he is so."

"Hum. So you think that he had great influence over Anna Sergheïevna?"

"Yes, but nobody can have it long," added Katia, lowering her voice.

"What makes you think so?"

"She is very proud—no, that is not what I want to say; she thinks a great deal of being independent."

"We all do that," replied Arcadi, and he asked almost immediately: "For what good?" Katia had the same thought. When young people see one another often, the same ideas come to them at the same moment.

Arcadi smiled, and drawing near Katia, said to her:

"Acknowledge that you fear her a little?"

"Whom?"

"Her," repeated Arcadi significantly.

"And you?" said Katia in her turn.

"And I also; observe that I say: and I also."

Katia threatened him with her finger.

"That surprises me," said she; "my sister has never been so well disposed towards you as now; she was much less so at your first visit."

"Indeed?"

"You have not noticed it? Does it not give you pleasure?"

Arcadi became thoughtful.

"How can I deserve Anna Serghëievna's good graces? Perhaps it is because I brought her some of your mother's letters."

"Yes; but there are other reasons that I shall not tell you."

"Why not?"

"I shall not tell you."

"Oh! I don't doubt that; you are very obstinate."

"Obstinate? it is true."

"And you observe well."

Katia gave a sidelong glance at Arcadi.

"Something vexes you a little? What are you thinking about?"

"I am asking myself whence your observing mind can come. You are so timid, so distrustful; you shun every one—"

"I have lived alone a great deal; that makes one reflect in spite of oneself. But you say that I shun every one. Is it right in you to say that?"

Arcadi gave Katia a grateful look.

"You are right," he replied; "but people in your position, I mean rich people, rarely have the talent of observing; as with kings, truth only comes to them by chance."

"But I am not rich—"

Arcadi was entirely taken by surprise, and did not comprehend her at first.

"So then, the fortune is all her sister's," he said to himself at last, and the thought was not disagreeable to him.—"How nicely you said that," he added aloud.

"What do you mean?"

"You said it well; without simplicity, without false shame, and without airs. By the way, I imagine that every woman who knows and says that she is poor must experience a sort of pride."

"I have never experienced anything like that, thanks to my sister; I do not know how it happened that I spoke to you of my position."

"That may be, but own that the feeling in question, I mean pride, is not quite unknown to you."

"How so?"

"For instance, and I hope that my question will not make you angry, would you consent to marry a rich man?"

"If I loved him very much—but no; I think that even in that case I should not marry him."

"Ah! see!" exclaimed Arcadi; then he added: "and why would you not consent?"

"Because even songs dissuade from an unequal marriage."

"You like perhaps to rule, or—"

"Oh no! why should I? On the contrary I should be quite disposed to submit, but inequality seems to me an insupportable thing. I can understand that to respect oneself and submit, may be happiness; but an inequality, a subordinate existence—No, I have enough of that."

"You have enough of that," repeated Arcadi. "Ah yes! it is not for nothing that you are of the same blood as Anna Sergheïevna. You have the same spirit of independence, but you are more of a dissembler. I am sure that you would never be the first to declare a feeling, however holy and powerful it might be—"

"But that seems to me quite natural," said Katia.

"You are both intelligent; you have as much, and perhaps even more, character than she—"

"Do not compare me with my sister, I entreat you," replied Katia hastily; "it is too unfavorable to me. You seem to forget that my sister has everything for herself, beauty, talent, and—you especially, Arcadi Nikolaïtch, it does not become you to say such things, and with such a serious air."

"What do you mean by 'you especially'? and why do you suppose that I am jesting?"

"Certainly you are jesting."

"You think so? And if I were sure of what I say? If I even thought that I could say much more?"

"I do not understand you."

"Truly? Come, I see that I have praised your talent for observation too highly."

"How?"

Arcadi did not reply to her and turned away; Katia found some more crumbs in her basket and began to throw them to the sparrows, but the motion which she gave to her hand was too violent, and the birds flew away before they had picked up anything.

"Katerina Sergheïevna!" said Arcadi suddenly; "it is doubtless a matter of indifference to you, but I declare to you that I prefer you not only to your sister, but to every one in the world—"

He rose suddenly and strode away, as though frightened at the words which he had just spoken.

Katia let her two hands and the basket fall on her knees, bowed her head and followed Arcadi a long time with her eyes. Her cheeks were slightly flushed, but her mouth was not smiling, and her eyes expressed a sort of astonishment ; she had the air of experiencing for the first time a feeling of the name of which she was still ignorant.

"You are alone?" said Madame Odintsof at her side. " I thought that Arcadi came with you."

Katia glanced at her sister, who, dressed with taste, even with elegance, stood in the path and touched Fifi's ears with the end of her parasol.

"Quite alone," said Katia.

"I can see that quite well," replied her sister laughing; "he has gone in then."

"Yes."

"You were reading together?"

"Yes."

Madame Odintsof took Katia by the chin and raised her head.

"I hope that you have not been disputing?"

"No," replied Katia, gently putting away her sister's hand.

"How gravely you reply to me! I expected to find him here and to offer to walk with him. He has asked me to do so for a long time. They have brought your boots from the city, go and try them on. I noticed yesterday that you needed them ; the boots which you are wearing are tarnished. I think that you are much too negligent in that respect, and yet you have a charming foot ! Your hand is beautiful too—but it is a little large, and so you ought to give more attention to your feet. But you are not a coquette."

Madame Odintsof left her, her elegant dress sweeping lightly behind her ; Katia rose from the bench, took the volume of Heine and returned to the house ; she did not go to try on her boots.

" A charming foot," she thought, as she slowly and lightly mounted the terrace whose steps were warm from the sun. —" Well, he will soon be at my charming feet."

But she had also a feeling of shame, and ran into the house.

Arcadi walked along the corridor to gain his room. The butler ran after him and informed him that Mr. Bazarof was waiting for him.

" Eugene ? " he answered almost with terror ; "has he been here long ? "

" He has just come, but he did not wish to be announced to Anna Serghéïevna, and was shown directly to your room."

" Can any misfortune have happened at home ? " said Arcadi to himself, and hastily mounting the stairs, he opened the door quite wide.

He was tranquillized as soon as he saw Bazarof, though a practised eye would doubtless have perceived that the always energetic but slightly thin features of his friend expressed a sort of inward agitation. He was seated on the window-sill, a dust-covered cloak on his shoulders, and his cap on his head ; he did not move, even when Arcadi threw himself on his neck with a cry of joy.

"Here is a surprise! By what chance?" cried Arcadi, walking up and down the room like a person who imagines that he is delighted and wishes to have it thought so.—"Is every one well at home, is everything going on well?"

"Everything is going on well at your home, but everybody is not well," replied Bazarof. "Come, keep calm, have a glass of kvass * brought for me, then sit down and listen to what I am going to tell you in a few words, but in terms which will, I hope, appear sufficiently clear to you."

Arcadi calmed himself, and Bazarof gave him an account of his duel with Paul Petrovitch. Arcadi was very much surprised and even affected by it, but he did not think it necessary to manifest it. He contented himself with asking if his uncle's wound were indeed slight, and Bazarof having replied that it was very interesting, but not from a medical point of view, he forced himself to smile, and inwardly felt shame and a sort of fright. Bazarof seemed to understand what was passing in him.

"Yes, yes," he said, "that is what it is to live under a feudal roof; one takes up the customs of the middle ages, one makes a bully of oneself. I am going now to see the old people again, but I have stopped here on my way—in order to tell you all about the affair, I might tell you, if I did not consider a lie as useless as a folly. No, I have come here, the devil knows why! Do you see, it is sometimes well to seize oneself by the forelock and drag oneself into the air like a radish which you pull up from your hotbed, and that is what I have just done.—But a fancy has taken me to look for the last time on the place which I have left, the hot-bed where I had taken root."

"I hope that those words do not concern me," said Ar-

* A drink made of barley.

cadi in an agitated tone; "I hope that you do not think of separating from me?"

Bazarof looked at him with a fixed and scrutinizing eye.

"Would you really be very much grieved about it? It seems to me that you are already separated from me. You are so neat, so fresh—I suppose that your affair with Madame Odintsof is getting on marvellously well."

"Of what affair are you speaking?"

"Was it not for that that you left the city, little bird? By the way, what have become of the Sunday-schools? Are you not in love? Or have you already arrived at the period of modesty?"

"Eugene, you know that I have always been frank with you. I swear to you, I take God as a witness, that you are in error."

"Hum! God as a witness—a new expression," muttered Bazarof. "Why do you take it up so hastily? It is absolutely a matter of indifference to me. A romantic person would exclaim: I feel that our roads begin to divide; I confine myself to saying that we are disgusted with one another."

"Eugene—"

"The evil is not great, my dear; one becomes disgusted with many other things in life. Now I think that we might be able to separate. Since I have been here, I have felt disgusted, exactly as though I had been gorging myself with Gogol's letters to the wife of the governor of Kaluga. I have not had the horses unharnessed."

"What an idea! it is impossible!"

"And why?"

"I do not speak for myself; but I am sure that Madame Odintsof will think it in the highest degree impolite, for she will very certainly wish to see you."

"As for that, I think that you are wrong."

"I am certain on the contrary, that I am right," replied Arcadi. "Why dissimulate? Since we are on the subject, did you not come here for her?

"Perhaps; but you are not less wrong."

However, Arcadi was right. Madame Odintsof wished to see Bazarof, and sent him word to that effect by the butler.

Bazarof changed his dress to present himself before her; his new coat being packed so that he could get it without disturbing anything.

Madame Odintsof did not receive Bazarof in the room where he had so unexpectedly declared his love, but in the drawing-room. She gave him the ends of her fingers with an affectionate air, but her face expressed an involuntary constraint.

"Anna Serghėïevna," Bazarof hastened to say, "first of all, I ought to tranquillize you. You see a man who is completely restored to reason, and who hopes that others have forgotten his follies. I am going away for a long time, and although I am not tender, as you know, I should not like to think that you remember me with displeasure—"

Madame Odintsof sighed deeply, like one who has just reached the summit of a high mountain, and a slight smile animated her features. She held out her hand a second time to Bazarof, and when he pressed it she responded to the pressure.

"May the one of us two that recalls the past lose one of his eyes," * said she, "the more, since, speaking conscientiously, I too have sinned, if not by coquetry, at least by—in some other way, in short. In a word, let us be friends as before. All that was but a dream, was it not? And who remembers a dream?"

* A Russian proverb.

"Who remembers it? Besides, love—is a factitious feeling."

"Indeed? I am charmed to learn it."

Thus said Madame Odintsof, and thus, on his side, said Bazarof; they each thought that they spoke the truth. How much truth was there in their words? They probably did not know themselves, and the author is also ignorant. But the conversation took a turn which seemed to indicate that they were fully and reciprocally confidential.

Madame Odintsof asked Bazarof what he had been doing at the Kirsanofs'. He came near telling her about his duel with Paul Petrovitch, but checked himself when he thought that she might suspect him of seeking to make himself interesting, and contented himself with telling her that he had passed the time in working.

"And I," replied Madame Odintsof, "at first I had the blues, God knows why! So much so that I thought of travelling. Imagine that! But I have recovered little by little; your friend Arcadi came, and I have returned to the beaten path, to my true *rôle.*"

"What is that *rôle,* if I may be permitted to ask?"

"The *rôle* of aunt, governess, mother, as you may choose to call it. By the way, do you know that I was for a long time unable to understand your close intimacy with Arcadi; I found him rather insignificant. But now I have learned to know him better, and I am convinced that he is very intelligent,—and especially young, very young—We are no longer that, we, alas! Eugene Vassilievitch!"

"Does your presence frighten him as much as ever?" Bazarof asked.

"Did?"—began Madame Odintsof, and immediately checking herself, added:

"He has become much more confident, and talks willingly with me. Formerly he fled from me. However, I must own that I did not seek his society. Katia and he are now warm friends."

Bazarof felt impatient. " Woman cannot dispense with artifice," said he to himself.

"You pretend that he avoided you," he replied with a cold smile, "but the timid love with which you have inspired him is doubtless no longer a secret to you ?"

· "How ! he also !" exclaimed Madame Odintsof involuntarily.

"He too," repeated Bazarof with a respectful bow. "Is it possible that you are ignorant of it, and that I am the first to tell you this news ?

Madame Odintsof cast down her eyes.

· "You are mistaken," she said.

"I do not think so : but perhaps I ought to have been silent."

Bazarof said to himself at the same time: "That will teach you to employ artifice."

"Why should you not have spoken of it ? But I think that in this circumstance also you have given far too great a significance to a passing impression. I begin to suspect that you are inclined to exaggeration."

"Let us speak of something else, Madame.'

"Why ?" she replied, but that did not prevent him from giving another turn to the conversation.

She never felt quite at her ease with Bazarof, although she was persuaded that all was forgotten, as she had told him. While exchanging with him the most simple words, even in jest, she had a slight feeling of fear. It is thus that on a steamboat at sea people talk and laugh carelessly, exactly as they do on terra firma ; but let the least mishap occur, the least unforeseen circumstance, and immediately can be read on all faces an extraordinary anxiety, bearing witness to the permanent consciousness of a permanent danger.

The conversation of Madame Odintsof and Bazarof did not last long. Anna Sergheïevna became more and more serious; she replied absently and ended by proposing to go to the parlor, where they found the princess and Katia.

"Where is Arcadi Nikolaïevitch," asked Madame Odintsof. On learning that he had disappeared an hour before, she sent some one to look for him.

After having run everywhere they found him seated on a bench at the bottom of the garden, his chin supported on his hánds, plunged in reflection. His thoughts were profound and serious, but not at all sad. He knew that Madame Odintsof was *téte-à-téte* with Bazarof, and he did not feel the least jealousy; on the contrary, his face was bright; he seemed decided to do something which rejoiced and at the same time astonished him.

XXVI.

Madame Odintsof's husband had not liked innovations, but he was always ready to accept "the wise fancies of a pure taste," and in consequence of that disposition he had had erected in the garden, between the orangery and the pond, a sort of Greek portico, built of bricks. The wall which formed the back of this structure contained six niches for statues which Madame Odintsof wished to have brought from foreign parts. These statues were to represent Solitude, Silence, Reflection, Melancholy, Modesty and Sensibility. One of them, the Goddess of Silence, represented with her finger on her lips, had been brought and put in her place; but the very day of her installation some boys of the domestics broke her nose, and although a house-painter of the neighborhood engaged to make another nose "twice as beautiful," Madame Odintsof had her taken away, and they put her in the corner of a threshing-room, where she remained for a long time, to the great terror of the superstitious peasants. For many years tufts of bushes had covered the front of the portico. Only the capitals of the columns appeared above this wall of verdure. Under the portico it was always very cool, even in the hottest part of the day. Anna Sergheïevna had never liked the place since she had found an adder there ; but Katia often came and seated herself on a large stone bench under one of the niches. Surrounded with shade and freshness, she read, embroidered, or gave herself up to the sweet and languid sensation of a profound calm, a sensation which every one must know, and whose charm consists in the silent and almost mechanical observation of the powerful wave of life which is constantly flowing around us and in us.

The day after Bazarof 's arrival, Katia was seated on her favorite bench, and Arcadi again found himself beside her. She had consented to go with him under the portico. It was not more than an hour before breakfast ; the heat of the day had not yet replaced the morning freshness. Arcadi's face preserved the same expression as on the evening before ; Katia seemed preoccupied. Her sister had called her into her private room immediately after tea, and, having first caressed her, which always frightened Katia a little, advised her to be more circumspect in her behavior to Arcadi, and especially to avoid any *tête-à-tête* with him, her aunt and all the household having noticed that she saw him too frequently. Besides, already, the evening before, Anna Sergheïevna had been provoked, and Katia herself felt agitated as though she had been guilty. In yielding to Arcadi's entreaty, she had promised herself that it should be for the last time.

"Katerina Sergheïevna," said Arcadi suddenly, with an

indescribable mingling of assurance and timidity, "Since I have had the honor of being under the same roof with you, I have talked with you on many subjects, and yet I have left one side one question—which is very important to me. You made the remark yesterday that they had changed me here," he added, at the same time seeking and avoiding Katia's interrogating look ;—"in fact I am modified in many things, and you know it better than any one, you to whom I in reality owe this change."

"I ?—You ?—" replied Katia.

"I am no longer the presumptuous boy that I was on my arrival here," replied Arcadi ; "it is not for nothing that I have finished my twenty-third year. I still think of being useful and consecrating all my strength to—to the triumph of truth ; but I no longer seek my ideal where I formerly sought it ; it seems to me—much nearer. Until now I did not understand myself. I imposed on myself problems above my strength. My eyes are at length opened, thanks to a feeling—Perhaps I do not express myself very clearly, but I hope that you will understand me—"

Katia did not reply, and ceased to look at Arcadi.

"I think," he resumed in a more agitated voice, while a finch sang its ceaseless song above his head in the foliage of a birch, "I think that it is the duty of every honest man to be frank towards those—those who—in a word, towards those who are dear to him, and that is why—I have decided—"

But here Arcadi's eloquence failed him ; his sentences became confused, he lost countenance, and was obliged to break off, while Katia's eyes were still dropped ; she did not understand what he wanted to get at, and yet she seemed to expect something.

"I foresee that I am going to surprise you," resumed Arcadi as soon as he had recovered himself—"the more

since this feeling refers in some way—in some way—mark
it well—to you. I think that I remember your reproaching
me yesterday with my want of seriousness," he added, with
the air of a man who, having entered a marsh, feels himself
sinking deeper and deeper at each step, and nevertheless
continues to advance in the hope of getting out more
quickly.—"That reproach is often addressed—to young
men, even when they cease to deserve it,—and if I had
more confidence in myself—" "Come to my aid! Do!"
thought Arcadi despairingly; but Katia remained immovable.

"And if I might hope—"

"If it were permitted me to have confidence in your
words," said Madame Odintsof suddenly, quite near them,
in her clear and calm voice.

Arcadi was silent immediately, and Katia turned pale. A
little path passed near the bushes which hid the portico;
Madame Odintsof was following it with Bazarof. Neither
Katia nor Arcadi could see them, but they heard their words
and even their breathing. The promenaders took a few steps
and stopped just before the portico, as though intentionally.

"Don't you see," continued Madame Odintsof. "You
and I were mistaken; we are neither of us in our first
youth, I especially; we have lived, we are both of us fa-
tigued, we are—why not acknowledge it? both intelligent;
we have begun by becoming mutually interested, our curiosity was aroused—then—"

"Then, I made a fool of myself," said Bazarof.

"You know that that was not the cause of our rupture.
It is certain that we did not read one another; we had too
—how shall I say it? too many features in common. We
did not understand it immediately. On the contrary, Arcadi—"

"You needed him?" asked Bazarof.

10

"Cease, Eugene Vasilievitch! You pretend that I am not indifferent to him, and in fact, it has always seemed to me that I pleased him. I know that I might be—his aunt; but I do not wish to hide from you that I have thought oftener of him for some time. His youth and his simplicity have a certain attraction for me."

"A certain charm—; that is the word that one uses in such a case," replied Bazarof in a hollow and tranquil voice, through which the tumult of his passion was still evident. —"Arcadi played at mysteries yesterday, and he did not talk either about you or your sister—it is a grave symptom!"

"He is exactly like a brother to Katia," said Madame Odintsof, "and that pleases me, although perhaps I ought not to allow such an intimacy between them."

"Is it indeed the sister that speaks in you at this moment?" replied Bazarof slowly.

"Of course—But why have we stopped? Let us continue our walk. What a strange conversation we are having, is it not? I should never have believed that I could come to saying such things to you! You know that—while fearing you, I have great confidence in you, because I know that, at the bottom, you are very good."

"In the first place I am not good at all; and in the second place, I have become very insignificant to you, and you tell me that I am good!—It is as if you put a crown of flowers on the head of a corpse."

"Eugene Vasilievitch, we are not masters—" replied Madame Odintsof.

But at that moment a puff of wind disturbed the leaves and carried away her words.

"But you are free?" said Bazarof some instants after.

That was all that could be heard of their conversation. The sound of their steps grew more and more distant—and silence was re-established.

Arcadi turned to Katia. She had still the same attitude; only her head was bent still lower.

"Katerina Serghe ïevna," said he in a trembling voice and with clasped hands; "I love you passionately and for my whole life, and I love only you in the world. I wanted to confess it to you, and if your reply were favorable, I wanted to ask your hand—because I am not rich and I feel ready for any sacrifice.—You do not reply? You do not believe me? You think that I speak thoughtlessly? But recall these last days. Can you doubt that all the rest,—understand me well,—all, all the rest has disappeared without leaving any traces? Look at me; say a single word to me—I love—I love you—believe me!"

Katia gave Arcadi a serious and limpid glance; after reflecting a long time, she replied with an imperceptible smile :—" Yes."

Arcadi leaped from the bench.

"Yes! you said yes, Katerina Serghe ïevna! what does that word mean? Must I understand by that that you believe in the sincerity of my words—or—or—I dare not finish—"

"Yes!" replied Katia, and this time he comprehended her.

He seized her large and beautiful hands and pressed them against his heart; he was suffocated with joy. His limbs tottered and he continually repeated: "Katia! Katia!" and she began to weep too, all the time laughing at her own tears. He who has not seen such tears in the eyes of the woman he loves, does not know to what point, overpowered by gratitude and passion, a man can be happy.

Early the next morning Madame Odintsof sent to Bazarof that she would like to see him in her study, and handed him, with a constrained laugh, a sheet of letter-paper folded double. It was a letter from Arcadi; he asked the hand of Katia.

Bazarof ran rapidly through the letter, and made an effort to restrain a feeling of wicked satisfaction.

"Admirable!" said he; "yet you pretended, only yesterday, that he felt for Katerina Sergheïevna only a fraternal love? What are you going to reply to him?"

"What do you advise me to do?" replied Madame Odintsof, still laughing.

"I suppose," said Bazarof, also laughing, though he felt no more like it than she, "I suppose you must give them your blessing. The match is very good in every respect; the fortune of the Kirsanofs is quite considerable, Arcadi is the only son, and his father is a good-natured man, who will not trouble him in any way."

Madame Odintsof took a few steps in the room; she grew red and pale by turns.

"You think so?" she replied; "I do not see any objection to it myself. It gives me pleasure for Katia—and for Arcadi Nikolaïevitch. I shall await, of course, his father's reply; I shall send Arcadi himself to get it. But all this proves that I was right yesterday evening when I told you that we were old, you and I—How is it that I did not suspect anything? that confounds me."

Madame Odintsof began to laugh again and immediately turned away.

"The youth of the present day is decidedly sly," said Bazarof, laughing in his turn. "Adieu," he added, after a moment of silence, "I congratulate you on terminating this affair in the most agreeable way possible; I shall rejoice over it from afar."

Madame Odintsof turned quickly back to him.

"Are you going? Why should you not stay *now*—stay—your conversation is amusing—one seems to be walking on the edge of a precipice. One is afraid at the first moment, and then one feels a boldness which is surprising. Stay."

" I am grateful for your invitation, as well as for the good opinion which you have of my little conversational talents. But I find that I have already too long haunted a world which is not mine. The flying-fish can hold itself for some time in the air, but it ends by falling again into the water; permit me also to plunge again into my natural element."

Madame Odintsof looked at Bazarof. A bitter smile contracted his pale face. "That man loved me!" she said to herself, and she held out her hand to him with affectionate pity.

But he had understood her.

" No!" said he, drawing back a step, "although I am poor I have never yet accepted alms. Good bye, and may you be well."

" I am sure that we are not seeing one another for the last time," replied Madame Odintsof with an involuntary impulse.

" What does not happen in this world!" replied Bazarof. Then having bowed to Anna Serghe͏̈ievna, he went out.

" You think then of making a nest for yourself?" he said to Arcadi, while packing his trunk. "You are right! it is a good idea; only you were wrong to finesse. I expected quite another direction from you; but perhaps you were astonished at it yourself?"

" In fact I did not expect it at all when I left you," replied Arcadi. "But you are hardly frank in telling me that it is a good idea, as if I did not know your opinion of marriage!"

" Oh! my dear fellow," replied Bazarof, "how you express yourself to-day! Do you not see what I am doing? I have discovered an empty place in my trunk, and am filling it up as well as I can with hay; just so one must do with the trunk of life ; you must fill it with whatever comes to hand, only so that it does not remain empty. Do not be offended, I beg of you ; you probably remember the opinion I have always had of Katerina Serghëievna. There are young girls at home who pass for wonders merely because they sigh at the right time ; but yours makes herself valuable by other merits, and she will know so well that you are her very humble servant ; besides, it is in the order of things."

Bazarof slammed down the cover of his trunk and stood up.

" Now I will repeat to you by way of adieu (for we need not deceive ourselves, we are separating forever, and you must know it as well as I—): you are doing wisely ; our rough, sad, vagabond existence does not suit you. You lack boldness, wickedness, but in return you are endowed with a youthful audacity and ardor. That does not suffice for the work which we others are pursuing. And then, you gentlemen cannot go beyond a generous indignation or a generous resignation, things which do not signify much. You think that you are great men, you think yourselves at the pinnacle of human perfection when you have ceased to beat your servants, and we, we ask only to fight with one another and to beat. Our dust reddens your eyes, our mire soils you ; you are truly not of our height ; you admire yourself complacently, you take pleasure in reproaching yourself; all that bores us ; we have other things to do than to admire or reproach ourselves ; we must have other men broken on the wheel. You are an excellent fellow, but you are none the less an affected lordling, a little liberal noble and *vola tou*, to speak like my noble father."

"You are bidding me good bye forever, Eugene ?" asked Arcadi sadly. " And is this all that you find to say to me ? "

Bazarof scratched his neck.

"I might add some sentiment, Arcadi, but I shall not do it. That would be making romance, sucking bonbons. Here is a last piece of advice: marry as soon as possible; arrange your nest well and have many children! They will certainly be talented, because they will come in season, not like you and I. Ah! I see that the horses are ready—I'm off! I have said good bye to everybody. Come! shall we embrace?"

Arcadi threw himself on the neck of his old master and friend, and a flood of tears flowed down his cheeks.

"There is youth!" said Bazarof tranquilly; "but I count on Katerina Serghe\ievna! She will console you in less than no time."

"Good bye brother!" he said to Arcadi when he had already climbed into the *telega*, and pointing to two crows seated side by side on the roof of the stable, he added: "There is a good example! do not fail to follow it."

"What do you mean?" asked Arcadi.

"What! I thought that you knew more of natural history than that. Don't you know that the crow is the most respectable of birds? it loves family life. Take it for a model! Addio, signor!"

The *telega* started and rolled off.

Bazarof had spoken truly. Arcadi in talking that very evening with Katia had completely forgotten his master. He began already to submit to her, and Katia was in no way surprised at it. The next day he was going to return to Marino to Nicholas Petrovitch. In order not to put a restraint upon the young people, whom for propriety's sake only she did not leave too long alone, Madame Odintsof generously carried off the princess, who was thrown by the news of the approaching marriage into a state of tearful irritation. As for herself, Anna Serghe\ievna feared for a mo-

ment that the sight of the happiness of the young people
would be a little painful to her ; but it was quite otherwise.
Instead of fatiguing, the sight interested and even touched
her. She was at the same time rejoiced and saddened by it.

"It seems that Bazarof was right," she said to herself,
"there is nothing in me but curiosity, only curiosity, and
the love of repose and selfishness—"

"Children !" she said hoarsely, "is it true that love is
a factitious sentiment ?"

Neither Katia nor Arcadi understood the question. Anna
Serghéïevna inspired them with a certain fear ; the conversation which they had quite involuntarily overheard would
not leave their minds. But she soon tranquillized them ;
and very naturally, for she became tranquil herself.

XXVII.

Bazarof's arrival rejoiced his parents the more because it
was unexpected to them. Arina Vlassievna was so agitated
by it that she could do nothing but run up and down through
the house ; her husband ended by comparing her to a par-
tridge ; the little turned up train of her short gown gave her,
in fact, some resemblance to a bird. Vasili Ivanovitch
himself grunted with satisfaction as he sucked the amber
mouth-piece of his pipe ; then seizing his neck with his
fingers he turned his head convulsively, as though to assure
himself that it was firmly in its place, and suddenly opening
his mouth quite wide, he began to laugh in a silent way.

"I have come for six weeks at least, my old man," said
Bazarof to him ; "I want to work and I hope that you will
leave me in peace."

"You will forget my physiognomy ; that is the extent to
which I shall trouble you !" replied Vasili Ivanovitch.

He did not fail to keep his promise. Having established

his son, as at first, in the cabinet, he seemed almost to hide from him, and prevented his wife from giving herself up to a too demonstrative tenderness towards him.

"I think," he said to her, "that we annoyed Enioushenka a little during his first visit; we must show ourselves wiser now.

Arina Vlassievna agreed with her husband, but she did not gain much by it, for she only saw her son at meal-time, and feared to address a word to him.—"Enioushenka,"— she would say to him, and he would not have time to turn around before, twisting her fingers in the cords of her reticule, she would stammer: "Nothing; nothing; it is nothing!—" Then she would go to Vasili Ivanovitch and say to him, her cheek supported by her hand :—"How could we know my dear, what Eniousha would rather have for dinner, *stshi* or *borstsh* * ?"—"Why did you not ask him ?" he would reply—"I was afraid of annoying him."

Bazarof soon ceased to keep himself shut up ; the fever for work to which he had been a prey was replaced by a sort of gloomy and uneasy ennui. A strange languor was noticeable in all his movements ; even his walk, hitherto so firm and rapid, changed visibly. He took no more solitary walks, and began to seek society ; he began to drink tea in the parlor, to stroll in the kitchen-garden with Vasili Ivanovitch, and to smoke with him in silence ; one day he asked news of Father Alexis. This change at first greatly rejoiced Vasili Ivanovitch ; but his joy was not of long duration.—"Eniousha distresses me," he said one day confidentially to his wife ; "not that he is discontented or irritable, that would not make me anxious ; but he is sad, melancholy : it is dispiriting. He is silent ; I should rather have him scold at us. In addition to that he is growing thin and his complexion is bad."—"O my God! my God!" replied

* The first of these soups is prepared with cabbage, the second with beets.

10*

the old woman sighing, "I would put a bag of relics around his neck, but he would not consent to it." Vasili Ivanovitch tried several times prudently to question Bazarof about his occupations, his health, Arcadi—but Bazarof replied with a bad grace, and ended by saying impatiently : — "One would say that you were walking around me on tiptoe. That way is even worse than the first.—" " Come ! come ! I will not do it any more," hastily replied poor Vasili Ivanovitch. Their political conversations were not more successful. One day having broached the great question of progress with reference to the approaching liberation of the serfs, he imagined that his son would be pleased; but the latter replied indifferently : —"Yesterday, as I passed behind the garden hedge, I heard some little serfs making themselves hoarse with shouting, instead of one of their old songs : 'The time of truth is coming, my heart feels love.' There is your progress !"

Bazarof went sometimes to the village, and would talk, in his usual way, with a mocking air, to the first peasant he met.—" Come," he would say, "show me your ideas ; they pretend that you constitute the strength and future of Russia : with you will begin a new epoch in our history ; you will give us our true language and good laws.—" The peasant either would say nothing or else would speak words like these : "We might, indeed, because, besides—according to the rule, for instance, which is given us.—" "Explain to me what your *mir***** is," Bazarof would ask ; "is it that which rests on three fishes ?"

"It is the earth that rests on three fishes," replied the peasant in a tone of conviction, and giving to his voice a patriarchal and good-natured whine ;—"and the will of the

* This word can mean "The universe," and "the communal assembly "—The old legends say that the universe is upheld by three fishes.

masters is powerful against our *mir*, you know; for you are our fathers. The more severe the master, the more amiable the peasant."

One day when he had just heard such a speech, Bazarof shrugged his shoulders contemptuously and turned away from the peasant, who tranquilly went into his house.

" What was he talking to you about ? " asked another serf, a middle-aged man of a surly countenance, and who had seen from his threshold the conversation with Bazarof; "was it of rents in arrear ? "

" Well, yes my brother ! " replied the first peasant, and his voice had now no trace of patriarchal whine ; it showed, on the contrary a rudeness full of disdain :—" he talks with me because his tongue itched, doubtless. The masters are all the same : do they understand anything ? "

" How should they understand anything ? " said his inter-locutor, and shaking off their caps, and letting down their belts, they began to talk together of their affairs and wants.

Alas ! the young man full of assurance, who had just left them shrugging his shoulders disdainfully, this Bazarof who knew so well how to talk to peasants (as he had boast-ed in a discussion with Paul Petrovitch), did not even sus-pect that they considered him a sort of buffoon.—

At last he found an occupation. One day Vasili Ivano-vitch dressed, in his presence, the wounded leg of a peasant ; the old man's hands trembled, and he had some difficulty in tightening the bandages ; Bazarof came to his aid. From that time he did not cease to assist his father in his task as doctor, without ceasing, nevertheless, to jest at the reme-dies which he himself advised, and at his father's eagerness to put them in practice. But these jests did not in the least disconcert Vasili Ivanovitch ; he found them on the contrary, quite to his taste. It was with real happiness that he listened to Bazarof, all the while smoking his pipe

and holding with two fingers the skirts of his old dressing
gown, and the more venomous the words of his son, the
more heartily the happy father laughed, showing all his
blackish teeth.   He went so far as to repeat his son's sayings, sometimes with the point left out or without the meaning his son had given; thus, for example, he repeated on all
occasions for several days : " This is for the dessert ! " only
because his son, on learning that he had gone to matins,
had employed that expression.—" God be thanked ! " he
said confidentially to his wife ; " Eniousha has forgotten
his humors !   How he has talked to me to-day ! "—But on
the other hand he did not feel easy in having such an as-
sistant ; that idea inspired him with a feeling of exalted
pride.   "Yes, yes," he said to a poor peasant woman,
wrapped in her husband's *armiak*,* and wearing a
horned *kitchka*,† to whom he gave a vial of Goulard water
or a little pot of hyoscyamus ointment ; " You ought to
thank God constantly, my dear, for having brought my son
here ; you are treated now according to the most learned
method of the day ; do you understand that !   The Emperor
of the French, Napoleon himself, has not a better physician."—The peasant woman to whom he addressed his ex-
hortation, and who had come to complain that she felt herself " raised up by little fists " (without being able to explain
the meaning of her words), listened to Vasili Ivanovitch,
bowing to the ground, and drawing from her bosom three
eggs, wrapped in the end of a napkin, which constituted
her fee.

Bazarof even drew a tooth for a foreign merchant, and
although this tooth was not particularly remarkable, Vasili
Ivanovitch preserved it as a curiosity, and repeated several
times, as he showed it to father Alexis :

* A coat of thick cloth.   † A peasant headdress.

"See, father, what roots! Eugene must have a famous wrist! I saw the merchant lifted into the air. It was magnificent! I really think that an oak could not have resisted him!"

"It is praiseworthy!" replied the priest, not knowing very well how to cut short the old man's ecstacy.

A peasant of the neighborhood came to Vasili Ivanovitch one day, bringing his brother, who had the typhus. The wretched dying man was stretched on a bundle of straw; his whole body was covered with blackish spots; he had been long unconscious. Vasili Ivanovitch regretted that they had not thought sooner of applying for medical aid for the unfortunate man, and declared that there was no possibility of saving him. In fact, the peasant could not be taken home; he died on the road in his *telega*.

Two or three days after, Bazarof went to his father and asked if he had not some caustic.

"Yes, but what do you want of it?"

"I need it to cauterize a little wound."

"Who is wounded?"

"I am."

"How! You? What is this wound? Show it to me."

"Here, it is on this finger. I went this morning to the village from which they brought us the peasant who died of the typhus. For some reason or other they wanted to perform an autopsy—It is a long time since I have performed that sort of an operation."

"Well, I asked the physician of the district to give me the charge of it, and I have cut myself."

Vasili Ivanovitch became suddenly pale, ran, without speaking a single word, into his cabinet, and returned with a piece of caustic. Bazarof wanted to take it and leave the room.

"For heaven's sake!" said Vassili Ivanovitch, "let me burn you."

Bazarof smiled.

" What a love of practice ! "

" Do not jest, I entreat you. Show me your finger. The wound is not large. Do I not hurt you ? "

" Bear on hard, don't be afraid."

Vasili Ivanovitch stopped.

" Perhaps it would be better to burn it with a hot iron ; what do you think ? "

" We should have done it sooner ; now, that would be no more efficacious than the caustic. If I have been harmed there is no longer a remedy."

" What !—no longer a remedy ? " stammered Vasili Ivanovitch.

" To be sure not ! it is more than four hours since I cut myself."

Vasili Ivanovitch again applied the caustic to the wound :

" The physician of the district had no caustic then ? "

" No."

" Great God ! it is incredible : every physician ought to be provided with it ! "

" If you could have seen his lancets ! " said Bazarof going out.

During the rest of that day and all the next day Vasili Ivanovitch made all sorts of pretexts for entering his son's room : and although he did not speak to him of his wound, and even forced himself to talk about insignificant things, he looked at him so fixedly and observed all his movements with so much anxiety, that Bazarof lost his patience and threatened to go away. Vasili Ivanovitch promised to torment him no more, especially as Arina Vlassievna, to whom he had, be it understood, confided nothing, began to insist on knowing why he seemed uneasy and did not close his eyes during the night. He kept his promise for two days, although his son's face, which he observed constantly by stealth, did not in any way reassure him; but on the the third day he could no longer contain himself; they were at the table, and Bazarof, who sat with his eyes cast down, did not eat anything.

" Why do you not eat, Eugene ? " asked his father, adopting an indifferent air. " These dishes seem to me very well cooked."

" I do not eat because I do not wish to eat."

" You have no appetite ? and your head," he added, " does it pain you ? "

" Yes. Why should it not ? "

Arina Vlassievna became attentive.

" Do not be angry, I entreat you, Eugene," continued Vasili Ivanovitch; " but permit me to feel your pulse."

Bazarof rose.

" I will tell you without your feeling my pulse that I have a fever."

" And you have chills, too ? "

" Yes. I am going to lie down a little while. Send me some linden-flower tea. I must have taken cold."

" It was you then that I heard coughing last night," replied Arina Vlassievna.

" I have taken cold," repeated Bazarof, going out of the room.

Arina Vlassievna went to prepare the tea, and Vasili Ivanovitch passed into the next room, where he clutched his hair without saying a word.

Bazarof remained lying down all the rest of the day, and passed the night in a heavy and fatiguing state of drowsiness. Opening his eyes with difficulty, towards one o'clock in the morning, he saw, by the light of the night lamp, the pale face of his father, who was at his bedside, and he begged him to retire; the old man obeyed, but re-entered almost immediately on tip-toe, and, cowering behind the

half-open door of a closet, continued to watch his son.
Arina Vlassievna, too, did not go to bed; she came every
moment to the door of the room to listen to Eniousha's
breathing, and to assure herself that Vasili Ivanovitch was
still at his post. She could only distinguish her husband's
broad, bowed back; but that sufficed to tranquillize her a
little. Bazarof tried to get up when it was day; he was
taken with dizziness, soon followed by bleeding from the
nose, and he went to bed again without delay. Vasili
Ivanovitch assisted him in silence; Arina Vlassievna approached and asked him how he felt. "I am better," he
replied, turning to the wall. Vasili Ivanovitch signed to
his wife with both hands to withdraw; she bit her lips to
keep herself from crying, and went out. Everything in the
house seemed in some way to be darkened; every face was
lengthened; a strange silence reigned, even in the yard;
they sent off to the village a crowing cock, who must have
been remarkably surprised by such a proceeding. Bazarof
remained in bed, with his face turned to the wall. Vasili
Ivanovitch spoke to him several times, but his questions
annoyed the sick man, and the old man remained motionless
in his chair, wringing his hands from time to time. He
went into the garden for a few minutes, and stood there
immovable as a statue; he seemed under the shock of an
unheard-of astonishment (the expression of surprise hardly
left his face); then he returned to his son, seeking to avoid
his wife. She succeeded at last in seizing him by the hand
and asking him in a convulsed, almost menacing tone:
"What is the matter with him?" Vasili Ivanovitch, to
reassure her, tried to smile, but to his own astonishment,
it was a burst of laughter that came from his lips. He had
sent to the city for a physician, in the morning; he judged
it proper to tell his son of it, in order that the latter might
not reproach him in the presence of his *confrère.*

Bazarof turned over suddenly on the sofa where he was lying, looked fixedly at his father, and asked for a drink.

Vasili Ivanovitch gave him some water, and profited by the occasion to put his hand on his son's forehead : it was burning.

" The old story," said Bazarof slowly and hoarsely ; " it is taking a bad form. I have taken the infection, and you will put me in the ground in a few days."

Vasili Ivanovitch tottered as though his limbs had been struck violently.

" Eugene," he stammered, " what are you saying ! It is a simple attack of chills."

" Come ! " replied Bazarof. " A physician is not permitted to say such things. I have all the symptoms of the typhus ; you know it well."

" The symptoms—of the typhus ?—Oh ! no—Eugene ! "

" What is that then ? " said Bazarof, and drawing up his shirt sleeve, he showed his father the ill-omened reddish spots which covered his skin.

Vasili Ivanovitch turned pale with terror.

" Let us admit—that it might—even be—something—like an epidemic infection—"

" It is a pyæmia," said his son.

"Yes—an epidemic infection."

" A pyæmia," repeated Bazarof distinctly and in a rude tone ; " you have then forgotten your little study books ? "

" Well ! well, as you please—but still we shall certainly cure you."

" That is all nonsense. Let us talk sense. I did not think to die so soon ; it is an incident which, I acknowledge, seems rather disagreeable to me. My mother and you will do well to have recourse to your religious feelings ; this is a fine occasion to put them to the proof."

He drank a little water—" I must ask you something

while my head is still under my control. To-morrow or the
day after my brain, as you know, will have handed in its
resignation. It is possible that even now I do not express
myself clearly. Just now I thought that I was chased by
red dogs, and you were lying in wait for me exactly as one
does for grouse. It seems as though I were drunk. Do
you understand me easily ?"

" Certainly, Eugene, you talk very sensibly, as usual."

" So much the better ; you told me that you had sent for
a physician—I have not hindered you from obtaining that
satisfaction—obtain one for me in your turn ; I want you to
send an express—"

" 'To Arcadi Nikolaïevitch ?" asked the old man eagerly.

" Who is that Arcadi Nikolaïevitch ?" replied Bazarof, as
if in a moment of wandering.—"Ah ! yes—that little bird !
No, leave him in peace ; he is now changed into a crow. Do
not open your eyes so ; it is not delirium yet. Send an express to Anna Serghéïevna Odintsof ; she is a proprietress of
the neighborhood. Do you know her ? (Vasili Ivanovitch
made a sign that he knew her.) Let her be told : Eugene
Bazarof salutes you and sends you word that he is dying.
You understand that ?"

" You shall be gratified—But how could you die, Eugene ?—
I make you a judge of it !—Where after that would there
be justice in the world ?"

" I don't know anything about that ; but send the
express."

" This very instant, and I will send her a letter."

" No ; it is useless. Send her my compliments ; that
will suffice. As for me, I am going to return to my red
dogs. It is strange ! I should like to fix my thoughts on
death, and I cannot ! I see a sort of spot—and nothing
more."

He turned back towards the wall with difficulty, and Va-

sili Ivanovitch left the room. He went into his wife's room
and fell on his knees before the images.

"Let us pray, Arina! let us pray to God!" he exclaimed
groaning; "our son is dying!"

The physician of the district, the same who had no caustic, arrived; and having examined the sick man, he advised
them to keep to an expectant mode of treatment, and added
some phrases calculated to give hope of a cure.

"You have then seen men who, in my position, did not
set out for the Elysian Fields?" asked Bazarof, and at the
same instant he seized the foot of a heavy table which was
near the sofa, and moved it from its place.

"The vigor," he said, "all the vigor is still there, and I
must die!—An old man has at least had time enough to
wear out, but I—Deny, deny—Let a man venture to deny
death! It is death that denies you and that is all! I hear
weeping!" he added, after a short silence; "it is my
mother—Poor woman—who will she now compel to eat her
famous *borstsh?* And you, too, Vasili Ivanovitch, I see
that you are whimpering? If Christianity is not sufficient
for you, try to be a philosopher; remember the stories!
You used to boast, I believe, of being a philosopher?"

"I a philosopher!" exclaimed Vasili Ivanovitch, and
tears streamed down his cheeks.

Bazarof grew worse from hour to hour; the progress of
the disease was rapid, as is almost always the case in sur-
gical infections. His head was still clear and he understood
what was said to him; he struggled still.—"I do not wish
to be delirious," he repeated to himself in a low tone
clenching his fists; "it is far too stupid!" And he added
immediately: "If you take ten from eight, how many will
remain?"—Vasili Ivanovitch walked the floor like a mad-
man, proposed all sorts of remedies, and would every moment cover up his son's feet. "He must be wrapped in

cold cloths—an emetic—mustard poultices on the stomach—bleeding!" he said with an effort. The physician, whom he had begged to remain, agreed with him, gave lemonade to the sick man, and asked for himself now a pipe, now something strengthening and warming, that is brandy. Arina Vlassievna remained seated on a little bench near the door, and only left her place for a moment at a time to go and pray. A few days before she had dropped her toilette glass, which had broken, a thing which she had always considered a most sinister omen; Anfisushka even did not know what to say to her. Timofeitch had gone with the dying man's message to Madame Odintsof.

The night was bad for Bazarof,—he was a prey to devouring heat. He became a little better in the morning; he asked Arina Vlassievna to comb his hair, kissed her hand and swallowed two or three spoonfuls of tea. Vasili Ivanovitch picked up a little hope.

"God be praised!" he repeated, "the crisis is declared—the crisis is past—"

"See," said Bazarof, "what a word can do! This word crisis has come to your mind, and it has quite consoled you. It is strange what an influence words have over men! Let one call a man an idiot without fighting him, and he is quite affected by it; let one compliment him on his talent without giving him money, and he feels happy."

This little speech reminded Vasili Ivanovitch of Bazarof's sallies when he was well, and he appeared enchanted by it.

"Bravo! that is perfectly true and well said. Bravo!" he exclaimed, pretending to clasp his hands.

Bazarof smiled sadly.

"What do you really think," he asked his father: "Is the crisis past or declared?"

"You are better—that is what I see, that is what rejoices me," replied Vasili Ivanovitch.

" Capital! It is always well to rejoice. But has any one been sent there?—You know?"

"Certainly."

The improvement was not of long duration. The paroxysms were renewed. Vasili Ivanovitch kept near his son; a peculiar anguish seemed to torment the old man. He tried several times in vain to speak.

"Eugene!" he exclaimed at length, "my child! my dear, my good son!" This unexpected appeal made an impression on Bazarof. He turned his head a little, tried evidently to throw off the weight which pressed upon his mind, and said: "What, my father?"

"Eugene," continued Vasili Ivanovitch, and he fell on his knees near Bazarof, although the latter had his eyes shut and could not see him.—"Eugene, you feel better, and you will recover by God's mercy—But profit by this instant, grant your poor mother and myself the greatest of satisfactions; fulfil the duties of a Christian! I have needed great courage to propose it to you—but it is still more terrible—It is for eternity, Eugene—think well of it—"

The old man's voice became choked, and a strange contraction passed slowly over his son's features, who continued to lie with his eyes shut.—"If that can give you any pleasure, I will consent to it," he said at last; "but it seems to me that there is no haste. You have just told me yourself that I was better."

"Better, yes, Eugene; but one cannot answer for anything. All depends on the will of God! and to fulfil a duty—"

"I will wait awhile," replied Bazarof; "you say yourself that the crisis has just begun. If we are mistaken, what does it matter! They can easily give absolution to sick people who are insensible."

"In the name of Heaven, Eugene—"

"I will wait; I want to sleep now. Do not bother me."
And he laid his head back on the pillow.

The old man rose, seated himself in his chair, and with his chin resting on his hand, began to bite his fingers.

The sound of a spring carriage, that sound which one notices so quickly in the midst of the silence of the country, suddenly struck his ear. The rolling of light wheels came nearer and nearer; one could already distinguish the breathing of the horses.—Vasili Ivanovitch leaped from his chair and ran to the window. A two-seated carriage, drawn by four horses, was entering the yard of his little house! Not knowing what it could mean, but seized with a paroxysm of unreflecting joy, he ran to the door. A servant in livery opened the carriage, and a lady got out wrapped in a black mantle and with her face hidden by a veil.

"I am Madame Odintsof," said she. "Is Eugene Vasilitch still alive? You are his father! I have brought a physician."

"God bless you!" exclaimed Vasili Ivanovitch, and seizing her hand, he pressed it convulsively to his lips, while the physician of whom Anna Sergheïevna had just spoken, a little man with spectacles and a German physiognomy, slowly descended from the carriage:—"He is still living, my Eugene is living and he will be saved now! My wife! my wife! An angel has come to us from Heaven—"

"What is the matter! Great God!" stammered Arina Vlassievna, who had rushed from the parlor, and, falling at the feet of Anna Sergheïevna even in the anteroom, she began to kiss her dress, like a maniac.

"What are you doing? what are you doing?" said Anna Sergheïevna; but Arina Vlassievna did not listen to her, and Vasili Ivanovitch ceased not to repeat: "An angel! an angel from Heaven."

"*Wo ist der Kranke?* Where is the patient?" asked the doctor at last with an impatient air.

These words recalled Vasili Ivanovitch to reason.

"Here! here! please to follow me, *Werthester Herr Collega,*" he added, recollecting his old calling.

"Eh!" said the German with a sour smile.

Vasili Ivanovitch took him into the cabinet.

"Here is a physician sent by Anna Serghe'evna Odint-sof," said he leaning down to his son's ear, "and she is here herself."

Bazarof suddenly opened his eyes.

"What did you say?"

"I told you that Anna Serghe'evna Odintsof was here, and that she had brought you this respectable doctor."

Bazarof's eyes wandered about the room.

"You shall see her, Eugene; but we must first talk a little with the doctor. I am going to give him the whole history of your disease, from the time that Sidor Sidoritch (that was the name of the physician of the district) left us; and we are going to have a little consultation."

Bazarof looked at the physician. "Well, get through with it as soon as possible, but do not talk Latin, for I know what is meant by: *jam moritur.*"

"*Der Herr scheint des Deutschen mächtig zu sein,*" said the disciple of Esculapius turning to Vasili Ivanovitch.

"*Ik—gabe*—speak Russian, that will do better;" replied the old man.

"Ah! so! ferry vell!" and the consultation began.

Half an hour after, Anna Serghe'evna, accompanied by Vasili Ivanovitch, entered the cabinet. The doctor had had time to whisper in her ear that the state of the sick man was hopeless.

She looked once on Bazarof, and stopped near the door, so terrible was the impression given her by that inflamed and already dying face, by those troubled eyes which regarded her fixedly. She felt frozen, seized with an overwhelming fear; the thought that she would have felt very differently if she had really loved him, rapidly crossed her mind.

"Thank you," he said with an effort, "I did not hope for it. It is a good action. We see one another yet once more, as you predicted."

"Anna Sergheïevna has had the kindness—"

"Father, leave us—Anna Sergheïevna, you will permit it? I think that now—"

By a movement of the head he seemed to tell her that she had nothing to fear from a dying man.

Vasili Ivanovitch went out.

"Thanks," repeated Bazarof; "it is quite royal. They say that sovereigns visit thus the bedsides of the dying."

"Eugene Vasilievitch, I hope—"

"No, Anna Sergheïevna, let us speak the truth. All is over for me. I have fallen under the wheel. You see that I was right not to trouble myself about the future. Death is an old story, and yet it is new for each one. I have no fear as yet,—then I shall lose my consciousness, and Fut! (he made a slight sign with his hand).— But what more can I say to you?—Tell you how I have loved you? There was no sense in that before, and now less than ever. Love is a form, and my own form is going to dissolve. I will tell you rather—how beautiful you are! And now you stand, there, as lovely as—"

Anna Sergheïevna started involuntarily.

"It is nothing, do not be disturbed—sit down over there —Do not come near me; the disease with which I am attacked is infectious."

Anna Sergheïevna rapidly crossed the room to him, and seated herself in a chair near the sofa.

"What generosity!" said Bazarof in a low tone; "how

near she is ! So young, so fresh, so neat, in this ugly room !
—Well ! good bye ! may you live long, that is what it is
best to do, and enjoy life while it is not too late. See what
a hideous sight: a worm half crushed and still writhing ! I
thought myself sure of accomplishing a great deal of work ;
to die, I ? Ah ! bah ! I have a mission ; I am a giant ! And
now the giant's whole mission consists in dying with decency,
although that does not interest anybody.—It matters little,
I shall not die like a dog."

Bazarof was silent and began to feel for his glass with his
hand. Anna Serghĕievna gave him a drink without remov-
ing her gloves, and holding her breath !

"You will forget me," he resumed ; "the dead are no
longer anything to the living. My father will tell you that
Russia has lost a man who was very precious to her !—That
is childishness ; but leave the old man his illusions—For a
child all amusements are good—you know ?—Console him
and my mother too. In your great world you will not find
such people, even if you seek for them lantern in hand.—I
necessary to Russia !—No, it seems not ! Who then is
necessary to her ? A shoemaker is a necessary man, a tailor
is necessary, a butcher—he sells meat—a butcher—Wait, I
am getting confused.—There is a wood there—"

Bazarof put his hand to his forehead.

Madame Odintsof leaned towards him.

"Eugene Vasilievitch, I am here still—"

He took away his hand and raised himself suddenly.

"Good bye !" he said with a sudden energy, and his eyes
shone for the last time.—"Good bye !—Listen—I did not
kiss you the other day—blow on the dying lamp, and let it
go out—"

Anna Serghĕievna pressed her lips to the brow of the
dying man.

"Enough !" he said, and his head fell back—"how the
shades—"

11

Anna Serghëievna went out noiselessly.

"Well ?" asked Vasili Ivanovitch in a low tone.

"He is asleep," she replied still lower.

Bazarof did not wake again. He lost his consciousness completely in the evening, and died the next day. Father Alexis performed the last offices. When they administered the extreme unction, when the consecrated oil flowed on his breast, one of his eyes opened, and one would have said that at the sight of this priest in his sacerdotal costume, of that smoking censer and those tapers lighted before the images, something which resembled a shudder of terror passed over his distorted face—but that lasted but an instant. When he had given the last sigh and the house resounded with groans, Vasili Ivanovitch was seized with a sudden transport.—"I vowed to rebel!" he cried in a hoarse voice, his clenched hands raised, as if he were threatening some one in the air ;—"and I will rebel! I will rebel!"

But Arina Vlassievna all in tears hung on his neck, and they fell together, with their faces to the ground, "exactly like two lambs," Anfisushka said afterwards in the ante-room, "like two lambs in the heat of the day ;" they prostrated themselves at the same time, and side by side.

But the heat of the day passes and evening comes, and then the night, the night which brings into a tranquil asylum all the careworn and the weary.

XXVIII.

Six months after, winter had come ; winter with the terrible silence of its frosts, the compact and creaking snow, the rosy rime on the branches of the trees, the pillars of thick smoke above the chimneys showing against a sky pale blue and cloudless, the eddies of warm air shooting out of opened doors, the fresh and nipped-looking faces of the passers by, and the hasty trot of horses half-frozen by the cold. A January day was drawing near its end; the coldness of the evening condensed still more the motionless air, and the blood-colored twilight was being rapidly extinguished. The windows of the house of Marino were lighted up, one after the other; Prokofitch, in a black coat and white gloves, placed with a very extraordinary air of dignity five covers on the dining room table. A week before, two marriages had taken place, silently and almost without witnesses, in the little church of the parish; Arcadi was united to Katia, and Nicholas Petrovitch to Fenitchka; and on this very day Nicholas Petrovitch was giving a farewell dinner to his brother, who was going to Moscow on business. Anna Sergheïevna had likewise gone to that city, after making rich presents to the young couple.

They sat down at table at three o'clock precisely; Mitia was among the guests; he had already a nurse in a *kokoshnik* * of silk stitched with gold; Paul Petrovitch was placed between Katia and Fenitchka; the new husbands were seated near their wives. Our old friends had changed a little lately; they had grown handsomer, or at least fatter; Paul Petrovitch alone had grown thin, but that added to his *distingué* appearance.—Fenitchka too was not the same. In a black silk dress, a large knot of velvet in her hair, a gold chain around her neck, she sat in a respectful immovability, not less respectful towards herself than towards all by whom she was surrounded. And she smiled as if she wanted to say: "Excuse me, I am not here for nothing." All the other guests had smiling faces, and seemed also to be asking pardon; all felt a little embarrassed, a little sad, and yet perfectly happy. Each had pleasant attentions for

* A head-dress of the Russian peasants.

his or her neighbor; the word seemed to be given that they should enjoy some comedy full of good nature. Katia was the most tranquil of all; she looked around her with confidence, and it was easy to see that Nicholas Petrovitch already loved her very fondly. He rose before the end of the dinner, a glass of champagne in his hand, and turning to Paul Petrovitch, said:

"You are leaving us—you are leaving us, my dear brother,—for a short time, I hope, but yet I cannot resist the desire of expressing to you what—I—what we—how much I—how much we—The trouble is that we Russians do not know how to make speeches! Arcadi, speak in my place."

"No, papa, I am not prepared."

"You are always better prepared than I! In short, my dear brother, permit me simply to embrace you and to wish you all possible happiness. Return to us as soon as you can."

Paul Petrovitch embraced every one, without excepting, be it understood, Mitia; he kissed Fenitchka's hand besides, which she held out to him awkwardly enough; then having drunk a second glass of champagne which had just been poured out for him, he exclaimed with a deep sigh:

"May you be happy, my friends. *Farewell!* " *

The little English word passed unperceived; all the guests were too much moved.

"To the memory of Bazarof," said Katia in her husband's ear, and she drank with him. Arcadi pressed Katia's hand, but did not dare to propose that toast.

It seems to me that all is ended. But some of my readers will perhaps desire to know what the different persons of whom we have just been talking are now doing. We we will ask nothing better than to satisfy them.

* In English in the original.

Anna Serghe茨evna was married quite recently; she has made a judicious marriage. The man whom she has taken for a husband is one of our future men of action, an intelligent lawyer, endowed with a very well developed practical turn of mind, with a firm will and a great facility of elocution; moreover, he is still quite young, good, and cold as ice. They live quite happily together, and will end perhaps by attaining domestic happiness, perhaps even love. The princess is dead, and forgotten from the day of her death. The Kirsanofs, father and son, are settled at Marino; their affairs begin to go a little better; Arcadi has become a good agriculturist, and the "farm" already brings in quite a considerable income. Nicholas Petrovitch has been chosen justice of the peace,* and fulfils his duties with the greatest zeal; he traverses unceasingly the district assigned to him, makes long speeches, for he thinks that the peasant needs to be well "argued with," that is, that it is necessary to repeat the same thing to him, to satiety; and yet, to tell the truth, he does not succeed in fully satisfying either the enlightened gentlemen who discuss "emancipation" at one time with affectation, at another with melancholy, or the unlearned masters who openly curse this unfortunate "*emuncipation.*" Both find him too tame. A son has been born to Katerina Serghe茨evna, and Mitia is already a lively little fellow who runs and chatters quite prettily. Fenitchka, now Fedossia Nikola茨evna, loves no one in the world, next to her husband and son, so much as her daughter-in-law, and when the latter sits down to the piano, she would willingly stay by her side all day. Do not let us forget Peter. He has become quite stupid and more inflated with importance than ever; but that has not prevented him from making quite an advantageous marriage; he has married

* Functionaries created temporarily and charged with smooth-ing the difficulties which the abolition of serfdom has caused be-tween the peasants and their old masters.

the daughter of a gardener of the city, who preferred him
to two other suitors, because they had no watch, while he
possessed not only a watch,—but even varnished boots !

One may meet at Dresden, on the Brühl terrace, between two and three o'clock, the most fashionable time for
promenading, a man of fifty, with very white hair, and who
seems to suffer from. the gout, but who is still handsome,
elegantly dressed, and has that peculiar stamp given by familiarity with the world.   This promenader is no other than
Paul Petrovitch Kirsanof.   He left Moscow on account of
his health ; he has settled at Dresden where he associates
principally with the English, and with Russian travellers.
With the former, his manners are simple, almost modest,
although always dignified ; they think him a little tiresome,
but consider him "a perfect gentleman."   More at his ease
with the Russians, he gives full play to his choleric temper,
mocks at himself, and does not spare the others ; but he
does it all with an amiable ease and without ever failing in
the proprieties.   He professes besides the opinions of the
Slavophiles and every one knows that in high Russian society, that manner of thinking is considered very " *distingué.*"   He reads no Russian books ; but one can see on his
bureau a silver ash-pan in the form of a peasant's *lapot.**
He is much sought after by our tourists.   Matveï Ilitch
Koliazin, who placed himself for the time *in the ranks
of the opposition*, paid him a solemn visit on his way
to the waters of Bohemia ; and the inhabitants of the city,
with whom, however, he has not been at all connected
seem to have a sort of veneration for him.   No one can obtain as easily as " *der Herr Baron von Kirsanow*" a ticket
of admission to the court chapel, a box, etc.   He always does
as much good as possible, and never fails to make some stir

* A shoe of birch bark.

about it. It was not in vain that he was formerly a lion ; but life is a burden to him, even more than he suspects. It is sufficient to see him at the Russian church, where, holding himself a little aloof, supported against the wall, he gets to dreaming, and remains motionless, his lips bitterly pressed together ; then, suddenly recovering himself, he begins to cross himself almost imperceptibly.

Madame Kukshin has also ended by leaving the country. She is actually at Heidelberg, and does not study the natural sciences any longer, but architecture. She has discovered, she says, new laws. As of old, she associates principally with the students and with the young Russian physicians and chemists of whom Heidelberg is full, and who, after stupefying the innocent German professors in the early part of their sojourn, by the soundness of their judgment, stupefy them still more a little while after, by their complete idleness and unexampled laziness. It is with two or three chemists of this type, not able to distinguish oxygen from azote, but criticising everything, and highly satisfied with themselves, that Sitnikof, accompanied by the *great* Elisevitch, and himself also preparing to merit that honorable title, is living on at St. Petersburg, and continuing, according to his own expression, the *work* of Bazarof. We are assured that he has been thrashed, lately, but not without taking his revenge; he has given out, in an obscure article, which has appeared in an obscure paper, that his aggressor was a coward. He calls that irony. His father makes him go and come as usual; his wife treats him as a fool and a literary man.

There is a little graveyard in one of the most remote corners of Russia. Like most of our graveyards it presents a most sad appearance; the ditches which surround it have been long since filled up and overrun with grass; the wooden crosses are overthrown, or scarcely hold themselves up, tottering under the little roofs, formerly painted, which surmount them; the tombstones are displaced as though some one had pushed them down; two or three trees, almost stripped of leaves, give a little shade; sheep graze among the graves.—However, there is one which the hand of man respects, which the animals do not trample under foot; the birds alone come to rest there, and sing every morning at daybreak. An iron railing surrounds it, and two young firs are planted at its two ends. This grave is that of Eugene Bazarof. Two persons, a husband and his wife, bending under the weight of years, often come from a little neighboring village to visit it; leaning on one another, they slowly approach the railing, fall on their knees, and weep long and bitterly, keeping their eyes long fixed on the mute stone which covers their son; they exchange a few words, wipe away the dust which covers the tombstone, straighten a branch of fir, then begin to pray again, and cannot make up their minds to leave the spot where they believe themselves nearer to their son, nearer to his memory.—Is it possible that their prayers, that their tears are in vain? Is it possible that pure and devoted love may not be all-powerful? Oh! no! However passionate, however rebellious the heart that rests in a tomb, the flowers that have sprung up over it look peacefully at us with their innocent eyes; they speak to us not only of eternal repose, of that perfect repose of "indifferent" nature; they speak to us also of eternal reconciliation, and of a life which cannot end.

THE END.